Empathy: Emotional, Ethical and Epistemological Narratives

At the Interface/Probing the Boundaries

Founding Editor

Rob Fisher (*Interdisciplinarian, Oxford, UK*)

Advisory Board

Peter Bray (*Programme Leader for Counsellor Education, School of Counselling, Human Services and Social Work Education and Social Work, University of Auckland, New Zealand*)
Robert Butler (*Professor/Chair, Department of History, Elmhurst College, USA*)
Ioana Cartarescu (*Independent Scholar, Bucharest, Romania*)
Seán Moran (*Waterford Institute of Technology, Ireland*)
Stephen Morris (*Author and Independent Scholar, New York, Illinois, USA*)
John Parry (*Edward Brunet Professor of Law and Associate Dean of Faculty, Lewis & Clark Law School, Portland, Oregon, USA*)
Natalia Kaloh Vid (*Associate Professor, Department of Translation Studies, Faculty of Arts, University of Maribor, Slovenia*)

VOLUME 123

The titles published in this series are listed at *brill.com/aipb*

Empathy: Emotional, Ethical and Epistemological Narratives

Edited by

Ricardo Gutiérrez Aguilar

BRILL
RODOPI

LEIDEN | BOSTON

Cover illustration: By Roberto R. Aramayo. Used with kind permission.

The Library of Congress Cataloging-in-Publication Data is available online at http://catalog.loc.gov
LC record available at http://lccn.loc.gov/2019935922

Typeface for the Latin, Greek, and Cyrillic scripts: "Brill". See and download: brill.com/brill-typeface.

ISSN 1570-7113
ISBN 978-90-04-37676-2 (paperback)
ISBN 978-90-04-39812-2 (e-book)

Copyright 2019 by Koninklijke Brill NV, Leiden, The Netherlands.
Koninklijke Brill NV incorporates the imprints Brill, Brill Hes & De Graaf, Brill Nijhoff, Brill Rodopi, Brill Sense, Hotei Publishing, mentis Verlag, Verlag Ferdinand Schöningh and Wilhelm Fink Verlag.
All rights reserved. No part of this publication may be reproduced, translated, stored in a retrieval system, or transmitted in any form or by any means, electronic, mechanical, photocopying, recording or otherwise, without prior written permission from the publisher.
Authorization to photocopy items for internal or personal use is granted by Koninklijke Brill NV provided that the appropriate fees are paid directly to The Copyright Clearance Center, 222 Rosewood Drive, Suite 910, Danvers, MA 01923, USA. Fees are subject to change.

This book is printed on acid-free paper and produced in a sustainable manner.

Contents

    List of Illustrations   VII
    Notes on Contributors   VIII

1   Introduction: The Joyful *Páthos* from Oxford   1
      Ricardo Gutiérrez Aguilar

2   In Search of Empathy in Prehistoric Times: Evolution and Revolution   7
      Josefa Ros Velasco

3   Empathy or Compassion? On Rational Understanding of Emotional Suffering   28
      Victoria Aizkalna

4   From Psychology to Morality: Sympathy, Imagination and Reason in Hume's Moral Philosophy   41
      Gerardo López Sastre

5   Existence as a Matter of Co-existence: Jean-Jacques Rousseau's Moral Psychology of *Pitié*   53
      Nina Lex

6   Empathy in Education: the Successful Teacher   73
      Giovanna Costantini

7   Anti-Utilitarian Empathy: an Ethical and Epistemological Journey   82
      Irina Ionita

8   Empathetic Art in a Paediatric Oncology Clinic   92
      Judy Rollins

9   Practicable Empathy in Acting: Empathic Projection in Sophocles' *Ajax*   106
      Christopher J. Staley

10   Empathy in Experimental Narratives   125
      Barış Mete

11   On the Bearability of Others-Being: Bartleby, Expression and Its Justification   142
     Ricardo Gutiérrez Aguilar

12   The Basis for Responsibility in Empathy: an Exploration   152
     Paulus Pimomo

13   Empathy and Historical Understanding: a Reappraisal of 'Empathic Unsettlement'   162
     Rosa E. Belvedresi

14   Empathy with Future Generations? A Historical Approach to Global Justice   178
     Johannes Rohbeck

Index of Subjects   203
Index of Authors   205

Illustrations

8.1 Kite Flying. © 2006, Joan Drescher. Used with permission. 96
8.2 Not Feeling Well. © 2006, Joan Drescher. Used with permission. 96
8.3 The Clinic. © 2006, Joan Drescher. Used with permission. 97
8.4 The Goldfish Tank. © 2006, Joan Drescher. Used with permission. 98
8.5 Healing Mandala. © 2006, Joan Drescher. Used with permission. 99
8.6 Coming Home Again. © 2006, Joan Drescher. Used with permission. 100
8.7 Chandy. © 2006, Joan Drescher. Used with permission. 101
8.8 Trio. © 2016, William Wegman. Used with permission. 103

Notes on Contributors

Victoria Aizkalna
Since she started taking an interest in Philosophy, her journey has taken her a long way from Metaphysics to Analytical Philosophy, and finally to the Philosophy of Mind. Studying and trying to understand the way people perceive and structure the information in their mind is her main fascination: how it can be used to improve the quality of intellectual and daily life, how it can be utilized in the field of education, and how it can help people understand each other on a compassionate and emphatic level. Understanding the way we think can help people overcome the barrier of the I–Them thinking, and change from Us versus Them thinking model, to I among Us. She started her academic journey at the University of Latvia, where she had an opportunity to connect with the international Philosophy community via the International Philosophy Olympiad (IPO-UNESCO). Alongside with it, she has been a part of multiple academic events and conferences as a co-organiser, and has been giving lectures and accommodated workshops on critical thinking and Analytical Philosophy.

Rosa E. Belvedresi
is currently Professor of Philosophy of History at Universidad Nacional de La Plata and a researcher at CONICET (Argentinean Council for Scientific Investigations). Her main academic interest is historical experience and its relationship to temporal consciousness, especially regarding the expectations of future.

Giovanna Costantini
is a teacher of English and English Speaking Countries Culture and Literatures in Rome. She graduated in Foreign Languages and Literatures in 2001 and in Science of Education in 2016. In 1998 and 2000, she had a leave for studies at the University of Miami and at Columbia University, for conducting her thesis research. She got a master's degree in Public Relations in 2002 and a master's degree in School Management and Administration in 2017 (Rome). In 2008, Costantini started teaching in Public Secondary schools, where she passed two teaching qualifications and a national competition. In 2014 and in 2016 she took part in the Food Conference and the Empathy Conference in Oxford (UK), organized by *Interdisciplinary-Net*. Her essay "Italian food: the Pride of a People without Borders" was published by Brill in the volume *Who Decides?* (2018). From 2014 to 2017 she cooperated with the University of International Studies in Rome as a subject matter expert and journal reviewer.

Ricardo Gutiérrez Aguilar
(MA in Philosophy, 2006; National Prize in Philosophy, 2008; MA in Teachers Training, 2008) is Assistant Professor and Researcher in Philosophy at the Logic and Theoretical Philosophy Department (Universidad Complutense de Madrid). He holds a PhD (2014) with an European Mention awarded by U.N.E.D. (Spain). He received the degree of Doktor der Philosophie from the Technische Universität zu Berlin (2014) as well. Pre-doctoral fellow at the *National Spanish Research Council* (C.S.I.C. – Instituto de Filosofía) under the tutorship of Prof. Dr. Roberto R. Aramayo (2007–2010), and a Marie Curie Early Stage Researcher at TU Berlin (Project ENGLOBE. Enlightenment and Global History – FP7-PEOPLE-238285)(2010–2013), Dr. Gutiérrez has focused his research interests mainly in Analytical Philosophy of History and Philosophy of Mind. Narratives and values encrypted in them – or the absence thereof – throughout the course of ordered events and actions and the subsequent critique of the historian's task with the help of ladden-institutional instruments centered his developments in those fields. Amongst Dr. Gutiérrez's most recent publications can be counted his *Virtud y Sistema. Juicio moral y filosofía de la Historia en Kant* [*Virtue and System. Moral Judgement and philosophy of History in Kant*] (Alamanda, 2018) and *Deuda y legado en la filosofía de la Historia de Schiller* [*Debt and Legacy in Schiller's philosophy of History*] (Herder, 2018). He is Member of the Editorial Board of *Con-textos Kantianos. International Journal of Philosophy* (WoS, SCOPUS International Journal) as well.

Irina Ionita
holds a PhD in Development Studies granted by the Graduate Institute of International and Development Studies in Geneva, Switzerland. She is currently working in Public Policy for elderly and Aging Programs, while specializing in Conflict Mediation.

Nina Lex
(Technische Universität Berlin), after finishing her studies in Philosophy, German Literature, and Art History, became a PhD candidate in the ITN-Marie Curie Fellowship Training Program (2010–2013). A former fellow of the DFH Scholarship, her work on a Theory of the Subject according to Jean-Jacques Rousseau profited from the exchange with a variety of research institutes, which included the Barnard College at the Columbia University in New York and the Instituto de Filosofía–CSIC in Madrid. She is a member of the IiAphR (Internationaler, interdisziplinärer Arbeitskreis für philosophische Reflexion) while her philosophical focus has meanwhile extended to work at the interface of philosophical theory, discursive practice and performative arts.

Gerardo López Sastre
is Professor of Philosophy at the Faculty of Humanities of Toledo, University of Castilla-La Mancha, Spain. He studied Philosophy at the Complutense University of Madrid and also completed his PhD there. He translated into Spanish the *Enquiry concerning the principles of Morals*, by David Hume (2007), the *Three Dialogues between Hylas and Filonus*, by Berkeley (1996), and the *Three Essays on Religion*, by John Stuart Mill (2014). He is the editor of the volume *David Hume. Nuevas perspectivas sobre su obra* (2005); and coedited the volumes *Cosmopolitismo y nacionalismo. De la Ilustración al mundo contemporáneo* (2010), and *Civilizados y salvajes. La mirada de los ilustrados sobre el mundo no europeo* (2016). His latest publications are the books *Hume. Cuándo saber ser escéptico* (2015), and *John Stuart Mill. El utilitarismo que cambiaría el mundo* (2017).

Barış Mete
is an Assistant Professor in the English Language and Literature Department of *Selçuk University* (Turkey) where he has been teaching Comparative Short Story, Contemporary British Novel and Literary Criticism. He had his BA in English Language and Literature and his MA in English Literature from Hacettepe University. He completed his PhD at the Middle East Technical University, again in English Literature. He has written articles on the twentieth-century British novel, particularly the works of John Fowles and Iris Murdoch and is now finishing a book on the Mimetic Theory of Art.

Paulus Pimomo
is Professor of English at Central Washington University (Ellensburg, USA). He was educated in northeast India and the USA, and has taught in both countries. He teaches Colonial/Postcolonial Studies, World Literature Theory, African American Literature and American Multicutural Literatures. His publications are in diverse fields, including on postcolonial studies (*Critical Quarterly*, UK, *Journal of Commonwealth and Postcolonial Studies*, USA), Literature, Empathy and Crises Studies (*Inter-Disciplinary Press*, UK), Indo/Naga Politics and Naga Cultural Studies (*Economic & Political Weekly* and others in India), and three English usage dictionaries for Japanese learners of English as second language, with Hidemi Masamura (Taishukan & Shogakukan, Japan).

Johannes Rohbeck
studied Philosophy and Political Science at the University of Bonn and at Freie Universität Berlin. Doctor in 1976, Prof. Rohbeck got his Habilitation (postdoctoral degree with lecture qualification) in Philosophy in 1985. From 1993 till 2012

held a position as Professor for Practical Philosopy and Didactics of Philosophy at Technische Universität Dresden. Between 2012 and 2018, Prof. Rohbeck held a Senior Professorship at this University. In the academic year 2018/19 he was Invited Professor at Universidad Carlos III Madrid (UC3M). Amongst his books published, *Egoismus und Sympathie* (1978), *Die Fortschrittstheorie der Aufklärung* (1987), *Technologische Urteilskraft* (1993), *Technik – Kultur – Geschichte* (2000), *Geschichtsphilosophie zur Einführung* (2004), *Marx* (2006), *Aufklärung und Geschichte* (2010), and *Zukunft der Geschichte* (2013) are of special relevance.

Judy Rollins
PhD, RN, President of Rollins & Associates research and consulting; Adjunct Assistant Professor in the Department of Family Medicine with a secondary appointment in the Department of Pediatrics at Georgetown University School of Medicine, Washington, DC; and Adjunct Lecturer at the Center for Arts in Medicine at the University of Florida, Gainesville, Florida. She is a nurse with a fine arts degree in Visual Arts, a master's in Child Development/Family Studies, and a PhD in Health and Community Studies. She has developed arts in healthcare programming in hospitals, hospice care, and the community, including Studio G, the artists in residence program in pediatrics at MedStar Georgetown University Hospital. Her writing and research interests include arts in healthcare, family-centered care, and psychosocial issues of care, with a focus on children with cancer. She is editor of *Meeting Children's Psychosocial Needs Across the Health-care Continuum*, now in its second edition; editor of *Pediatric Nursing*; North America regional editor of *Arts & Health*; and a Scholar at the Institute for Integrative Health, Baltimore, MD.

Josefa Ros Velasco
is Teaching Assistant and RCC Postdoctoral Fellow in the Department of Romance Languages and Literatures at Harvard University. She is conducting a multidisciplinary research on the evolutionary role of boredom from a philosophical-anthropological point of view to argue against the widespread understanding of boredom as a pathological personality trait whereby medicalization of such a common, daily annoyance is legitimized. As part of this approach, she is examining how the comprehension of boredom in terms of a mental disease has gradually formed historically as a result of the act of taking at face value the metaphor of boredom as an illness, especially represented in nineteenth-century Western literature and philosophy. Dr. Ros Velasco holds a PhD in Philosophy with International Mention at the Excellent Program of Doctorate in Philosophy at Universidad Complutense de Madrid (UCM) as an FPU scholar; MA in Contemporary Thought; and MA in Teachers Training. She

was visiting researcher at Zentrum für Kultur und Technikforschung at Stuttgart Universität (Germany) as a Deutscher Akademischer Austauschdienst scholar, and at the Deutsches Literatur-Archiv Marbach as a DLA and MECD fellow. She is a member of the research groups Saavedra Fajardo Library for Hispanic Political Thought at UCM; *History and Videogames* at the University of Murcia; and History and Philosophy of Emotions at CCHS-CSIC. She is the editor or author of the books *Feminism. Past, Present, and Future Perspectives* (Nova, 2017), *Contemporary Approaches in Philosophical and Humanistic Thought* (Aracne, 2017), and *Hans Blumenberg. Literatura, estética y nihilismo* (Trotta, 2016), and of academic papers such as "Hans Blumenbergs' Philosophical Anthropology of Boredom" (Karl Aber, 2018), "Boredom: humanizing or dehumanizing treatment" (Vernon, 2018), and "Boredom: A Comprehensive Study of the State of Affairs" (*Themata*, 2017). She is currently working in her next books: *La enfermedad del aburrimiento* (2019), *Boredom is in your mind* (Springer, 2019), *The Culture of Boredom* (Brill, 2019), and *The Faces of Depression in Literature* (Peter Lang, 2019).

Christopher J. Staley
is a PhD student in Theatre and Performance Studies at the University of Pittsburgh (USA). MFA in Acting from the American Repertory Theatre/Moscow Art Theatre Institute for Advanced Theatre Training at Harvard University; BS in Theatre and Psychology from Skidmore College. Research interests include the intersections of performance studies, cognitive science, and existential psychology. Chris has presented "Lorca's Corpses and their Mothers: Death and the Maternal in the Rural Tragedies" for the Kristeva Circle 2017 Conference, and "Demonstrating the Actor's Process: Empathic Projection in Sophocles' *Ajax*" for the University of Pittsburgh Department of Classics Conference on "Empathy, Sympathy, and Compassion: The Dynamics of Other-Oriented Emotions." As a theatre practitioner, he has performed at the American Repertory Theater, Indiana Repertory Theater, Moscow Art Theatre, Opera Carolina, and others. Training includes SITI Company intensives at Skidmore College, a summer intensive with the Suzuki Company of Toga in Japan, and participation with the Watermill Center International Summer Program. Chris is an acting teacher, director, and avid yoga instructor.

CHAPTER 1

Introduction: The Joyful *Páthos* from Oxford

Ricardo Gutiérrez Aguilar

> There is a problem here. But it is not so much a problem for my account of the appreciation of works of fiction as one for theories of emotion. What are admiration and pity? Believing that someone is admirable or that she suffers misfortune is not *sufficient* for admiring or pitying her (whether or not it is necessary); one can hold such beliefs without experiencing the emotion. Perhaps the emotions involve mere dispositions to feel in certain ways, or dispositions to react in certain ways to certain stimuli, dispositions of which one may or may not be aware [...] Whatever it is that combines with the appropriate belief to constitute the emotion (in those instances in which such a belief is involved), I suggest that some such state or condition, or one that is naturally taken [...] keep[s] our conception of quasi emotion flexible enough to accommodate any reasonable theory of emotion.
>
> WALTON, KENDALL L., *Mimesis as Make-Believe*[1]

∴

Looking back, it could be said that we've come a long way since July 2016. On a hazy, English summer afternoon, this present editorial project came about under such special circumstances to attend to that emotion we usually call 'empathy' – a theme apparently not fit for table talk. Moreover, empathy is sometimes – for unfathomable reasons – a surprisingly evasive emotion. It is indeed a problem open to discussion. It can be particularly problematic since, for one thing, it is in appearance the emotion responsible for stitching together a shared experience with our common fellow. It is the emotion essential to

---

1 Walton, Kendall L., "Psychological Participation", in *Mimesis as Make-Believe: On the Foundations of Representational Arts* (Cambridge-MA-London: Harvard University Press, 1990), 251–252.

bridging the gap between subjects – to making a community. We do not *naturally* live (nor want to live) alone: we do not want to take that state or condition as natural; not in the flesh; not even lost in our thoughts. This familiar and demanding condition is so fundamental that it poses a threat to perspective – perhaps even more so than when the haze in Oxford is so thick. But we do not want to take it for granted – that natural state which is already trivialised – and we do not want to think alone.

Thus, when this collective work was initially conceived in that faraway conference room, its future could not fully be projected. It has since evolved into the challenge to compile some of the proposed answers that had their origins there in 2016, but that are today in 2019 by all means actualised to the utmost extent – so much so that we dare to commit them to writing. They remain, though, answers that have their place of reference in the welcoming chambers of *Mansfield College*, at the University of Oxford (UK). *The Empathy Project* (an interdisciplinary academic initiative promoted by Dr Robert Fisher, founder of its network) held its third Global Meeting within the premises of *ye olde* constituent college at Mansfield Road from Thursday 14th to Saturday 16th of July 2016.[2] Hosted by Susan Fairbarn in the role of the Conference Leader, around 40 scholars hailing from the most distant corners of the world shared on those days their good measure of the very condition being studied. We spoke *about, on,* and *with* emotion – and we did it with joy. Whether having landed from Australia, India, Turkey, the U.S.A., or from so many of the places interconnected by the familiar paths that intimately unite our Europe (from Germany, Greece, Ireland, Italy, Spain, etc.), the attendees proffered both facts and intuitions, dedicating those three days to thoroughly rounding out the so-called 'problem' of the elusive emotion of empathy. Each of us gave her/his 'pound of insights'. Whether scattered and drinking coffee under the shelter of the hall in The Tower, or gathered dining and chatting in The Chapel, we strove to highlight what is otherwise clearly evident. While we of course sought each to advance our best hypotheses on the subject as well, we also looked for the common ground between both the results of our

---

[2] The project was ambitious in its aims. It consisted of a wide variety of academic interests around the idea and concept of 'otherness' that were not limited to 'empathy-questioning'. Emotion was augmented by the problematisation of rights and feeling. The third Global Meeting on Empathy was just one of three parallel academic initiatives conducted by the *Inter-Disciplinary.Net* (*IDNet*) in Oxford that comprised the 7th Global Conference on *Strangers, Aliens and Foreigners: A Cultures, Traditions, Societies Project*, and the 1st Global Meeting on Torture. (We, as 'others', are eminently and in the first place beings capable of sensation: *sentient beings*.)

conducted research and our experiences: Digital Media ideas on the subject worked just fine elbow to elbow with those proposed by fields like Nursing or Health and Social Care; and Psychiatry, Psychology and Philosophy got along quite well with the lines of inquiry of Education, Literature and Dramatic Performance, for example. As if collectively taking on the shape of a prism, all contributions officiated like facets of the same body – a delineated space not void, but rather full – and encompassed ever more suitable signs, symbols and expressions to incarnate the concept being pursued. Lastly, we intended to come back home if not having found the intellectual consensus on our 'empathetic' concerns, then at least *having been found* – having coincided at the crossroads of *páthos*, of affect and being affected – by others' speeches and personalities.

This book is in some way none other than the written emblem – perhaps a true milestone, or at the very least a meaningful souvenir – commemorating that at once now-distant and still-near success.[3]

Sympathy, Empathy and Their Ilk

'Empathy' threatened (and whenever it reaches out to connect with someone, still threatens) to be a term too close to the chest to be properly grasped by plain, cold-blooded, intellectual articulations, but which is nevertheless too fundamental to dismiss as a mere functional tool that can be substituted by others of equal value. For example, consider the case made by our moral judgments. They count on empathy in order to praise or blame, to call out liars and hypocrites – and we certainly do judge morally on a daily basis.

Empathy is thus central, ultimately, to our judgments of others. But as Walton says, believing that someone is admirable (praiseworthy) or that he/she is suffering misfortune (pitiable) is not sufficient for admiring or pitying him/her; whether or not it is necessary to in fact have that belief, that certitude – to have that feeling. This latter can be a 'necessary condition' to a praxis, but it is not the only one. To praise or to pity are actions undoubtedly in need of the subjective certitude of the feeling – the alleged motivational drive. You cannot use the term and refer to the practice without incorporating the subjective state

---

[3] A mention is needed to those that helped in the first stages of this editorial project: first, to Sean Moran in Oxford; after Oxford, due mention to Lisa Howard, whose invaluable assistance cannot be highlighted enough; and last but not least – before Oxford – to Ioana Cartarescu, who as Coordinating Assistant circumnavigated the necessary bureaucracies that finally made possible all of us gathering in England.

of 'feeling pity', nor 'praise someone' without admiring him/her – otherwise what you really practice is 'being an hypocrite', i.e. you are a user of the practice of 'hypocrisy'. They are complex devices (if we are allowed to call a concept a device), however – we have them in layers. The feeling accompanying the judgment, constituting it, is just one of those layers. They are complex states and conditions in which whatever it is that combines with the feeling to constitute the emotion has to accommodate *a reasonable theory for its applicability*. 'Reasonability' is the key here. It is a term usually attached to judicial vocabulary, close to 'warrant'. Here, closer to 'theory', the term presents discursive reasons as a type of justification. It is not sufficient on its own – but it does work as a criterion. In fact, such a component is central to empathy to so deep an extent as to demand the kind of public justification we have strived to achieve in each navigation around the concept. For it is here that 'sympathy' and 'empathy' part ways. Their proximity has always been a matter of theoretical concern. Here we should blatantly differentiate the foundations of an idea of empathy that severs it from its closest acquaintance, sympathy – and a good part of current discussions on the topic is intended to clarify once and for all both terms on the basis of that categorical difference. Professor Linda Zagzebski can help us at this point to better articulate it:

> The class of moral judgments I want to focus on are what I call *ground level moral judgments*. These judgments can be identified by two important features. First, they are "here and now" judgments. That is, they are made in a context in which the person making the judgment is confronted with the object [another person] of the judgment. Second, they utilize what I call "thick affective concepts." These concepts mostly coincide with what Bernard Williams calls "thick evaluative concepts." Examples of ground level judgments include, "She is pitiful," "He is contemptible," "That remark is rude," [...][They] combine descriptive and evaluative aspects in a way that cannot be pulled apart [...][They] have both cognitive and affective aspects that cannot be pulled apart.[4]

Investigating these judgments is the domain of praxis. Appreciating emotion has to do with the ability and practice of being sensitive to the vicarious experience of personal states that are capable of founding and making possible the recognition of another human being as a subject of special rights: the right

---

4 Zagzebski, Linda, "Emotion and Moral Judgment", in *Philosophy and Phenomenological Research*, vol. 66, no. 1 (2003): 108–109. My italics. In this passage, Zagzebski references Williams, Bernard, *Ethics and the Limits of Philosophy* (London: Harvard University Press, 1985.)

to be appraised, the right to be defended from contempt or harm or humiliation – but all of this goes beyond the mere concept of a subjective state. The justification needs to be public in the sense a dialogue would entail. Furthermore, these cognitive judgment criteria are independent of time and space. We can be empathetic with fictions and protagonists of the past, 'here and now'. We can recognize them. Public justification is meant to work like a two-way warrant. It is a sort of credential, a safeguard. The justification – the reason(s) – is a word shared communally. The Greek word *dialogue* [διάλογος] exposes its inner meaning quite well: symmetrically, the word that parts the speakers is the same that connects them. It is like a rope that links the parties holding it, even as they perhaps pull in different directions. At its ends, two or more speakers tread on common ground and pledge to respect each other. They are separated and united by reasons, by words shared. But reasons must be transparent to this end; they must go public to work in this manner. It is an openness of the criteria to judge others worthy of the empathic motions of feelings. Emotions are nothing but articulated systems. They substantiate a 'reasonable theory' by virtue of which the appellative function of language motions, by means of which an imaginative projection leading to objectivity is made:

> In the fields of developmental psychology and socialization research, it has long been agreed that the emergence of children's abilities to think and interact must be conceived as a process that occurs *in the act of taking over another person's perspective* [...] [T]aking up this person's view and steering it toward certain significant objects, is interpreted by these theories to be an indication of a phase of experimentation in which a child tests out the independence of another perspective on the surrounding world.[5]

'To think' has to do with 'to interact'. The child tests out his/her own judgments in the confrontation with the 'possible Other'. Empathy, as we shall see in the forthcoming pages, assumes then a theory of reference in which that very reference as an individual is bestowed with personality by means of a 'charitable act' (as Donald Davidson would say), but an act to which (in reverse) the charitable person is afterwards committed. An act based on the concept of a 'duty-right'.

---

5   Honneth, Axel, *Reification: A New Look at an Old Idea*, edited and introduced by Martin Jay (Oxford-New York: Oxford University Press, 2008), 41.

In what follows, the contributors to this volume will surely enlighten the 'naturally taken' and 'personally given' character of such a miracle.

Madrid
21 November 2018

Bibliography

Honneth, Axel, *Reification: A New Look at an Old Idea*, edited and introduced by Martin Jay (Oxford-New York: Oxford University Press, 2008).

Walton, Kendall L., *Mimesis as Make-Believe: On the Foundations of Representational Arts* (Cambridge-MA-London: Harvard University Press, 1990).

Williams, Bernard, *Ethics and the Limits of Philosophy* (London: Harvard University Press, 1985).

Zagzebski, Linda, "Emotion and Moral Judgment", in *Philosophy and Phenomenological Research*, vol. 66, no. 1 (2003): 104–124.

CHAPTER 2

In Search of Empathy in Prehistoric Times: Evolution and Revolution

Josefa Ros Velasco

Abstract

Empathy is normally defined as the psychological identification with the feelings, thoughts or attitudes of another. Stated differently, empathy is the ability to understand what another person is experiencing and put oneself in someone else's position. This contribution attempts to be a reflection on the evolutionary and 'revolutionary' role of empathy in human evolution by paying attention to the conditions of possibility and the presence of empathic behaviours in pre-*sapiens*' prehistory. On the basis of the knowledge provided by specialists in multiple disciplines such as neuropaleontology, prehistoric ethnology, psychology and philosophical anthropology, we will first establish how different levels of empathy were possible in our ancestors as cognitive and social complexity was gradually developed over time and which factors were responsible for and made possible our current ability to empathise. Following from the above, we will address the understanding of the biological and sociological evolutionary function of empathy, that is to say, what was – or/and is – the role of empathy in the evolution towards the species *Homo sapiens*. The aim of this exercise is not only to get to know more about the nature of empathy and its anthropogenesis but to show that the role of empathy in our global time remains the same in evolutionary terms, i.e., to promote both the mutual understanding and cooperation necessary for the prosperity of peoples and the realisation of private interests.

Keywords

anthropogenesis – consciousness – empathy – *Homo sapiens* – human evolution – language – paleoneurobiology – philosophical anthropology – prehistory – pre-*sapiens* – proto-culture – theory of mind

> I was experiencing empathy and wondering how other people feel and what they're suffering. I never wanted to feel empathy. It's a lot easier to feel alienated. It's easier to be mechanical. It's a challenge for me to try to be human.
>
> BRIAN HUGH WARNER, *Marilyn Manson*[1]

∴

1   Preparations for the Journey to Prehistoric Empathy

Messinian Age, 7 Ma, our relative Toumaï (*Sahelanthropus tchadensis*) walks along the marshy areas of the current Djurab Desert, Chad. Nomad, semi-bipedal brachiator, of simian appearance … Was the TM 266-01-0606-1 able to empathise? And, if so, for what purpose/s? Could this distant ancestor feel empathy with his peers or even species other than his own?

Not all species are able to empathise or to reach the same level of empathy. It is not the same to perceive the physical (*somatic empathy*) or emotional states of others by *contagion* as to identify with them (*sympathetic concern*), to consciously attend to them (*emotional empathy*), to intentionally put oneself in their shoes (*cognitive empathy/perspective-taking*) or to deliberately use empathy for own benefit (*Machiavellian intelligence*).[2] The matter becomes increasingly complicated when we talk about empathy among species.[3] Moreover, even if empathy is possible, it may serve different biological and social purposes in evolutionary terms: from maintaining durable relationships and inhibit aggression to anticipate others' behaviours and avoid cheating. Empathy seems to be part of the life of many species for many reasons. What was/were the case/s of our ancestors? And how can we know about that?

Research in recent years has focused on possible brain, genetic and hormonal processes underlying the experience of empathy[4] and has proved that

---

1 Ashare, Matt, "Omega Man", in *CMJ New Music Monthly*, no. 64 (1998): 58.
2 Smith, Adam, "Cognitive Empathy and Emotional Empathy in Human Behavior and Evolution", in *The Psychological Record*, vol. 56, no. 1 (2006): 3–21.
3 Bradshaw, John W. S. and Paul, Elizabeth S., "Could Empathy for Animals have been an Adaptation in the Evolution of Homo sapiens?", in *Animal Welfare*, vol. 19, no. 2 (2010): 107–112.
4 Decety, Jean, "The Neuroevolution of Empathy", in *Annals of the New York Academy of Science*, vol. 1231, no. 1 (2011): 35–45; Decety, Jean, *et al.*, "A Neurobehavioral Evolutionary Perspective on the Mechanisms underlying Empathy", in *Progress in Neurobiology*, vol. 98, no. 1 (2012): 38–48.

observing others' states activates some parts of the neuronal network involved in processing such states in oneself.[5] In this regard, fMRI has been employed to investigate the *anatomy* of empathy. However, fMRI is not so useful to understand 'the brains of the past' since they do not fossilise and have to be reproduced by using MRI and PET. Much of this information helps us to know, by comparing past brains with current ones, if our predecessors' brain anatomy were ready for empathy.

Neuropaleontology is just a first stop on the journey to the search for empathy in our ancestors. Thanks to this discipline we know emotional empathy had an earlier phylogenetic origin than cognitive empathy. Even so, it has important limitations. To determine emotional intelligence, so necessary in the evolution of empathy, we need to pay attention to other sources of information: We have to 'see' and 'hear' what our relatives could do, i.e., to make general inferences on the basis of overall archaeological records.[6] Does empathy leave any archaeological trace? Of course, it does. We can search them, for example, on the correlate of their social life: from types of settlements to cave paintings.

Yet, we have to take the leap from physical evidence to plausible reasoning. The question of empathy in prehistoric times does not admit only one, definitive answer. It is perfectly legitimate to offer perspectives, on the basis of our present knowledge, and establish probable connections, dealing with various interpretations at the same time. To reach a meaningful understanding of this topic we can rely on speculations, narrations and other plausible constructions, as long as they do not contradict what the science has proven.[7] This being so, to get to *what could be* when little evidence is available we need our common sense and to empathise with our predecessors. We will play with all these tools to trace the presence and evolution of empathy in pre-*sapiens* and *sapiens*' prehistory. If we agree with the statements of our methodology, i.e., the principle of insufficient reason, then and only then will we be ready to progress through this journey.

Before doing that, let me record that we will work with the slightly modified definition of empathy by de Waal and Preston, as a form of intersubjectivity in

---

5 Lamm, Claus; Batson, Daniel and Decety, Jean, "The Neural Substrate of Human Empathy: Effects of Perspective-taking and Cognitive Appraisal", in *Journal of Cognitive Neuroscience*, vol. 19, no. 1 (2007): 42–58.

6 Holloway, Ralph, "Evidence for POT Expansion in early Homo: a Pretty Theory with Ugly (or no) Paleoneurological Facts", in *Behavioral and Brain Sciences*, no. 18 (1995): 191–193.

7 *vid.* Kant AA VIII: 109. Critical Edition of Kant's works is quoted according to the *Akademische Ausgabe* by volume (8) and page (109). Indications to authors in this sense are online in *Kant Forschungsstelle* (Mainz Universität, http://www.kant-gesellschaft.de/de/ks/Hinweise_Autoren_2018.pdf. Viewed on the 18th November 2018).

which the observer participates in the feelings of the other at different degrees as a result of a combination of evolutionary ancient emotional responses and more recent anatomical and neurological innovations unique to primates and highly refined in human beings.[8] Among the many levels of empathy and processes associated to it,[9] we will focus on the 'road' from the 'bottom-up' (contagion to Machiavellian intelligence) to draw the evolution of this ability. We will pay attention firstly to the most ancient phylogenetically empathic states to move towards more complex forms of empathy that also include the former, rudimentary levels of empathy – take in mind the image of a Russian doll.[10]

2   Reading the Signs of Empathy

From Contagion to Emotional Empathy in Pre-Homo Species

The abovementioned ethnologist and biologist, de Waal, claimed that human beings, apes, elephants and dolphins were the most capable species for high degrees of empathy.[11] However, many other species can experience more primitive levels of empathy related to emotional contagion (same state as a result of observing other's state), sympathy (sorry and care for) or emotional empathy (attended, conscious perception of others' states). If Toumaï was on the borderline between apes and humans it is reasonable to think that he experienced some degree of empathy with other apes, and even with those monkeys with which he had shared so much, so long ago. But which one?

Much depends on his little brain. It was only 350 cm^3, similar to that of modern chimpanzees. Despite its size, Toumaï's brain showed clear allometric trends in the white matter[12] translated into cerebral specialisations.[13] His brain concentrated high levels of cerebral tissue in its frontal lobes. Although little

---

8   Preston, Stephanie D. and De Waal, Frans, B. M., "The Communication of Emotions and the Possibility of Empathy in Animals", in *Altruistic love: Science, Philosophy, and Religion in Dialogue*, edited by Stephen G. Post, *et al.* (Oxford: Oxford University Press, 2002), 284–308.

9   *vid.* Table 2 in Preston and De Waal, "Empathy", 3.

10 De Waal, Frans B. M., "Putting the Altruism Back into Altruism: the Evolution of Empathy", in *Annual Review of Psychology*, no. 59 (2008): 279.

11 De Waal, Frans B. M., *The Age of Empathy: Nature's Lessons for a Kinder Society* (New York: Harmony Books, 2009).

12 Arsuaga, Juan L. and Martínez Mendizábal, Ignacio, *Chosen Species: The Long March of Human Evolution* (Marblehead: Wiley & Sons, 2011).

13 Arsuaga, Juan L. and Martín-Loeches, Manuel, *El sello indeleble. Pasado, presente y futuro del ser humano* (Barcelona: Random House, 2013).

or nothing is known about the impact those modifications had on this specimen in terms of empathy, it has been widely recognised that all these changes were decisive for Toumaï to go from emotional contagion to some degree of sympathy.

A brain capable of withstanding the heavyweight of further emotional empathic behaviours must be equipped with a complex network of cells whose activity enables high levels of consciousness and *recursion* or *intentionality* – at least a second level to be able to pay attention to the own perception of others' states. Not to talk of cognitive empathy, which requires a Theory of Mind (mind-reading capacity) to interpret the intention of others and predict their behaviours.[14] This is not exactly the case of Toumaï. He could have a minimum degree of recursion that together with the possibility of possessing VEN s[15] puts us on the track that this ancestor was somewhat empathic by contagion or sympathy. *Sahelanthropus tchadensis*' brain was prepared for social complexity and rapid computation of social information. He had a minimal degree of self-consciousness, a capacity for causal inferences, a certain degree of social inhibition and kind of social specialisation.[16] Despite being able to show some signs of empathy, this specimen would neither have shown a fully fledged ToM nor self-consciousness. What about his successors?

Much has been said about the possibility that the following hominid in the line is *Orrorin tugenensis* (6,1-5,7 Ma). The *Millenium ancestor* must be like their very predecessors. However, the fact that no single piece of the skull has been found makes it difficult to speculate about their brain ability, perhaps a little bit more evolved than Toumaï's one, as well as their capacity for empathy. Besides that, Orrorin is thought to be a potential ancestor of *Ardipithecus kadabba* (5,8 Ma), a relative about whom much more can be said.

A comparison between *kadabba*'s skulls and those from their ancestors reveals that their brain underwent changes. All the same, such physiological changes could not result in a more empathic creature on their own. Nevertheless, paleontologists explain that this specimen had a quite stable life in small groups in which their members did not have too many conflicts but cooperated

---

14   Seyfarth, Robert M. and Chaney, Dorothy L., "Affiliation, Empathy, and the Origins of Theory of Mind", in *Proceedings of the National Academy of Sciences*, vol. 110, no. 2 (2013): 10349–10356; Dunbar, Robin, *Gossip, Grooming and the Evolution of Language* (Cambridge: Harvard University Press, 1998).

15   Allman, John, *et al.*, "The von Economo Neurons in Frontoinsular and Anterior Cingulate Cortex in Great Apes and Humans", in *Brain Structure and Function*, no. 214 (2010): 495–517.

16   Arsuaga and Martín-Loeches, *El sello indeleble*, 210.

with each other.[17] In this sense, according to the statement that they had a glimmer of proto-culture, maybe a higher level of empathy was responsible for promoting cooperation instead of confrontation.

Kadabba's immediate successor, *Ardipithecus ramidus* (4,4 Ma), was also described as 'relatively peaceful.'[18] But, besides that, *Ardi* was a faster learner. The HAR1F gene, responsible for brain development during pregnancy and formation of new synaptic connections during adulthood, was promoting an accelerated evolution. Additionally, the CaMK2 gene, related to synaptic plasticity and transmission, began to get more presence in their brains.[19] This all contributed to the expansion of the neocortex over time to an extent that Ardi's congeners were capable for an emerging, incipient proto-language of gestures, vocalisations and facial expressions to communicate needs and intentions.[20] It seems quite obvious that the act of wanting to make themselves understandable each other responds to a process of becoming more empathic – we may call this *empathisation* and the result would be the *Homo empathicus narrativus*.[21]

A higher capacity for socialisation and empathy would be yet to come after Ardi, i.e. in australopithecine species. First specimens of *Australopithecus*, named *anamensis*, lived a 'stable'[22] life 4,2 Ma, partly as a result of the changes in their environment, partly due to the growing complexity of their brains. Occasional scavenging involved the acquisition of DHA that promoted the internal expansion of the cerebral cortex in our 500 cm^3-brain-size relatives.[23] Despite having a brain like a chimpanzee, in terms of size, it was significantly restructured: The frontal lobes became more complex morphologically, the parietal association areas increased[24] and Broca's and Wernicke's areas,

---

17   Arsuaga, Juan L. and Martínez Mendizábal, Ignacio, *Atapuerca y la evolución humana* (Barcelona: Fundación Caixa Cataluña, 2004).

18   De Waal, Frans B. M., "The Antiquity of Empathy", in *Science*, no. 336 (2012): 874.

19   Agustí, Jordi; Bufill, Soler Enric and Mosquera Martínez, Marina, *El precio de la inteligencia: La evolución de la mente humana y sus consecuencias* (Barcelona: Crítica, 2012).

20   Ros Velasco, Josefa, "The Evolution of Language: An Anthropological Approach. Language in Prehistory", in *Evolutionary Anthropology*, vol. 25, no. 2 (2016): 79–80.

21   Coulehan, Jack, "Empathy and Narrativity: A Commentary on 'Origins of Healing: An Evolutionary Perspective of the Healing Process'", in *Families, Systems, & Health*, vol. 23, no. 3 (2005): 261–265. Before a proto-language had come into play, another common, social practice betrayed an empathic behavior, the act of *grooming* that served to enhance friendship, loyalty and societal cohesion. *vid.* Dunbar, *Gossip*.

22   Arsuaga, Juan L., *El primer viaje de nuestra vida* (Madrid: Planeta, 2012).

23   Gazzaniga, Michael, *Human: The Science Behind What Makes Us Unique* (New York: Harper, 2009).

24   Agustí, Bufill Soler and Mosquera Martínez, *El precio de la inteligencia*.

responsible for manual control and language, were developed.[25] The recipients of these changes would be those species closer to the *Homos* such as *bahrelghazali* (4 Ma), *afarensis* (e.g. *Lucy*, 3,9 Ma), *deyiremeda* (3,3 Ma), *africanus* (e.g. *Taung child*, 3 Ma), *garhi* (2,5 Ma) or *sediba* (2 Ma). Surely, the latest *Australopithecus* had some level of operational intelligence and were self-aware to the extent of recognising their own bodies, cravings and moods, enabling more intricate emotional empathic behaviours.

This is perhaps the reason why, at this point, *pre-humans* began helping each other in food transportation,[26] in giving birth[27] and started to reciprocally exchange their foodstuff[28] after 'gender-based division of labour'[29] took place. Related males gathered with a small female harem to feed, sleep and move around to make life easier for these mothers by sporadically assisting them in caretaking.[30] Not just that, specific social caring interactions were attributed, even still in initial stages, to grandmothers.[31]

These all were signs of a growing empathic ability to understand the needs of others and how assisting in such requirements could help their own performance and subsistence. Almost on the verge of the leap forward *Homo* species, our ancestors were able to think of themselves as a *self*, knowing the difference between their *self* and the *others' selves*. Soundly, we cannot assume they were able to realise that others selves were aware of the same fact. The australopithecine proto-culture heirs marked the commencement of *Homo* species' evolution 2,4 Ma with a great ability to empathise beyond emotional empathy.

Cognitive Empathy in Homo *Species*

The Stone Age began with the advent of the first *Homos* that exceeded the limitations of *Australopithecus*: *Homo rudolfensis* and *Homo habilis*. The *handyman* had a brain truly similar to that of their predecessors, 510–600 cm³ (KNM-ER 1813 and OH 24/*Twiggy*, respectively). The greatest difference is in

---

25 Arsuaga and Martínez Mendizábal, *Chosen Species*.
26 *Ibid.*
27 Fischman, Joshua, "Putting a New Spin on the Birth of Human Birth", in *Science*, no. 264 (1994): 1082–1083.
28 Roth, Gerhard and Dicke, Ursula, "Evolution of the Brain and Intelligence", in *Trends in Cognitive Sciences*, vol. 9, no. 5 (2005): 250–257.
29 Blumenberg, Hans, "Biotopwechsel, aufrechter Gang, generatives Verhalten", *Deutsches Literatur Archiv (DLA)*, 03: 023868.
30 Arsuaga and Martínez Mendizábal, *Chosen Species*.
31 Roth and Dicke, "Evolution of the Brain and Intelligence."

rudolfensis' 800 cm³-brain size.³² *Rudolfensis* underwent aggressive *encephalisation*, as the specimen KNM-ER 1470 shows, resulting in a greater brain complexity internally ('wiring') and externally (brain matter). In *rudolfensis*, genes regulating the number of brain cells and their connections, named MCPH1, developed strongly.³³ This species had a greater amount of nerve tissue beyond what was necessary for the very survival. Consequently, their capacity for abstract thinking made possible empathise in a closer level to ours. They had a knack for looking the others as *others selves* and understanding the reciprocity of this act and its implications by being attentive to their own thought.

This, of course, affected their daily performance. It is known that *rudolfensis* was more inclined towards scavenging.³⁴ Females spent their time looking after the children, whose infancy was longer than that of *Australopithecus*,³⁵ with the help of the oldest relatives and also males when freed from the sporadic hunting task.³⁶ *Rudolfensis* was more flexible with regard to their own behaviour and that of others: they were more adjustable and creative in successfully tackling their environment and proto-society.

The last African *rudolfensis* had evolved, biologically and socially, to the extent that it is necessary to use another nomenclature for 1,9 Ma specimens: *Homo ergasters*, quite often also called *Homo erectus* as their Asian 'cousins' or African *Homo erectus*.³⁷ Firstly named *Telanthropus capensis* and then known for the 11–12 years-old *Turkana Boy* (also *Nariokotome Child* or KNM-WT 15000), *ergaster* had superior cognitive abilities in comparison with their ancestors. This species lived in a very unstable world and required great care to survive. Firstly, the latest *ergasters* developed such a brain size into the uterus that mothers had to give birth before their children's brains were fully formed for foetuses' head to be able to cross the birth canal.³⁸ They were born

---

32 Lieberman, Daniel E.; Wood, Bernard A. and Pilbeam, David R., "Homoplasy and Early Homo: an Analysis of the Evolutionary Relationships of H. habilis sensu stricto and H. rudolfensis", in *Journal of Human Evolution*, no. 30 (1996): 97–120.

33 Gazzaniga, *Human*.

34 Carbonell, Eudald, *Las primeras ocupaciones de los continentes* (Barcelona: Ariel, 2005).

35 Locke, John L. and Bogin, Barry, "Language and Life History: A new Perspective on the Development and Evolution of Human Language", in *Behavioral and Brain Science*, no. 29 (2006): 259–325.

36 Carbonell, *Las primeras ocupaciones*.

37 *Ibid.* Some *rudolfensis* moved out of Africa and settled in various parts of Asia 1,8 Ma. They evolved into the species *Homo erectus*. Others came back to Africa after a long time and many others never went out. They were those who led to the subsequent populations towards *sapiens*.

38 Arsuaga, *El primer viaje*.

absolutely dependent. That means a higher development of the intelligence but also a need for more care time. Secondly, the *working man*'s childhood was close to ours in terms of outbreak and length – proportionally to their life expectancy of 40.[39] Premature birth and prolonged infancy prompted cognitive and social changes translated into smarter individuals and more protective social environments.

It is also important the way in which such a care Took place. The majority of a group of 20 members were caregivers. Hunting forced them to maintain a life of nomadism, but bit by bit the settlements would be longer-lasting.[40] Females remained in them taking care of their children, together with those unfit for hunting – still too young, already too old, the wounded, the sick.[41] Males went out, looking for meat and staying overnight in caves when the preys were far from *home*. Division of labour and seasonal hunting of large animals had much to do with both female and male empathy, but also other factors did such as, for example, the use of fire and its promotion of socialisation.[42]

Sitting around it the day was longer, with more hours to be awake and interact, in longer summers. At night, a controlled fire would become the meeting place for telling stories responsible for transmitting experiences and knowledge;[43] since this species probably speak some kind of proto-language![44] Language is essential to talk about complex levels of empathy[45] as to speak to a peer it is necessary to understand and feel the same they are understanding and feeling.[46] According to Dunbar, communication helped to create a sense of emotional and cognitive solidarity among the members of the 'clan', giving cohesion and coherence to it, maintaining alliances strong, especially when males were hunting.[47] If they talked about what was happening is because they were able to understand they all were aware of their *self* and other *selves*.

---

39   Locke and Bogin, "Language and Life History."
40   Lumley, Henry, *La Grand Histoire des premiers hommes européens Broché* (Paris: Odile Jacob, 2007).
41   Bloom, Michael V., "Origins of Healing: An Evolutionary Perspective of the Healing Process", in *Families, Systems, & Health*, vol. 23, no. 3 (2005): 251–260.
42   Barnard, Alan, *Language in Prehistory* (New York: Cambridge University Press, 2016).
43   Wiessner, Polly W., "Embers of Society: Firelight talk among the Ju/'hoansi Bushmen", in *Proceedings of the National Academy of Sciences*, vol. 111, no. 39 (2014): 14027–14035.
44   Barnard, *Language in Prehistory*.
45   Buck, Ross, "Communicative Genes in the Evolution of Empathy and Altruism", in *Behavior Genetics*, vol. 41, no. 6 (2011): 876–888.
46   Barnard, *Language in Prehistory*.
47   Dunbar, *Gossip*.

Women, overall, may have tended to talk about themselves and others,[48] which not only implies the ability to empathise but also promotes it.

Likely, last *ergasters* were able to sense their peers' affective and emotional states just by looking at their eyes, to think about such a sensation and the fact of being thinking about such a sensation. This level of empathy allowed them to promote a supportive behaviour of mutual care. Arsuaga firmly asserts this when ensures that our ancestors took care of those mentally and physically handicapped.[49] However, the first evidence of this belongs to other species that populated Europe 500,000 ka, *Homo heidelbergensis*. We will get back to this later, but *heidelbergensis* did share very similar characteristics with the last specimens of the species we are about to introduce: *Homo antecessor*, *ergasters*' successors.

Antecessor was described as a link between *ergaster* and *heidelbergensis* (in Europe) and *rhodesiensis* (in Africa). Their origins have been attributed to both a second *out of Africa*[50] at some point Beyond *ergaster* and a moving of Asian *erectus*' 'sons'. Whatever, *antecessor* seems to be a predecessor of *sapiens* and the analysis of their capacities, quite similar to those of *heidelbergensis*, are very helpful to understand the concrete examples I want to introduce on those handicapped. 900,000 ka, *antecessor's* feedback loops between left and right hemispheres were more powerful and also the functions of the medial prefrontal cortex, responsible for self-reference and inner speech processes, and the anterior cingulate area, in charge of social relationships, emotions and inner world.[51]

In *ergaster* something was missing to equalise our empathy: they would have been able to neither consciously, deliberately empathise with others for an intentional purpose nor to project their thought forward and backward, i.e., to empathise with their past and future unknown peers[52] (mental time travel theory).[53] The first one would be earmarked for *Homo antecessor* and the second for *Homo rhodesiensis* and *sapiens*. *Antecessors*' mental life went through all the different conscious phases modern human beings do. They had a *core consciousness*,[54] or *phenomenic*

---

48 Locke and Bogin, "Language and Life History".
49 Arsuaga, *El primer viaje*.
50 Agustí, Jordi and Antón, Mauricio, *La gran migración* (Barcelona: Crítica, 2011).
51 Arsuaga and Martín-Loeches, *El sello indeleble*.
52 Gibbons, Ann, "Empathy and Brain Evolution", in *Science*, no. 259 (1993): 1250–1252.
53 Suddendorf, Thomas; Addis, Dona Rose and Corballis, Michael C., "Mental Time Travel and the Shaping of the Human Mind", in *Philosophical Transactions of the Royal Society of London B: Biology Science*, no. 364 (2009): 1317–1324.
54 Agustí, Bufill Soler and Mosquera Martínez, *El precio de la inteligencia*.

consciousness,[55] that involves most basic mental-state consciousness connected to attention and selection, perceptions, emotions, thoughts and memories, i.e. the genuine consciousness directed outward without any kind of reflection – what Sartre called *la pensée irréfléchie*.[56] Core consciousness is not unique to humans but necessary to talk of more complex, conscious systems such as self-consciousness, metaconsciousness or reflexive-self-consciousness. *Antecessor* was the first one with such an *extended consciousness*.[57] They could describe a situation in which they reflexively recognised being perceiving something, i.e., they could say themselves that the private mental state they were experiencing was own. This is the consciousness that experiences itself or *what we think when we think that we are thinking* of something: when our thought is the object of our attention.[58]

Such a level of consciousness involved the *interpreter*, the fundamental support of emotional but overall cognitive empathy. The interpreter is a rhetorical figure to explain the experience of the *self*. It builds a narrative of our actions, emotions and thoughts and unifies our past and future story.[59] The interpreter is a capacity of self-representation, an autobiographical memory that is possible because of the development of language, through *inner speech* or *subvocal speech*.[60] This mental function is directly related to the full capability to perfectly discriminate between the *self* and others *selves* and to move from the self-perspective to that of the other consciously, deliberately. Also, it leads time traveling ability that *ergaster* lacked.

As we said earlier, this would be also the case of *heidelbergensis*. They evolved into *Homo neanderthalensis* and Denisovans, not into *Homo sapiens*, but, again, this is seamless to our case. Our 1200 cm^3 brain size European relatives had a capacity for symbolic thinking. Among those who got into Spain, the *pre-Neanderthals* from Sima de los Huesos, there were three specimens

---

55   Zahavi, David and Parnas, Josef, "Phenomenal Consciousness and Self-awareness: A Phenomenological Critique of Representational Theory", in *Journal of Consciousness Studies*, vol. 5, nos.5–6 (1998): 687–705.
56   Sartre, Jean-Paul, *The Transcendence of the Ego: An Existentialist Theory of Consciousness* (New York: Hill and Wang, 1991).
57   Morin, Alain, "Levels of Consciousness and Self-awareness: A Comparison and Integration of various Neurocognitive Views", in *Consciousness and Cognition*, no. 15 (2006): 358–371.
58   Metcalfe, Janet, "Evolution of Metacognition", in *Handbook of Metamemory and Memory*, edited by John Dunlosky and Rober A. Bjork (New York: Psychology Press, 2008): 29–46.
59   Gazzaniga, Michael, *The Mind's Past* (California: University of California Press, 1998), 174.
60   Agustí, Bufill Soler and Mosquera Martínez, *El precio de la inteligencia*.

that reveal the *conscious* empathic behaviour that also characterised *antecessors*: *Elvis*, *Miguelón* and *Benjamina*.

Elvis (400,000 ka, Pelvis 1) represents a collection of fossils consisting of a pelvis and some parts of a trunk, which shows that the specimen to whom they belonged suffered a locomotor disability called spondylolisthesis. The *grandpa of Atapuerca* was a very old individual of 45–50 with a degenerative lumbar kyphosis because of which his backbone did not have a normal curvature. His hip inclination would have caused so much pain to Elvis that he would not have been able to move as the rest of his group. Surely, he needed some type of cane and he moved very slowly. However, despite being a 'burden' for his group, slowing down their migrations, such a family never abandoned him, which seems to be a clear evidence of complex empathy.[61] Some authors ensure that despite his precarious living conditions, Elvis received care from his family because he was able to do sedentary tasks and to look after the children. Also, his life experience may have been considered a source of wisdom.[62] In this regard, their family could consciously keep him alive for a matter of *interest*.

The almost perfectly preserved skull of Miguelón (400,000 ka, Skull 5) shows that this individual suffered from a dental infection that put an end to his life by septicaemia at age 35. Before he died, his family looked after him for a while so that his affected bone had time to heal. His symptoms during that time could include fever, shortness of breath, rapid heartbeat, low blood pressure, shaking chills, fatigue, drowsiness, delirium and mental confusion.[63] So, why was this individual kept alive? Quite likely, his infection and subsequent pain would not make him very valuable for sedentary tasks and care – overall if it was the case of suffering from altered states of consciousness, which may even constitute a danger to others. Why did they take care of Miguelón?

Benjamina (530,000 ka, Skull 14) was a little girl with craniosynostosis, a condition in which one or more of the fibrous sutures in an infant skull prematurely fuses by turning into bone (ossification), thereby changing the growth pattern of the skull. Benjamina's cranium did not grow normally and she

---

61   Bonmatí, Alejandro, *et al.*, "Middle Pleistocene Lower Back and Pelvis from an Aged Human Individual from the Sima de los Huesos Site, Spain", in *Proceedings of the National Academy of Sciences*, vol. 107, no. 43 (2010): 18386–18391; Bonmatí, Alejandro, "El caso de Elvis el viejo de la Sima de los Huesos", in *Revista de Humanidades*, no. 10 (2011): 138–147.

62   Arsuaga, *El primer viaje*; Arsuaga and Martín-Loeches, *El sello indeleble*.

63   García, Ana, *et al.*, "Orofacial Pathology in Homo heidelbergensis: The case of Skull 5 from the Sima de los Huesos Site (Atapuerca, Spain)", in *Quaternary International*, no. 295 (2013): 83–93.

suffered from migraines and vomiting, psychometric and behaviour disorders and some form of mental retardation and optic atrophy. Despite her shortcomings, Benjamina received care from her group to the extent that she survived 10 years.[64]

Undoubtedly, for the group to consciously see some advantage in looking after a disabled child or adult it was necessary a high capacity for complex, intentional empathy. In particular, Benjamina was assisted all the time, as she would have needed special long-term care, instead of being abandoned to a certain death. Her family was willing to bear the burden of her disability in their continuous displacements and to sacrifice part of their food to feed a member who would never be *helpful* in practical terms. This is not strictly true: caring of the weak could increase the reputation of those in charge of individuals like Benjamina or Miguelón in a complex social structure. Mothers and young females could demonstrate their abilities as future mothers to males by taking care of the weak.[65] Other members, as the wounded and elders, from their part, could prove their worth in helping mothers and young females to look after others to ensure their own care.

What differentiates these cases from those in which primates behave *altruistically* – for example, when "a female chimpanzee reacts to the screams of her closest associate by defending her against an aggressive male, thus taking great risk on her behalf" or when a group adopt orphans "who may devote years of costly care to unrelated juveniles"[66] – is that they do not think about this phenomenon and its advantages consciously. Both are thinking of rewards, but the former innately and the latter deliberately. This is the result of internally telling oneself: *I'm going to behave in such a manner to obtain something from my group*.

Our immediate predecessor, *Homo rhodesiensis* (600,000 ka) was in the same conditions there in Africa. Also known as *Kabwe 1* or *the Broken Hill skull*, perhaps what made the difference between them and us in terms of ability to empathise was the complexity of the purposes of their empathic behaviour when our brain reached its definitive complexity 200,000 ka. In brief, the jump from *rhodesiensis* to the first *sapiens* would crystallise in the existence of a collective

---

64 García, Ana, *et al.*, "Craniosynostosis in the Middle Pleistocene Human Cranium 14 from the Sima de los Huesos, Atapuerca, Spain", in *Proceedings of the National Academy of Sciences*, vol. 106, no. 16 (2009): 6573–6578; García, Ana, *et al.*, "The Earliest Evidence of True Lambdoid Craniosynostosis: The Case of 'Benjamina', a Homo heidelbergensis Child", in *Child's Nervous System*, vol. 26, no. 6 (2010): 723–727.
65 Bradshaw and Paul, "Could Empathy for Animals."
66 De Waal, "The Antiquity of Empathy", 875.

consciousness about the intrinsic value of their own species and the ability to use perspective-taking not only individually but collectively to take advantage of the fact of knowing others' mental states. This would explain why they began to bury their dead and created shared myths and metaphysical orders. They also became cognitively empathic with other animals by thinking as them to facilitate hunting and making them think as humans to avoid becoming preys (ToM for animals), to the point of domesticating them over time.[67] Primitive *sapiens* were able to consciously think about empathy and perspective-taking and its possibilities as a group. The statement, in this case, would be: *We're going to behave in such a manner to obtain something from other groups.*

Moreover, *sapiens* could/can *use* the knowledge about their peers' to *influence* their actions and thoughts, to *convince*, in their own advantage,[68] what is different from simply behaving consciously in an empathic manner just expecting a reward. Our species would have specialised in using empathy to predict others' intentions and manipulate them and even in simulating fictitious versions of the beliefs, desires, character traits and contexts of another individual or collective to see what emotional feelings came out and use such an insight to deceive the peers. Perhaps empathy is different in *sapiens* because we have reached the level of what Whiten and Byrne called Machiavellian intelligence[69] – and only perhaps this was a reason for the withdrawal of the other *Homo* species, *Homo neanderthalensis* and Denisovans.

Slightly simplified, this is a tentative proposal on the evolution of empathy from contagion to Machiavellian intelligence throughout Hominisation. Yet we have to see the reasons behind the adoption of higher levels of empathy over time, the pressures influencing such a possible evolution to a point in which our ability to empathise may lead us to both the most prosocial and the most antisocial behaviour.

3 Anthropogenetic Reasons for Empathy

Some people believe that empathy, as well as solidarity or altruism, is a means to an end, so it meets a certain function, even in its most basic forms.[70]

---

[67] Bradshaw and Paul, "Could Empathy for Animals".
[68] Dunbar, *Gossip*.
[69] Whiten, Andrew and Byrne, Richard, *Machiavellian Intelligence: Social Expertise and the Evolution of Intellect on Monkeys, Apes, and Humans* (Oxford: Oxford University Press, 1988).
[70] De Waal, "Putting the Altruism."

Charlton explained that sufficiently developed animals do experience, at least, contagion, sympathy and even emotional empathy if they are able to pay attention to others' emotions.[71] This is the level of empathy that, since it is not self-conscious, does not open the door to freely choose what to do with it. It simply leads an impulse in response to some kind of biological (reproductive) and evolutionary (survival) pressures. This was also the case of our pre-*sapiens* relatives.

Firstly, empathy before and after first *Homo* species seems to mainly respond to a maternal, emotional – even unconscious – impetus for caring.[72] As De Waal claims, the evolution of empathy is thought to go back to mammalian maternal care.[73] This usually explains why women tend to be more empathic than men.[74] Our female ancestors were primary caregivers of children and then *nurturers of the group*. They seem to have been the *Homo empathicus* par excellence.[75] At the very beginning, they looked after their children and some others to demonstrate their skills as mothers to males. With the advent of *Homo* species, they started to consciously rear their children and the weakest peers in the settlements ensuring their own reputation and the unity of the group. In complex *Homo* 'societies', caretakers would have attended to the most vulnerable, the defenceless or the 'hopeless', even with more devotion than to any other: they were the favourites.[76]

It was because of this act of empathy promoted by 'the mothers' and supported by 'the outcasts' in search for acceptation the weak could survive and put an end to *the law of the strongest*. Thanks to the 'culture of care' those who could neither take for themselves the right of the strongest nor become the breadwinners found a compensation mechanism to gain the right to survival through empathy and mutual support.[77] Furthermore, this became a matter of sexual selection. Hunters must adapt to their weak-caregivers-peers' pace of life on returning 'home' to win the goodwill of females who would select

---

71 Charlton, Bruce, "Evolution and the Cognitive Neuroscience of Awareness, Consciousness and Language", in *Cognition*, no. 50 (2000): 7–15.
72 Bradshaw and Paul, "Could Empathy for Animals"; Decety, *et al.*, "A Neurobehavioral Evolutionary Perspective."
73 De Waal, "The Antiquity of Empathy."
74 *Ibid.* Also Baron-Cohen, Simon, *The Essential Difference: The Truth about the Male and Female Brain* (New York: Basic Books, 2003).
75 Bloom, "Origins of Healing."
76 Blumenberg, Hans, "Die Lieblinge der Mütter in den Höhlen", *Deutsches Literatur Archiv*, 1.2: UNF 162.
77 *Ibid.*

their mates depending on how empathic they were able to be.[78] Under different pressures, their ability to empathise was much more led toward understanding animal mind and behaviour "to take on the perspective of potential prey in tracking"[79] and not to "lessen the likelihood of falling prey to animal hunters."[80]

Empathy seemed to have put an end to the basic problem of human beings: the fragmentation of the group in the weak and the strong.[81] Nothing could be more untrue. With the consolidation of the group, the family, and the subsequent collective consciousness, the problem was transferred from the ingroup to the outgroup.[82] Survival and sexual pressures then together with pre-socio-cultural ones put our most recent prehistoric relatives in the position of having to make use of the knowledge achieved on others' states of mind for their collective-interests. Here I see that our former ability to use animals' minds reading to make them preys was extrapolated to humans.[83]

As new pressures appeared in *sapiens*' life the power of empathy would increase, as well as cognition, to the extent of becoming both the best hope and the greatest danger concerning collective survival: a "simultaneously prosocial and cruel" disposition.[84] With regard to empathy, things went awry when we started to put ourselves in the others' position to take advantage of their weaknesses. Understanding others' position implies knowing their shortcomings. The primitive, naive empathy ceased to be such when *economy* replaced *ecology*.[85]

What is/are the reason/s for empathy today? If empathy can develop man into a wolf to a man, what is the function of empathy currently? At this point, empathy no longer responds to a survival or reproductive function but to a

---

78   *Ibid.*
79   Sarnecki, John, "The Emergence of Empathy in the Context of Cross-Species Mind Reading", in *Origins of Mind*, edited by Liz Swan (Dordrecht: Springer, 2013), 129.
80   *Ibid.*, 135.
81   Ros Velasco, Josefa, "La debilidad como ejemplo en la antropología de Hans Blumenberg", in *Predicar con el ejemplo. Ser y deber (de) ser en lo público*, edited by Ricardo Gutiérrez Aguilar (Barcelona: Bellaterra, 2019).
82   Richerson, Peter J. and Boyd, Robert, *Not by Genes Alone: How Culture Transformed Human Evolution* (Chicago: University of California Press, 2005).
83   Sarnecki, "The Emergence of Empathy."
84   Young, Alan, "Empathy, Evolution and Human Nature", in *Empathy from Bench to Bedside*, edited by Jean Decety (Boston: The MIT Press, 2011), 29.
85   Blumenberg, Hans, "Alle Tierpopulationen haben Ökologien, nur die menschlichen Populationen haben Ökonomie", in *Deutsches Literatur Archiv*, 01 (1968–1988): 019592.

wish to have a better standard of living ('over-survival'/beyond-survival). Since then, it is our responsibility to tip the balance towards creation or collapse in the use of our empathic abilities. We have to *morally* choose what to do with our empathy. With de Waal, we cannot say that humans behave like apes because precisely they have nothing to choose and seems to be even more empathic than us in both behaviour and brain organisation.[86] Will human beings have to become *mechanical animals*[87] to avoid misuses of empathy and ensure the survival of humankind?

What if the matter of empathy is much simpler? Agreeing again with de Waal, "although empathy [...] is likely to be adaptive, not each and every application of this capacity needs to be for it to retain overall adaptive value";[88] it could be even just the opposite. Perhaps the explanation of empathy is much simpler and species behave empathically just because this kind of social behaviour is endogenously rewarding and stimulate "dopamine release within the mesocorticolimbic dopamine system", as Decety claims.[89] The obvious conclusion is that empathy does not allow to be fully apprehended by rationalisations.[90]

Bibliography

Agustí, Jordi and Antón, Mauricio, *La gran migración* (Barcelona: Crítica, 2011).

Agustí, Jordi; Bufill Soler, Enric and Mosquera Martínez, Marina, *El precio de la inteligencia: La evolución de la mente humana y sus consecuencias* (Barcelona: Crítica, 2012).

Allman, John; Hakeem, Atiya Y. and Watson, Karli K., "Two Phylogenetic Specializations in the Human Brain", in *The Neuroscientist*, no. 8 (2002): 335–346.

Allman, John; Hakeem, Atiya Y.; Manaye, Kebreten F.; Semendeferi, Katerina; Erwin, Joseph M.; Park, Soyoung; Goubert, Virgine and Hof, Patrick R., "The von Economo

---

86   De Waal, "The Antiquity of Empathy."
87   A recall to the album *Mechanical Animal* (1998), by Marilyn Manson.
88   De Waal, "The Antiquity of Empathy", 875.
89   Decety, *et al.*, "A Neurobehavioral Evolutionary Perspective", 42.
90   This chapter addresses some points concerning empathy presented in my doc. diss. *Boredom as selective pressure in Hans Blumenberg* (UCM, 2017). I would like to express my gratitude to the DAAD, the DLA and the MECD, the projects FFI2012-32611-FFI2016-75978-R and FFI2016-78285-R, and the RCC and the RLL at Harvard University. To Ricardo Gutiérrez Aguilar, for reminding me what matters.

Neurons in Frontoinsular and Anterior Cingulate Cortex in Great Apes and Humans", in *Brain Structure and Function*, no. 214 (2010): 495–517.

Arsuaga, Juan L. *El primer viaje de nuestra vida* (Madrid: Planeta, 2012).

Arsuaga, Juan L. and Martínez Mendizábal, Ignacio, *Atapuerca y la evolución humana* (Barcelona: Fundación Caixa Cataluña, 2004).

Arsuaga, Juan L. and Martínez Mendizábal, Ignacio, *Chosen Species: The Long March of Human Evolution* (Marblehead: Wiley & Sons, 2011).

Arsuaga, Juan L. and Martín-Loeches, Manuel, *El sello indeleble. Pasado, presente y futuro del ser humano* (Barcelona: Random House, 2013).

Ashare, Matt, "Omega Man", in *CMJ New Music Monthly*, no. 64 (1998): 56–89.

Barnard, Alan, *Language in Prehistory* (New York: Cambridge University Press, 2016).

Baron-Cohen, Simon, *The Essential Difference: The Truth about the Male and Female Brain* (New York: Basic Books, 2003).

Bloom, Michael V., "Origins of Healing: An Evolutionary Perspective of the Healing Process", *Families, Systems, & Health*, vol. 23, no. 3 (2005): 251–260.

Blumenberg, Hans, "Alle Tierpopulationen haben Ökologien, nur die menschlichen Populationen haben Ökonomie", in *Deutsches Literatur Archiv*, 01 (1968–1988): 019592.

Blumenberg, Hans, "Biotopwechsel, aufrechter Gang, generatives Verhalten", in *Deutsches Literatur Aarchiv*, 03: 023868.

Blumenberg, Hans, "Der Möglichkeiten der Anthropogenese", in *Deutsches Literatur Archiv*, 01 (1968–1988): 8678–8679.

Blumenberg, Hans, "Die Lieblinge der Mütter in den Höhlen", in *Deutsches Literatur Archiv*, 1.2: UNF 162.

Bonmatí, Alejandro, "El caso de Elvis el viejo de la Sima de los Huesos", in *Revista de Humanidades*, no. 10 (2011): 138–147.

Bonmatí, Alejandro; Gómez Olivencia, Asier; Arsuaga, Juan L., Carretero, José Miguel; García Téllez, Ana; Martínez Mendizábal, Ignacio; Lorenzo, Carlos; Bermúdez de Castro, José María and Carbonell, Eudald, "Middle Pleistocene Lower Back and Pelvis from an Aged Human Individual from the Sima de los Huesos site, Spain", in *Proceedings of the National Academy of the Sciences*, vol. 107, no. 43 (2010): 18386–18391.

Bradshaw, John W. S. and Paul, Elizabeth S., "Could Empathy for Animals have been an Adaptation in the Evolution of Homo Sapiens?", *Animal Welfare*, vol. 19, no. 2 (2010): 107–112.

Buck, Ross, "Communicative Genes in the Evolution of Empathy and Altruism", *Behavior Genetics*, vol. 41, no. 6 (2011): 876–888.

Carbonell, Eudald, *Las primeras ocupaciones de los continentes* (Barcelona: Ariel, 2005).

Charlton, Bruce, "Evolution and the Cognitive Neuroscience of Awareness, Consciousness and Language", in *Cognition*, no. 50 (2000): 7–15.

Coulehan, Jack, "Empathy and Narrativity: A Commentary on 'Origins of Healing: An Evolutionary Perspective of the Healing Process' ", in *Families, Systems, & Health*, vol. 23, no. 3 (2005): 261–265.

De Waal, Frans B. M., "Putting the Altruism Back into Altruism: the Evolution of Empathy", *Annual Review of Psychology*, no. 59 (2008): 279–300.

De Waal, Frans B. M., *The Age of Empathy: Nature's Lessons for a Kinder Society* (New York: Harmony Books, 2009).

De Waal, Frans B. M., "The Antiquity of Empathy", in *Science*, no. 336 (2012): 874–876.

Decety, Jean, "The Neuroevolution of Empathy", in *Annals of the New York Academy of Sciences*, vol. 1231, no. 1 (2011): 35–45.

Decety, Jean; Norman, Greg J.; Bernston, Gary G. and Cacioppo, John T., "A Neurobehavioral Evolutionary Perspective on the Mechanisms underlying Empathy", in *Progress in Neurobiology*, vol. 98, no. 1 (2012): 38–48.

Dunbar, Robin, *Gossip, Grooming and the Evolution of Language* (Cambridge: Harvard University Press, 1998).

Fischman, Joshua, "Putting a New Spin on the Birth of Human Birth", in *Science*, no. 264 (1994): 1082–1083.

García, Ana; Arsuaga, Juan L.; Martínez Mendizábal, Ignacio; Lorenzo, Carlos; Carretero, José Miguel; Bermúdez de Castro, José María and Carbonell, Eduald, "Craniosynostosis in the Middle Pleistocene Human Cranium 14 from the Sima de los Huesos, Atapuerca, Spain", in *Proceedings of the National Academy of Sciences*, vol. 106, no. 16 (2009): 6573–6578.

García, Ana; Martínez Lage, Juan; Arsuaga, Juan L.; Martínez Mendizábal, Ignacio; Lorenzo, Carlos and Pérez Espejo, Miguel Ángel, "The Earliest Evidence of True Lambdoid Craniosynostosis: the Case of 'Benjamina', a Homo heidelbergensis Child", in *Child's Nervous System*, vol. 26, no. 6 (2010): 723–727.

García, Ana; Arsuaga, Juan L.; Martínez Mendizábal, Ignacio; Mantín Francés, Laura; Martirón Torres, María; Bermúdez de Castro, José María; Bonmatí, Alejandro and Lira, Jaime, "Orofacial Pathology in Homo heidelbergensis: The Case of Skull 5 from the Sima de los Huesos Site (Atapuerca, Spain)", *Quaternary International*, no. 295 (2013): 83–93.

Gazzaniga, Michael, *The Mind's Past* (California: University of California Press, 1998).

Gazzaniga, Michael, *Human: The Science Behind What Makes Us Unique* (New York: Harper, 2009).

Gibbons, Ann, "Empathy and Brain Evolution", in *Science*, no. 259 (1993): 1250–1252.

Holloway, Ralph, "Evidence for POT Expansion in Early Homo: a Pretty Theory with Ugly (or no) Paleoneurological Facts", in *Behavioral and Brain Sciences*, no. 18 (1995): 191–193.

Kant, Immanuel, *Kant's Gesammelte Schriften*, edited by the Preußische Akademie der Wissenschaften in 29 vols. (Berlin: Walter de Gruyter, 1900-).

Kant, Immanuel, *Anthropology, History and Education* (New York: Cambridge University Press, 2007).

Lamm, Claus; Batson, Daniel and Decety, Jean, "The Neural Substrate of Human Empathy: Effects of Perspective-taking and Cognitive Appraisal", in *Journal of Cognitive Neuroscience*, vol. 19, no. 1 (2007): 42–58.

Lieberman, Daniel E.; Wood, Bernard A. and Pilbeam, David R., "Homoplasy and early Homo: an Analysis of the Evolutionary Relationships of H. habilis sensu stricto and H. rudolfensis", in *Journal of Human Evolution*, no. 30 (1996): 97–120.

Locke, John L. and Bogin, Barry, "Language and Life History: A new Perspective on the Development and Evolution of Human Language", in *Behavioral and Brain Sciences*, no. 29 (2006): 259–325.

Lumley, Henry, *La Grand Histoire des premiers hommes européens Broché* (Paris: Odile Jacob, 2007).

Metcalfe, Janet, "Evolution of Metacognition", in *Handbook of Metamemory and Memory*, edited by John Dunlosky and Robert A. Bjork (New York: Psychology Press, 2008), 29–46.

Morin, Alain, "Levels of Consciousness and Self-awareness: A Comparison and Integration of Various Neurocognitive Views", in *Consciousness and Cognition*, no. 15 (2006): 358–371.

Preston, Stephanie D. and De Waal Frans B. M., "The Communication of Emotions and the Possibility of Empathy in Animals", in *Altruistic love: Science, Philosophy, and Religion in Dialogue*, edited by Stephen G. Post, Lynn G. Underwood, Jeffrey P. Schloss and William B. Hurlbut (Oxford: Oxford University Press, 2002), 284–308.

Richerson, Peter J. and Boyd, Robert, *Not by Genes Alone: How Culture Transformed Human Evolution* (Chicago: University of California Press, 2005).

Ros Velasco, Josefa, "The Evolution of Language: An Anthropological Approach. Language in Prehistory", in *Evolutionary Anthropology*, vol. 25, no. 2 (2016): 79–80.

Ros Velasco, Josefa, *El aburrimiento como presión selectiva en Hans Blumenberg*, PhD Dissertation (Universidad Complutense de Madrid, UCM, 2017).

Ros Velasco, Josefa, "La debilidad como ejemplo en la antropología de Hans Blumenberg", in *Predicar con el ejemplo. Ser y deber (de) ser en lo público*, edited by Ricardo Gutiérrez Aguilar (Barcelona: Bellaterra, 2019).

Ros Velasco, Josefa, *La enfermedad del aburrimiento. El camino de la medicalización y sus alternativas* (2019)(forthcoming).

Roth, Gerhard and Dicke, Ursula, "Evolution of the Brain and Intelligence", in *Trends in Cognitive Science*, vol. 9, no. 5 (2005): 250–257.

Sarnecki, John, "The Emergence of Empathy in the Context of Cross-Species Mind Reading", in *Origins of Mind*, edited by Liz Swan (Dordrecht: Springer, 2013), 129–142.

Sartre, Jean-Paul, *The Transcendence of the Ego: An Existentialist Theory of Consciousness* (New York: Hill and Wang, 1991).

Seyfarth, Robert M. and Chaney, Dorothy L., "Affiliation, Empathy, and the Origins of Theory of Mind". *Proceedings of the National Academy of Sciences*, vol. 110, no. 2 (2013): 10349–10356.

Smith, Adam, "Cognitive Empathy and Emotional Empathy in Human Behavior and Evolution", in *The Psychological Record*, vol. 56, no. 1 (2006): 3–21.

Suddendorf, Thomas; Addis, Dona Rose and Corballis, Michael C., "Mental Time Travel and the Shaping of the Human Mind", *Philosiphical Transactions of the Royal Society of London B: Biology Science*, no. 364 (2009): 1317–1324.

Whiten, Andrew and Byrne, Richard, *Machiavellian Intelligence: Social Expertise and the Evolution of Intellect on Monkeys, Apes, and Humans* (Oxford: Oxford University Press, 1988).

Wiessner, Polly W., "Embers of Society: Firelight talk among the Ju/'hoansi Bushmen", in *Proceedings of the National Academy of Sciences*, vol. 111, no. 39 (2014): 14027–14035.

Young, Alan, "Empathy, Evolution and Human Nature", in *Empathy from Bench to Bedside*, edited by Jean Decety (Boston: The MIT Press, 2011), 21–37.

Zahavi, David and Parnas, Josef, "Phenomenal Consciousness and Self-awareness: A Phenomenological Critique of Representational Theory", *Journal of Consciousness Studies*, vol. 5, nos. 5–6 (1998): 687–705.

CHAPTER 3

Empathy or Compassion? On Rational Understanding of Emotional Suffering

Victoria Aizkalna

Abstract

The subject of empathy and the role it has in forming a well-functioning society has become widely discussed since the advances of modern technology of functional magnetic resonance imagery (fMRI) give us the possibility to *read* human brain and track what parts of brain respond to certain stimuli. High, therefore, is the temptation of falling into a rabbit hole of labeling certain parts of physical human brain to be the key to understanding of a complex world of human mind and consciousness, of feelings and emotions. In the present article the focus is on understanding phenomenon of empathy, and also to the downsides of the cult of empathy. Saying this, by no means I want to diminish the value of findings and discoveries of neurosciences, however I am going to argue that mapping the brain is not the key to understanding mind, and that empathy is not the key to the solution of conflicts, nor it leads to stronger societal bonds. What does, then? There is no one, nor two or three good answers. There are plenty of ways to approach the subject, and any of them are right and wrong to certain extend. However, it might be safe to say that going back to the *roots* is the place to begin. Complex mechanism of society is based on interpersonal relationships of individuals. Individuals are shaped by the society they live in. To understand how this process intertwines and where is the place for the empathy, if it is at all needed, in the present article is approached through the phenomenon of conceptual schemes and consciousness in the theories of Donald Davidson and Daniel Dennett. Through understanding of the ways of processing and storing information for further use and decision-making, we will see what are the dangers of over-using empathy, and argue for usefulness of rational compassion.

Keywords

conceptual schemes – consciousness – empathy – rational compassion – internal process – psychopathy

Introduction

"Scratch an 'altruist', and watch a 'hypocrite' bleed" – said Michael Ghiselin once.[1] What does this mean and how is it related to the subject of empathy? Does that mean that human beings can only care about themselves without ulterior motive? Would that make human kind to be monstrous creatures, willing to sacrifice others for own pleasure or benefit? Or are things not quite as simple as that? Perhaps, it is fairly safe to claim that human nature is not all black and white: that human can either only be altruists, disregarding own profits, or to be completely selfish, disregarding the well-being of others. However, for the purposes of the present articles we are not going to focus on the subject of the evolution, but rather we are going to explore the subjects of empathy and rational compassion, the difference between them and their role in social interactions though the phenomenon of conceptual schemes to make a step towards understanding the scale of importance and reliability of empathy in social encounters. The article, being an ambitious attempt to give a diversified overview of empathy and the hidden hazards of it, and to advocate for a rational compassion as an alternative, the present article is interdisciplinary, contains references to neuroscience, psychology and psychiatry since the subject of empathy is complex and multi-dimensional, and to get a glimpse of the different aspects, it is important to establish interdisciplinary connections regarding the subject.

In the matter of the role of empathy in interpersonal relations and in its effect on an individual, not only the definition of empathy or the extent of it should be established. In order to enable the process of understanding of the complexity of the matter and to make a step towards certain clarity, we will address empathy from the perspective of Philosophy of Mind, in particular we will use the concept of the conceptual schemed in an interpretation of Daniel Dennett, with the links to Donald Davidson's theories.

In past several decades the subject of empathy and its role in interpersonal and intercultural communication has become widely discussed among social scientists, philosophers, psychologists, journalists and even politicians (for instance, Barack Obama's speech where the former president of the USA has claimed that the "empathy deficit is more serious than federal budget deficit).[2]

---

[1] Ghiselin, Michael T., *The Economy of Nature and the Evolution of Sex* (Berkeley, CA: University of California Press, 1974), 247.

[2] "It seems like we've got an empathy shortage, an empathy deficit. More serious than the federal budget deficit ... We've become so cynical that it almost seems naive to believe that we can understand each other across the gulf of race, or class or region or religion ..." –Barack

In its very essence, the idea appears to have a potential of being panacea for many, if not most, of the problems that modern society is facing: intolerance, violence, discrimination, – hostility against everyone who is not one-of-us, be that gender, nationality, religious believes, body type, or any other quality that can be used for distinguishing a person from *others* or what is more essential: from *us*. If we actually *feel* what the other one is feeling, the assumption is that witnesses, influenced by the feelings of the suffering of the other person that they feel into, are more likely to interfere with injustice, violence, or any other type of harmful behavior against an individual or a group of individuals that are being victimized. It is not enough to have good intention of helping the other, but it has to be put into action to achieve good results, as Hume had claimed. However, Hume's description of 'sympathy' is not identical to modern definition of 'empathy.' Understanding of feelings and experience of others can be useful and can serve for the purpose of the ethical assessment for the individual, however, according to Hume, this experience should not be decisive. Further in the article it will be analyzed in more details whether empathy can be held as a reliable argument or ethical guidance of the moral justice. Although now it can be mentioned, that stimulated emotional response to the experience of the others caused by empathic identification with the other, can be misguiding, and furthermore, it can be used to achieve immoral goals by manipulating individuals to make impulsive decision while being under the strong influence of emotional response, rather than analyzing the situation rationally and coming to be a better and more adequate, rational solution.

Empathic response according to Adam Smith, implied not mere *imagination* of having the experience of suffering of another, but rather identifying self with the other and the feelings they experience *as if we are them*.[3] The grief of *the other* becomes a grief of the *individual* as if his/her own. Therefore, the experience is not in the least selfish. This, however, raises an important question: with what amount of others one individual can identify him/herself with? It is essential to emphasize, that the statement Adam Smith has made

---

Obama on the 21st January 2002 Speech at the Rockefeller Memorial Chapel for the Martin Luther King Day. (https://www.youtube.com/watch?v=CAbQvJrDVv0). Viewed on the 16th October 2018.

3 *vid.* Smith, Adam, *The Theory of Moral Sentiments* (London: Penguin Classics, 2010). In the present article, sympathy and empathy are used in the identical sense, and are interchangeable; it does not, however, mean that the author is not aware of certain difference between the terms, but rather due to a fact that the term sympathy in works of such philosophers as Hume and Adam Smith possess qualities that contemporary researches attribute to empathy.

comes from the 18th century. Even if from purely theoretical or philosophical point his argument sounds consistent and logical, and practiced consistently by all the individuals it would, perhaps, lead to the world with a lesser amount of suffering: identifying self with each suffering individual would serve as a strong motivation to take good actions for the good result. However, the issue here is with the accessibility of the information in 18th century and in the 21st. Even if it does not directly reflect on the quality of the argument of the complete identification, it does, as aforementioned, raise an important question: how many others one individual can identify with? Does someone, who is perceived as an outsider (outsider as an individual outside of one's 'community': be that someone with different believes, values, or any other separating qualia) is possible to identify with to the same extent as with someone towards whom an individual experience certain affectionate feelings, be that parental or romantic feelings, friendship or any other affections of the positive connotations?

This will be discussed further, in the context of Donald Davidson's theories.

First, Dennett

Before pursuing with an overview of conceptual schemes, perhaps it is adequate to explain a direction of the further argument: why is it important to address Philosophy of Mind when talking about such phenomenon as empathy. Here one can be quick with an answer: to understand how and why to use or not use empathy, or how to make a moral judgment, it is necessary to take a step back and up to analyze what influences decision-making process, but not purely from psychological and *mechanical* position where it can be measured in a laboratory, but from philosophical perspective. Humans are able to analyze data before decision making due to being conscious and possessing an ability of critical thinking, therefore it would not be enough to measure and determine what part of a physical brain is activated when an individual experiences certain emotions and feeling. To be able to make a judgment and build arguments one has to take a meta position and try to establish connection between external stimuli and internal responses, the correlation between those and the positive or negative outcome of uncritical or critical decision making.

Mind is – according to Daniel Dennett – a product of environment and culture an individual is raised and lives in. Deprived of social life and culture, a human is to be deprived of an opportunity to develop a kind of mind as is accepted to perceive to be human one. For instance, Dennett mentions children raised by animals.[4] Not being exposed and accustomed to human language nor to cultural traditions and habits, these individuals have not developed conceptual schemes that would allow them to integrate and successfully function in a human society as a productive member, who is capable of critical thinking and of rational decision-making. Human mind, therefore, can be described as a collective product of external influence of the surroundings that shape an individual, culture and a language it is exposed to. Conceptual schemes are created through the experience of external stimuli and expand with each extension of individual experience and knowledge (e.g. an individual is exposed and learns a new language. Experience of this type is to create a new conceptual scheme).

Perhaps, since the term 'experience' has been mentioned so many times in the present article it might be useful for the purpose of avoiding misconception and misunderstanding in the further discussion to make an attempt to define the meaning in which the term is used in the present discussion. For this, we shall refer to Daniel Dennett's definition of the intentional stances. In his *Brainstorms* (1981),[5] intentional stances play the key role in connecting mental states to abstract phenomenons, but also in processing constructive (physical) stances. Human mind, unlike any other living forms' mind, has a need for explanation and understanding of a creation and functionality of an object in order to process it. First presented in the *Beloit College* lecture from the 23rd February 2011, Daniel Dennett used a curious example, comparing an anthill to the Sagrada Família – The Basílica i Temple Expiatori de la Sagrada Familia, a Roman Catholic church located in Barcelona (Spain) and designed by architect Antonio Gaudi. If one is curious enough to look for photos or can recall the images in their mind, the similarities between both objects cannot be neglected. However, for a human mind to produce such a product as the aforementioned Sagrada Família, for instance, the understanding of multiple concepts is necessary (such as *religion, architecture, church, anthill,* and others). For ants, on the other hand, the concept of functionality is not the condition for creation and usage of an anthill.[6]

---

4 Dennett, Daniel C., *Kinds of Minds: Towards An Understanding Of Consciousness* (New York: BasicBooks, 1996), 153.
5 Dennett, Daniel C., *Brainstorms: Philosophical Essays in Mind and Psychology* (Cambridge-MA: The MIT Press, 1981).
6 The original title of the conference for the cicle of conferences was "A Human Mind as an Upside-Down Brain." The idea has been developed more recently in Dennett, Daniel C., *From Bacteria to Bach and Back: The Evolution of Minds* (New York: W. W. Norton & Company Inc., 2017).

Based on the aforementioned, the term 'experience' is used here as a description of a complex intentional process of connecting abstract and physical stances – through understanding their functionality – with mental states. Learning behavior of other individuals and attempts to understand their mental states require vast intentional process and are not predetermined, based on Dennett's theory. Inability to interpret or explain certain type of behavior or unclarity is temporary, and if an object is observed through intentionality (connecting to own *experience*), model of certain behavior be determined and defined.[7]

Human mind has ability to connect abstract and physical stances, which gives humans a possibility to observe and understand motived of certain behaviors, which gradually brings us back to the main subject of the present paper: empathy and it's role in human interactions. However, before we pursue with the discussion about empathy *per se*, it is useful for the discussion to clarify one more term that was mentioned earlier: *behavior*. Dennett defines behavior as pre-determined on a genetic level, those expressions of behavior that possess "truly rational models" necessary for the survival of the species.[8] For instance, during the process of evolution, turtles have "learned" to grow a shell to protect themselves from the external dangers and from an evolutionary perspective this is highly rational behavior. To take an example from human behavior, one of the most widely used is, perhaps, an example of a crying baby: since it has not yet developed other means to communicate its needs, is not capable to provide for its own needs nor capable of protecting itself, a baby has to make a loud noise to attract attention of an adult that can protect them, and ensure baby's survival.

Also, when we address the matter of experience, we can not neglect that an individual is exposed to external impact whether they are conscious of it and experience it, or if they do not have access to certain experience due to being exposed to events while not being conscious. As Daniel Dennett says in his book:

> There is much that happens to me and in me of which I am not conscious, which I do not experience, and there is much that happens in and to me of which I am conscious. That of which I am conscious is that to which I have *access*, or (to put the emphasis where it belongs), that to which *I* have access. Let us call this sort of access the access of personal

---

7   Ross, Don; Thompson, David and Brook, Andrew, *Dennett's Philosophy* (Cambridge-MA-London: The MIT Press, 2000), 57.
8   *Ibid.*

consciousness, thereby stressing that the subject of that access (whatever it is) which exhausts consciousness is the person, and not any of the person's parts.[9]

According to the quote, the only experience an individual is able to access and therefore also to use is conscious experience, which has involved intentional process of connecting external physical and abstract objects with mental stances that has allowed a mind of an individual to create meaningful connection that affect also human behavior and perception of others.

At this point, we can address a statement that the human mind is a product of a culture and an environment an individual is exposed to. As it was discussed earlier, behavior is treated as a pre-determined, genetically programmed for survival, while the mind is responsible for creating connections between external physical and abstract stances and mental stances, creating experience. Conceptual schemes *store* the experience and we can assume that they do expand with every new gained experience which allows and individual to establish stronger connection between external stances and mental stances. With gaining more conscious experience, an individual extends own ability to understand more complex concepts and, perhaps, make more rational decisions since a decision would be based on more data than the one of a less experienced or less rational individual.

Here, however, appears a new temptation to continue an argument and insist on building it in favor of empathy: the more experienced an individual is, the better an individual can understand and, perhaps, experience, mental stances of other individuals. However, here it is important to distinguish ability to *understand* and *experiencing the same emotion* which empathy requires. Understanding of the emotional and/or mental stance of an individual does not require from an individual to force themselves into the same mental or emotional stance. We are not going to discuss the possibility of experiencing the same emotional stance as another individual. Perhaps, it might be possible with completely identical individuals, who were exposed to the same culture, have created the same mental stances while experiencing the same physical and abstract stances. In the present paper, of the interest is the relationship between empathy and rational compassion, and what issue both pose.

Mind is a product of a culture and environment one is exposed to, where an individual creates experience. Since experience is constructed out of concepts

---

9   Dennett, *Brainstorms*, 150.

that internal processes connected to mental stances, it can be connected to a language one is exposed to. Here we will address Donald Davidson's theory of conceptual schemes to empathize issues of transferability of emotions and ability to experience the same feelings as another individual.

Second, Davidson

Donald Davidson's approach to conceptual schemes is mainly based on a language, since concepts are linguistic phenomenons. In his book *On the Very Idea of a Conceptual Scheme* (2001) Davidson explores issues of translatability and defines two main phenomenons: partial and complete non-translatability of conceptual schemes.[10] Completely non-translatable schemes are those schemes that differ to the extent where they have nothing in common and translation is not possible. In such a case, neither of the languages posses predicates of experience that are present in another language. That can lead to a complete dismissal of one of the languages: if the concepts are not translatable, are they even real? Davidson claims, that if a concept is not translatable, it is not possible to accept that a concept is meaningful. How can it relate to the question of empathy?

Considering afore discussed Davidson's understanding of concepts as linguistic phenomenons, we can state that emotions are also linguistic concepts that express mental stances. Since mental stances are affected by external impact (physical and abstract stances) it is safe to assume that if one of the external stances varies in different cultural environments, mental stance will be affected differently as well. Being a product of a culture, human mind, therefore, will experience distinguishing external stances with different mental responses that are appropriate in the culture where an individual has been raised. Therefore, the extend of experiences emotions also varies, even if experienced emotions are conceptually similar, but this difference already denies an ability of experiencing empathy: an individual who belongs to a different culture can only experience the stance that is familiar to them, not what another individual experiences, even if the concept of a certain emotion is translatable. So, the identification with another individual's emotions, who does not share an individual's conceptual scheme and does not belong to the same 'community', will not be complete.

---

10 Davidson, Donald, "On the Very Idea of a Conceptual Scheme", in *Proceedings and Addresses of the American Philosophical Association*, no. 47 (1973–1974): 5–20.

However, experiencing full identification with the other's emotions possess certain issues also when it comes to individuals who share conceptual scheme. Paul Bloom, Canadian-American psychologist, in *Against Empathy: The Case of Rational Compassion* (2016) brings up multiple issues empathy poses including undeniable bias that individuals experience towards representatives of certain groups.[11] It is more likely that the jury – in the USA legal system – will feel more empathic towards an accused if a defendant is good-looking, has a respectable background or appeals to the jury on a personal level. A defendant who fits into certain negative stereotypes, does not have appealing looks nor right background, or belongs to a certain race or religion, is more likely to be found guilty and get a harsher sentence.

Furthermore, Bloom empathizes that an individual can feel empathic towards a limited number of others. It is easier to focus empathy if an individual can relate to feelings based on own experience, or is provided with a back story of a subject. For example, when charity campaigns take place in order to collect funds for a support of victimized group, for a region that has suffered from a natural disaster or is at war, it has become apparent that using an image of a suffering child is more effective in getting more resonance and response from a society than providing numbers of victims and costs of destruction. This leads us to another issue that empathy poses. Since it is apparent that certain images and other external stimuli can cause stronger emotional, empathetic response, it can be used for manipulating human minds in order to get rash and irrational, emotional response to a situation.[12] Bloom claims, that strong feeling of empathy is likely to lead to a rash decision and even to violence: an individual, experiencing pain of a victim of a violent crime, can have an impulse to seek for revenge since in their conceptual scheme causing pain to innocent individuals is not acceptable and should be punished.

Also, empathy can prevent an individual from action. Being overwhelmed by emotions of another individual, an individual can be incapacitated which can lead to serious consequences. Bloom mentions several examples. For instance, a psychologist who is highly empathic towards his patients is not capable of providing any help and guidance for resolving an issue, since he will be drowned in it himself.[13]

Besides this, empathy requires a lot of mental resources from an individual and is not sustainable long-term. Using psychological terms, it leads to

---

11   Bloom, Paul, *Against Empathy: The Case for Rational Compassion* (London: Penguin Books, 2016).
12   *Ibid.*, 26, 51.
13   *Ibid.*, 37, 144.

emotional exhaustion according to Bloom. Experiencing struggles of others and more often than not feeling inability to provide any help while being overwhelmed by emotions can leave an individual internally empty: an individual perceives external stimuli that address mental stances responsible for providing help, protection, or other similar response of justice, emotional comforting and etc., takes a lot of internal resources from an individual and shifts the focus of own well-being.

Rational compassion – on the other hand – calls for rational analysis of the situation. It does not exclude emotional experience though. Processing and analyzing external stimuli and data, an individual can feel compassion and yet be able to give appropriate response to a situation, be that comfort of a crying child, support of a charitable organization, or political vote. Unlike empathy, rational compassion does not require from an individual to experience whatever emotional stance is another individual experiences, but to be able to understand the stance and provide rational analysis of a situation. Rational compassion, therefore, can serve as a sustainable tool for interpersonal relations since it is less affected by biases that an individual might express towards representatives on another 'community.' However, an argument against empathy can cause some misunderstanding regarding the stance on the value of emotional response and the consequences of the lack of such. In past several decades, psychiatry has advanced a lot in studying and analyzing human psyche, identifying various conditions, including one that is of particular interest in the present paper: psychopathy. These findings can not be neglected by philosophical society: once a condition is identified and conceptualized, multiple questions come along with them, including those on the value of empathy and potential dangers of its absence.

Neuroscientists, due to technological advances in the field of neuroscience have been able to link feeling of empathy to a part of brain called cerebral cortex, and amygdala. Apparently, if it does not function correctly, an individual is deprived from the ability to feel empathy. This inability (or is it sort of emotional disability?) is linked to such mental disorders (or we can call them conditions) as psychopathy, sociopathy and narcissism. Jon Ronson in *The Psychopath Test* (2012) researches into the individuals who express traits of low or no empathy and are diagnosed with psychopathy.[14] For the purpose of his research Ronson interviewed Robert B. Hare, a researcher in the field of criminal psychology, author of the *Hare Psychopathy Checklist*, which is used for the

---

14 Ronson, Jon, *The Psychopath Test: A Journey Through the Madness Industry* (London: Picador, 2012).

identification of psychopaths. The list consists of twenty points one of which is lack of empathy (it also includes lack of remorse, poor behavior control and other). In the interview, Hare shared the findings of his own research on psychopathy, confirming that psychopaths' brain is indeed different. Amygdala – a part of brain responsible for the emotional response, to put it simply–, in psychopaths' brain when being exposed to unpleasant stimuli (electric shock) did not respond in the way it supposed to respond in a *normal* brain.

> [A]mygdala, the part of the brain that should have anticipated the unpleasantness and sent the requisite signals of fear over to the central nervous system, wasn't functioning as it should. [...] Bob learned something that Elliot Barker wouldn't for years: psychopaths were likely to reoffend.[15]

In case when an individual does not experience feelings of empathy when being exposed to images depicting violent scenes, neither s/he experiences fear of pain or punishment, an individual, according to the research conducted by Ronson and other expert researchers in the field of criminal psychology – for example, Christopher Berry-Dee, known for his best-selling books *Talking with Serial Killers* (2003) and *Talking with Psychopaths and Savages* (2017)[16] – are likely to be of danger to society. According to them, inability to feel empathy does not affect one's intellectual abilities. An individual who does not experience empathy can be of high intelligence, and might use his/her mental capacity against others, regardless of their belonging to his/her community in order to gain personal profit.

Description of psychopathy can serve as a strong argument for empathy: without it a human being turns into anti-social, primal predator, who disregards rules of the society to pursue personal benefits. He uses his cold, cunning minds against others, and, assuming that such an individual possesses high intelligence, is capable of understanding human emotions if only conceptually, which enables him to use this knowledge against other members of society, posing danger to its other members. However, these statements are not accurate in an account of value of empathy in this specific case. Paul Bloom in *Against empathy* ... emphasized that it is not empathy or lack of such is the

---

15   *Ibid.*, 98. Elliot Barker is a Canadian psychiatrist, famous for organizing The Oak Ringe Program.
16   *vid.* Berry-Dee, Christopher, *Talking with Serial Killers: The Most Evil People in the World Tell Their Own Stories* (London: John Blake Publishing Ltd., 2003); Berry-Dee, Christopher, *Talking with Psychopaths and Savages: A Journey into the Evil Mind* (London: John Blake Publishing Ltd., 2017).

reason for an individual to become a dangerous, anti-social element of the society. Environment an individual is expose to is more likely to stimulate proneness to violence than lack of empathy. Empathy – Bloom argues – can provide strong insight into internal processes of another individual and their mental stances which can be used in order to deliberately cause harm.

Rational compassion should aim on providing an individual with an insight to another individual's mental stance, and seeking for the most appropriate actions in a certain situation. Rational compassion does not exclude the possibility for an individual to experience empathy, but serves as a better stance for decision making since it allows an individual to maintain ability of rational thinking and rational behavior. In a dangerous situation, rational compassion can lead to a better risk-calculation, content behavior and provide sustainable solutions. Also, since individuals' conceptual scheme expands due to gaining new experience, the response to the situation and provided solutions might improved as an individual's mind develops his conceptual schemes. It means that, unlike empathy that is purely based on emotional response and does not require a development of a human mind, rational compassion is affected by conceptual schemes.

Therefore, it can be concluded that empathy as a concept of experiencing another individuals' mental stance, is not a tool for solving and overcoming societal issues. Strong empathic response can cause more damage, while rational compassion can help to keep mental stance emotionally stable and capable of rational decision-making.

Conclusions

To sum up, it can be said that human mind is a complex phenomenon and experiences various internal processes to create connection between external stimuli and mental stances. Conscious mind creates experiences and is shaped by culture and environment it is exposed to, and human culture and environment are essential in order for a human mind to develop. Not being exposed to any human culture, for instance, children that have been raised by animals, can never integrate into a human society. All human experience, gained under the influence of the culture, is structured in human mind as conceptual schemes that help distinguish different mental stances and establish connections between concepts, and therefore, expanding conceptual schemes affects rational compassion and quality of decisions.

Empathy, being tempting and popular concept, has various issues that can cause issues if it is used for decision-making and as a tool to overcome societal problems. Empathy, being rooted in emotional response to an external situation, is not rational and does not allow an individual to analyze a situation rationally to make the most suitable decision. Empathy can be used for manipulation and to achieve desirable results, and therefore should be treated with caution and should not be cultivated as a solution for misunderstanding. Rather development of conceptual schemes through gain of a new experience, including experience of another cultures, religions, races, can be more beneficial in social situations.

Bibliography

Berry-Dee, Christopher, *Talking with Serial Killers: The Most Evil People in the World Tell Their Own Stories* (London: John Blake Publishing Ltd., 2003).

Berry-Dee, Christopher, *Talking with Psychopaths and Savages: A Journey into the Evil Mind* (London: John Blake Publishing Ltd., 2017).

Bloom, Paul, *Against Empathy: The Case for Rational Compassion* (London: Penguin Books, 2016).

Davidson, Donald, "On the Very Idea of a Conceptual Scheme", in *Proceedings and Addresses of the American Philosophical Association*, no. 47 (1973): 5–20.

Dennett, Daniel, *Brainstorms: Philosophical Essays in Mind and Psychology* (Cambridge-MA-London: The MIT Press, 1981).

Dennett, Daniel, *Consciousness Explained* (New York: Back Bay Books, 1992).

Dennett, Daniel, *Kinds of Minds: Towards An Understanding Of Consciousness* (New York: BasicBooks, 1996).

Dennett, Daniel C., *From Bacteria to Bach and Back: The Evolution of Minds* (New York: W. W. Norton & Company Inc., 2017).

Ghiselin, Michael T., *The Economy of Nature and the Evolution of Sex* (Berkeley-CA: University of California Press, 1974).

Hume, David, *Treatise of Human Nature* (London: Penguin Classics, 1986).

Obama, Barack, *The 21st January 2002 Speech at the Rockefeller Memorial Chapel for the Martin Luther King Day*. Viewed on the 16th October 2018. https://www.youtube.com/watch?v=CAbQvJrDVvo.

Ronson, Jon, *The Psychopath Test: A Journey Through the Madness Industry* (London: Picador, 2012).

Ross, Don; Thompson, David and Brook, Andrew, *Dennett's Philosophy* (Cambridge-MA-London: The MIT Press, 2000).

Smith, Adam, *The Theory of Moral Sentiments* (London: Penguin Classics, 2010).

CHAPTER 4

From Psychology to Morality: Sympathy, Imagination and Reason in Hume's Moral Philosophy

Gerardo López Sastre

Abstract

Hume's point of departure in the moral field is the existence of what he calls benevolence, sympathy or humanity, the psychological mechanism that makes us aware of other people's feelings and causes us to worry about them. For Hume, a person originally framed to have no concern for his fellow creatures would be a monster, what we would call a psychopath today. Most people in real life gain pleasure from seeing others' happiness and feel uneasy when they are in the presence of their pain. But this sympathy is not impartial, as is clear from the fact that it operates according to the degree of familiarity we have with others. We sympathize more with people close to us than with those that are not, more with people we know than with strangers, more with our fellow countrymen than with foreigners. However, this psychological fact should not shape our moral judgements. The moral point of view needs the exercise of our imagination. Sometimes we have to imagine we are closer to others to pass a moral judgment on them. At other times we have to forget they belong to the past. Consequently, using our imagination to experience different situations, we arrive at a 'steady and general point of view.' And we have to use our reason as well, since discovering the usefulness of a quality or behavior (and this presence of utility pleases, that is, generates our sympathy) can sometimes be difficult. To say it in other words, we can discover that our original or spontaneous sympathy was wrong.

Keywords

Hume – moral psychology – benevolence – sympathy – empathy – imagination – reason – moral judgement

I have decided to write about Hume's moral philosophy because I think his most significant points are correct. I agree with him that the point of departure of ethics must be an empirically-based moral psychology. This means that we first have a subjectivist stance, but we will see that it evolves or progresses from there to a common standpoint. In this respect, some moral elements can be of universal value. Moral values do not exist independent of the human mind. Although they are not objects in the external world, that does not mean they are completely subjective. We could say they are intersubjective, created from the fact that all of us share the same human frame, one that makes us approve of what is useful or agreeable to ourselves or to others, and disapprove of what is useless or disagreeable.[1] I will try to demonstrate this by giving some examples and making comparisons with other philosophers. At the same time, I am conscious that many aspects I defend here will need additional qualification, but I have been hampered by space constraints. In any case, I have decided to follow Hume's words very closely and, as a result, I cannot be very wrong in my thesis. With these warnings in mind we can begin with two examples.

The first is a story that Jonathan Glover recalls in his book *Humanity: A Moral History of the Twentieth Century*. It is the anecdote of a woman who lived close to the Mauthausen concentration camp and saw people that had been shot taking several hours to die. Her reaction was to write a letter to protest: "One is often an unwilling witness to such outrages. I am anyway sickly and such a sight makes such a demand on my nerves that in the long run I cannot bear this. I request that it be arranged that such inhuman deeds be discontinued, or else be done where one does not see it."[2]

In the second imaginary example I have added some details to one created by the philosopher Bernard Williams. In his book *Morality: An Introduction to Ethics* he asks us to think about the gangster movie stereotype. He is a ruthless figure, but cares about his mother or his lover. He is able to think in terms of the interests of others. We could assume he robs banks to buy a mink coat

---

[1] For a presentation of Hume's moral theory I would recommend the book by James Baillie, *Hume on Morality* (London: Routledge, 2000); for a presentation of Hume's philosophy that is much more general than the title suggests see Miller, David, *Philosophy and Ideology in Hume's Political Thought* (Oxford: Clarendon Press, 1981).

[2] Glover, Jonathan, *Humanity: A Moral History of the Twentieth Century* (London: Pimlico, 2001), 379–380. We can appreciate here that as the psychologist Steven Pinker writes: "distress at another's suffering is not the same as a sympathetic concern with their well-being. Instead it can be an unwanted reaction which people may suppress, or an annoyance they may try to escape." (Pinker, Steven, *The Better Angels of Our Nature: Why Violence Has Declined* (New York: Penguin, 2011), 575). One of the alternatives the letter proposes – the discontinuing of the shootings – could be considered a product of a feeling of compassion, but it could also be a proposal based on her egoistical objective of no longer being disturbed. The second alternative clearly has this end as her objective.

or a diamond necklace for his mistress or to pay for all kinds of gifts for his elderly mother. Then he would have to admit that he is perfectly capable of experiencing sympathy. What happens is that he experiences it in a terribly partial way, ignoring the damage his acts cause to the victims of his crimes. But this means that to persuade such a gangster to behave morally, we do not need to make him experience a feeling he did not know previously. What we have to do is to try to convince him to further extend the sympathy he already possesses. We could say he needs to learn to adopt a more impartial perspective than the one he has had in the past. He has to learn to consider others' emotions and welfare. We could add that sometimes he must simply realize that others exist; because what often happens is that he does not even spend a second thinking about their concerns or anxieties. As Bernard Williams concludes:

> The model [the example] is meant to suggest just one thing: that if we grant a man with even a minimal concern for others, then we do not have to ascribe to him any fundamentally new kind of thought or experience to include him in the world of morality, but only what is recognizably an extension of what he already has.[3]

What can we learn from these cases? This brute fact that we worry about other people is the point of departure of Hume's moral psychology. He writes that: "Every thing, which contributes to the happiness of society, recommends itself directly to our approbation and good-will. Here is a principle, which accounts, in great part, for the origin of morality."[4] Why are we constituted in such a way? Hume does not have an answer to this question, and the truth is that he does not worry about it:

> It is needless to push our researches so far as to ask, why we have humanity or a fellow-feeling with others. It is sufficient, that this is experienced to be a principle of human nature. We must stop somewhere in our examination of causes; and there are, in every science, some general principles, beyond which we cannot hope to find any principle more general. No man is absolutely indifferent to the happiness or misery of others. The first has a natural tendency to give pleasure; the second, pain. This every

---

3   Williams, Bernard, *Morality: An Introduction to Ethics* (Cambridge: Cambridge University Press, 1993), 12.
4   Hume, David, *An Enquiry Concerning the Principles of Morals*, section V, edited by Tom L. Beauchamp (Oxford and New York: Oxford University Press, 1998), 109.

one may find in himself. It is not probable, that these principles can be resolved into principles more simple and universal, whatever attempts may have been made to that purpose. But if it were possible, it belongs not to the present subject; and we may here safely consider these principles as original.[5]

That is why I was talking of a 'brute fact.' It is something we find in our make-up or constitution: "there is no human creature to whom the appearance of happiness (where envy or revenge has no place) does give no pleasure, that of misery, uneasiness."[6] With this thesis, Hume was opposing a well-known theory of his time (but not only of his time!), one that we should call 'egoism', the idea that we only worry about ourselves and that people *only* do what it is in their self-interest. In his more pessimistic moments, Hume comes close to admitting that we often act from selfish motives:

> Political writers have established it as a maxim, that, in contriving any system of government, and fixing the several checks and controls of the constitution, every man ought to be supposed a *knave*, and to have no other end, in all his actions than private interest. By this interest we must govern him, and, by means of it, make him, notwithstanding his insatiable avarice and ambition, co-operate to public good.[7]

---

[5] Hume, *An Enquiry*, footnote 19, 109.

[6] *Ibid.*, 120; and compare the beginning of *The Theory of Moral Sentiments* by Adam Smith: "How selfish soever man may be supposed, there are evidently some principles in his nature, which interest him in the fortune of others, and render their happiness necessary to him, though he derives nothing from it, except the pleasure of seeing it. Of this kind is pity or compassion, the emotion which we feel for the misery of others, when we either see it, or are made to conceive it in a very lively manner. That we often derive sorrow from the sorrow of others, is a matter of fact too obvious to require any instances to prove it; for this sentiment, like all the other original passions of human nature, is by no means confined to the virtuous and humane, though they perhaps may feel it with the most exquisite sensibility. The greatest ruffian, the most hardened violator of the laws of society, is not altogether without it." (Smith, Adam, *The Theory of Moral Sentiments: The Glasgow Edition of the Works and Correspondence of Adam Smith*, vol. I, edited by D. D. Raphael and A. L. Macfie (Indianapolis: Liberty Fund, 1984), 9). On the proximity (and differences) between Hume's and Smith's ideas *vid.* Rasmussen, Dennis C., *The Infidel and the Professor: David Hume, Adam Smith, and the Friendship that Shaped Modern Thought* (Princeton: Princeton University Press, 2017).

[7] *vid.* Hume, David, "Of the Independency of Parliament," in *Essays Moral, Political and Literary*, edited and with a Foreword, Notes and Glossary by Eugene F. Miller (Indianapolis: Liberty Classics, 1985), 42.

Although Hume admits this is a just *political* maxim, he says at the same time that it is false in *fact*.[8] What he wants to say is that we cannot be confident in morality as the cement of society. It is true that our prompt to action is often self-interest, and that general benevolence or humanity (because for Hume these are interchangeable words) is not a historically important force, but this does not mean it does not exist. Instead, while attempting to find the principles of morals, we have to ponder the existence of what we could call moral indifference and in other cases plain immorality. But, at the same time, the observation of human nature shows we are not indifferent to society's interests. We have to consider the following facts:

1. When we are told a story, go to the theater or read a book, we "frequently bestow praise on virtuous actions, performed in very distant ages and remote countries; where the utmost subtilty of imagination would not discover any appearance of self-interest."[9]
2. A generous or noble deed, performed by an adversary or enemy can command our moral approbation at the same time that we are conscious that it is contrary to our particular interests.[10]

Hume, therefore, considers that even if our view of human nature is quite pessimistic (as he sounds in the above-quoted text), we have to recognize this minimum:

> there is some benevolence, however small, infused into our bosom; some spark of friendship for human kind; some particle of the dove, kneaded into our frame, along with the elements of the wolf and serpent. Let these generous sentiments be supposed ever so weak; let them be insufficient to move even a hand or finger of our body; they must still direct the determinations of our mind, and where every thing else is equal, produce a cool preference of what is useful and serviceable to mankind, above what is pernicious and dangerous.[11]

When this does not happen, we would not be before a human being, but before what Hume calls a 'fancied monster':

> Let us suppose a person originally framed so as to have no manner of concern for his fellow-creatures, but to regard the happiness and misery

---

8 *Ibid.* It is Hume who uses the italics.
9 Hume, *An Enquiry*, 106.
10 *Ibid.*
11 *Ibid.*, 147.

of all sensible beings with greater indifference than even two contiguous shades of the same colour. Let us suppose, if the prosperity of nations were laid on the one hand, and their ruin on the other, and he were desired to choose; that he would stand, like the schoolman's ass, irresolute and undetermined, between equal motives; or rather, like the same ass between two pieces of wood or marble, without any inclination or propensity to either side. The consequence, I believe, must be allowed just, that such a person, being absolutely unconcerned, either for the public good of a community or the private utility of others, would look on every quality, however pernicious, or however beneficial, to society, or to its possessor, with the same indifference as on the most common and uninterested object.[12]

However, this is not an alternative to which the theorist of morals must defend themself, because it is easy to conclude that this person, having broken their links with others' feelings, is mentally sick, a psychopath, a person with a deficit in cerebral brain function. Such a figure is not enviable at all and more likely to cause grief or horror than anything else.[13] But it is a figure that can show us the origin of morality, the fact that we are affected by others' happiness or unhappiness. This is not a theory Hume invented, however, as it was upheld by a wide variety of philosophers. Outside Europe, for example, we find it in the ancient Chinese philosopher Mencius. He writes that "All humans have hearts that are not unfeeling toward others," and the reason he gives to support this thesis is the famous example of someone who suddenly sees a young child on the verge of falling into a well. He states that:

---

12   *Ibid.*, 120. And Hume is clearly right. As a contemporary psychology researcher writes: "toddlers do seem to care about others. Some experiments explore this by getting adults to act as if they are in pain (such as the child's mother pretending to get her finger caught in a clipboard) and then seeing how children respond. It turns out that they often try to soothe the adults, making an effort to make their pain go away. Other studies find that toddlers will help adults who are struggling to pick up an object that is out of reach or struggling to open a door. The toddlers do so without any prompting from the adults, not even eye contact, and will do so at a price, walking away from an enjoyable box of toys to offer assistance. They really do seem to want to help." (Bloom, Paul, *Against Empathy: The Case for Rational Compassion* (London: Penguin, 2016), 171); and see for more details and experiments Bloom, Paul, *Just Babies: The Origins of Good and Evil*, (New York: Broadway Books, 2013).

13   See Williams, *Morality*, 9–10.

anyone in such a situation would have a feeling of alarm and compassion – not because one sought to get in good with the child's parents, not because one wanted fame among one's neighbors and friends, and not because one would dislike the sound of the child's cries.[14]

A famous second example by Mencius is the following: asked by a king about whether he would be able to be a true king and protect his people, he answers 'yes', and that his certainty is based on this story. Mencius knows that one day the king saw a person leading an ox. He was going to sacrifice him to consecrate a bell with his blood. The king ordered that the ox be released because he could not bear its frightened appearance, *like an innocent going to the execution ground*. But in this case, he was asked, "should we dispense with the anointing of the bell? And the king answered, 'How can that be dispensed with? Exchange it for a sheep'."[15] We can ask ourselves whether there is any morality or any moral progress here. If the king could not bear the ox's suffering, how is it that he can bear the sheep's? Mencius's answer is that the key is that the king has seen the ox, but not the sheep that is going to die in its place, and he explains: "Gentleman cannot bear to see animals die if they have seen them living. If they hear their cries of suffering, they cannot bear to eat their flesh. Hence, gentlemen keep their distance from the kitchen."[16] This reminds us,

---

14 For the reference I am using the following edition translated with introduction and notes by Bryan W. Van Norden, in Mencius, *Menzi with selections from traditional commentaries*, Book 2, Part A, Chapter 6 (Indianapolis-Cambridge: Hackett, 2008), 46. On the same page the commentator asks the reader to note that Mencius does not say that every human would act to save the child, but that everyone would have at least a momentary feeling of compassion, which is clearly not the same thing. Another consideration I would like to insist on is that it seems we cannot conclude that this adult empathizes in a psychological way with the child. One could experience the impulse to save a child who is drowning in a lake without previously experiencing in a vicarious way anything like the unpleasant sensation of drowning. Perhaps this is the kind of consideration that makes Hume use, together with the word 'sympathy', the words 'benevolence' and 'humanity'. We could add the qualification that acting in accordance with empathy and compassion is not always moral. I can experience great empathy and compassion towards the students who in an exam review ask me to raise their marks (I have also been a student!), but it may not be fair (that is, moral) to accept their request (for all this *vid.* Bloom, *Just Babies*, 44–47). Then it seems clear that morality is not the same as compassion (and that, in fact, morality and compassion can sometimes collide), although it also seems clear that morality would not exist if we did not care for others.
15 See Mencius, *Menzi,* 9.
16 *Ibid.*

rightfully, of the popular expression 'out of sight, out of mind' and because of it, this feeling the King experiences is only the beginning of morality, the point of departure. Mencius wants the king to understand that once he has the feeling he has to extend it, deploy it in a consistent manner. He has to realize that if his kindness reaches animals, the benefits of his government must reach all the people. Morality admits no exceptions. But, of course, before reflexively extending the feeling, we have to possess it. It is very interesting to compare Mencius's ideas with a passage in Rousseau's *Discourse on the Origin and Basis of Inequality Among Men*:

> We find, with pleasure, the author of the Fable of the Bees obliged to own that man is a compassionate and sensible being, and laying aside his cold subtlety of style, in the example he gives, to present us with the pathetic description of a man who, from a place of confinement, is compelled to behold a wild beast tear a child from the arms of its mother, grinding its tender limbs with its murderous teeth, and tearing its palpitating entrails with its claws. What horrid agitation must not the eyewitness of such a scene experience, although he would not be personally concerned! What anxiety would he not suffer at not being able to give any assistance to the fainting mother and the dying infant!/Such is the pure emotion of nature, prior to all kinds of reflection! Such is the force of natural compassion.[17]

For this reason, and always thinking of Mencius, François Jullien writes:

> to be human, as it should be, is to make this sensitivity to others around me effective – which is virtual in me. Later commentators will find nothing better to characterize this *sense* of the human than to illustrate it in relation to the body. In Chinese medical treatises, the same term of *ren* (composed of man and number two) serves to designate, in a negative

---

[17] I owe this comparison between Mencius and Rousseau to the excellent book by François Jullien, *Dialogue sur la morale* (Grasset: Le Livre de Poche, 1995). The fragment quoted is in page 24. Speaking of that spontaneous and immediate reaction concerning a child who is about to fall into a well described by Mencius, Jullien writes that "we cannot suppose that it is the product of some internalization: nor of the resentment of the weak (as in Nietzsche), neither of a class interest (as in Marx), nor of the function of the Father (as in Freud). It is ideologically pure, free from all alienation. It is because of this that it can serve as a touchstone of morals." (*Ibid.*, 44). The quotation from Rousseau is taken from the translation by G. D. H. Cole's public domain, http://www.aub.edu.lb/fas/cvsp/Documents/DiscourseonInequality.pdf879500092.pdf. Viewed on the 28th August 2018.

way, the numbness of the extremity of the limbs, hands or feet. As the vital energy "no longer passes through them," one has the impression that they don't belong to us and one no longer feels them. To be no-*ren* is to be numb. On the contrary, to be *ren*, to be human, is to take the conscience out of numbness in relation to others, to be receptive to what happens to them, to feel strengthened the vital link with them.[18]

In short, as Mencius knew very well, once we become aware of that feeling of concern for someone that at a certain moment can seize us, what we need to do is systematize it. This is also what Hume proposes: to work on what we could call a primary sentiment. As he writes in the *Treatise*:

> In general, all sentiments of blame or praise are variable, according to our situation of nearness or remoteness, with regard to the person blam'd or prais'd, and according to the present disposition of our mind. But these variations we regard not in our general decisions, but still apply the terms expressive of our liking or dislike, in the same manner, as if we remain'd in one point of view. Experience soon teaches us this method of correcting our sentiments, or at least, of correcting our language, where the sentiments are more stubborn and inalterable. Our servant, if diligent and faithful, may excite stronger sentiments of love and kindness than *Marcus Brutus*, as represented in History; but we say not upon that account, that the former character is more laudable than the latter. We know, that were we to approach equally near to that renown'd patriot, he wou'd command a much higher degree of affection and admiration. Such corrections are common with regard to all the senses; and indeed 'twere impossible we cou'd ever make use of language, or communicate our sentiments to one another, did we not correct the momentary appearances of things, and overlook our present situation.[19]

One is the viewpoint of our interests, which can generate our predominant psychological affections, the other is the point of view of morals. Moral sentiments are the product of a modification or correction of the sentiments generated from our interest or from our own particular point of view; or in any case they are feelings we arrive at when we adopt a perspective that is different

---

18   Jullien, *Dialogue*, 83.
19   Hume, David, *A Treatise of Human Nature*, Book III, Part III, Sect. I, edited by L. A. Selby-Bigge, 2nd edition with text revised by P. H. Nidditch, (Oxford: Oxford University Press, 1978), 582.

from the consideration of how the actions evaluated stand in relation to ourselves. In this respect, insofar as they are different feelings, they can produce their own language, the language of morals:

> When a man denominates another his *enemy*, his *rival*, his *antagonist*, his *adversary*, he is understood [...] to express sentiments, peculiar to himself, and arising from his particular circumstances and situation. But when he bestows on any man the epithets of *vicious* or *odious* or *depraved*, he then speaks another language, and expresses sentiments, in which, he expects, all his audience are to concur with him. He must here, therefore, depart from his private and particular situation, and must choose a point of view, common to him with others: He must move some universal principle of the human frame, and touch a string, to which all mankind have an accord and symphony [...] The humanity of one man is the humanity of every one; and the same object touches this passion in all human creatures.[20]

This is what allows morals to be universal. Moral judgements are made from a general point of view. They are made considering what we feel when we view actions (as manifestations of characters) from what Hume calls a 'general survey.'[21] This view is not always easy to attain. In fact, it is not putting myself in someone else's shoes nor changing my perspective to choose that of another person, the actor. No, it is choosing a common point of view. In this respect it seems to me that what Hume is proposing is a radical change from our primary sympathy, because it is clear that we sympathize more with our acquaintances than with strangers; with our countrymen than with foreigners. But Hume remarks that, "notwithstanding this variation of our sympathy, we give the same approbation to the same moral qualities in *China* as in *England*. They appear equally virtuous, and recommend themselves equally to the esteem of a judicious spectator."[22] Therefore, morals require the use of the imagination, as in the case of the appreciation of beauty. A beautiful countenance is the same whether it is far away or close, and we can say that because we can imagine that the pleasurable effect would be the same if we were to get closer.[23] It is the same when Hume talks about 'virtue in rags.' We morally appreciate a person whose character would benefit the interest of society even though particular

---

20   Hume, *Enquiry*, 148.
21   Hume, *Treatise*, 614.
22   Hume, *Treatise*, 581.
23   *Ibid.*, 582.

accidents prevent this character from exercising their capacities, and this is because we can imagine what their effects would be if there were no impediments.[24] Hume's conclusion is summarized as "the imagination adheres to the *general* views of things, and distinguishes betwixt the feelings they produce from those which arise from our particular and momentary situation."[25] Is there a good recipe that can help us to arrive at these "general views of things"? The exchange of ideas, the dialogue with other people can serve this purpose: "The intercourse of sentiments, therefore, in society and conversation, makes us form some general unalterable standard, by which we may approve or disapprove of characters and manners."[26]

And if imagination is important, we can say the same of reason. If I have the desire to help someone, reason will tell me the best way to do it, and it is because I know about this medium leading to this end that I will appreciate it from a moral stance. Conversely, reason can correct our feelings, for example, telling us that we have reached a wrong conclusion. In our case, for example, using an inadequate medium. In an example that Hume uses, I can morally approve the act of given alms to common beggars (it would be a natural reaction), but if I discover that by it I am making begging a profession and not really helping people to improve their lives, I will change my feeling of moral approval about this act.[27] Consequently, reason is what would later be called an 'instrumental reason' because the moral standpoint must take the long-term consequences of human behavior into account, and this is something our immediate sympathy does not do. However, as Hume writes, "where a passion is neither founded on false suppositions, nor chuses means insufficient for the end, the understanding can neither justify nor condemn it." And he continues with a statement that has become famous: " 'Tis not contrary to reason to prefer the destruction of the whole world to the scratching of my finger. 'Tis not contrary to reason for me to chuse my total ruin, to prevent the least uneasiness of an *Indian* or person wholly unknown to me."[28] It is true that these choosings would not be against reason, but from the perspective of our philosopher they would be less human, as they would go against our sense of humanity, against "the benevolent concern for others" we possess. And, furthermore, this concern can increase in ourselves thanks to our social life and others' support and approval. In this respect, we create what Hume calls "the

---

24   Ibid., 584–585.
25   Ibid., 587.
26   Hume, *Enquiry*, 116.
27   Ibid., 81.
28   Hume, *Treatise*, 416.

party of human kind against vice or disorder."[29] Could we think of a more interesting view of morality?

Bibliography

Baillie, James, *Hume on Morality* (London: Routledge, 2000).

Bloom, Paul, *Just Babies: The Origins of Good and Evil* (New York: Broadway Books, 2013).

Bloom, Paul, *Against Empathy: The Case for Rational Compassion* (London: Penguin Books, 2016).

Glover, Jonathan, *Humanity: A Moral History of the Twentieth Century* (London: Pimlico, 2001).

Hume, David, *A Treatise of Human Nature*, edited by L. A. Selby-Bigge, 2nd edition with text revised by P. H. Nidditch (Oxford: Oxford University Press, 1978).

Hume, David, *Essays Moral, Political and Literary*, edited and with a Foreword, Notes and Glossary by Eugene F. Miller (Indianapolis: Liberty Classics, 1985).

Hume, David, *An Enquiry concerning the Principles of Morals*, edited by Tom L. Beauchamp (Oxford and New York: Oxford University Press, 1998).

Jullien, François, *Dialogue sur la morale* (Grasset: Le Livre de Poche, 1995).

Mencius, *Menzi with selections from traditional commentaries*, translated with Introduction and Notes by Bryan W. Van Norden (Indianapolis-Cambridge: Hackett, 2008).

Miller, David, *Philosophy and Ideology in Hume's Political Thought* (Oxford: Clarendon Press, 1981).

Pinker, Steven, *The Better Angels of Our Nature: Why Violence Has Declined* (New York: Penguin Books, 2011).

Rasmussen, Dennis C., *The Infidel and the Professor: David Hume, Adam Smith, and the Friendship that Shaped Modern Thought* (Princeton: Princeton University Press, 2017).

Rousseau, Jean J., *Discourse on the Origin and Basis of Inequality Among Men*, translation to English by G. D. H. Cole's, lodged in this public domain, http://www.aub.edu.lb/fas/cvsp/Documents/DiscourseonInequality.pdf87950092.pdf. Viewed on the 28th August 2018.

Smith, Adam, *The Theory of Moral Sentiments: The Glasgow Edition of the Works and Correspondence of Adam Smith*, vol. 1, edited by D. D. Raphael and A. L. Macfie (Indianapolis: Liberty Fund, 1984).

Williams, Bernard, *Morality: An Introduction to Ethics* (Cambridge: Cambridge University Press, 1993).

---

29   Hume, *Enquiry*, 150.

CHAPTER 5

Existence as a Matter of Co-existence: Jean-Jacques Rousseau's Moral Psychology of *Pitié*

Nina Lex

Abstract

With Rousseau's depiction of the human capacity for pity, he can be seen as a forerunner or even starting point for the later and even current discourse on empathy. In particular my contribution wants to shed light on how Rousseau, by emphasizing the emotion in general and in contrast to the domination of the belief in *ratio*, marks the essence to make 'the human' in depth understandable. When referring to his terminology of pity, compassion or commiseration a theory unfolds where being human is intrinsically linked to sensitivity – not only but also and crucially through empathy, namely pity. A social realm is set within, that itself, while implicitly embodying a basic normativity, becomes also a factor for explicitly deriving norms through the inter-subjective rationalisation it determines. The self-mastering of the autonomous individual, embodied by Émile as a prototype, reflects therefore a freedom – even or especially moral freedom – where the other is understood as genuine and not only random part of a self-concept. Empathy as the social realisation of the self therewith not only makes us acting human, but is the crucial entity to *be* human, when *being* human is understood through subjectivity, morality and rationality.

Keywords

pity – compassion – commiseration – Inter-subjectivity – morality – rationality – sensitivity – alienation – virtue

1   Amour de soi

In Rousseau's book *Essai sur l'origine des langues* [*Essay On the Origin of Languages*], he introduces a striking emblematic picture about (*wo-*)man's[1] development of language, that hints already to an articulation in language of receptivity, understanding and interpretation, including the form of speech known as listening that enables the other to appreciate that he or she has been the target of empathy, stating that "*le premier mot ne fut pas chez eux, aimez-moi, mais, aidez-moi.*"[2] Of course, Rousseau is well known to have given preference to the sentiment before reason, but especially when regarding him as the forerunner of all subsequent and also modern contributors to the discourse on empathy, this suggestive metaphorical reflection on the relational quotient of a genuine sentiment and its moral implication in terms of a social determination demands a deeper and more detailed examination to unfold the rich heritage that he has left us to spell out. Even his primacy of feeling is in its essence not as easy to depict as many of his critics and mockers may suggest. But as this is nonetheless the starting point to grasp Rousseau's complex concept of the intertwinement of feeling, *ratio* and reciprocity to form humans moral psychology, we need to fully understand, what the notion of the sentiment provides in this very context.

Addressing the topic of empathy, it might be helpful to begin with sorting the actual references of the term. While Rousseau is – also as a matter of historical status quo of the terminology – not yet explicitly referring to empathy in the same sense as our current discourse picks it up, he sets up his framework with the genuine meaning of feeling and sensitivity itself:

> Exister pour nous c'est sentir ; et nôtre sensibilité est incontestablement antérieure à nôtre raison même. [...] Ces sentiments, quant à l'individu, sont l'amour de soi même, la crainte de la douleur, l'horreur de la mort, le désir du bien être.[3]

---

1 Rousseau is more or less explicitly excluding women from his focus. Despite not expressly formulating a gender topic, it is clear in his writings that his universalist view on equality is not as universally and equally expressed as his theory would allow it. In this regard, I want to understand his analysis as an impulse for further and even broader explanation of what his idea could mean when consequently thought through into systematic detail. I myself when referring to a generalised content, will however stick to the male form only because of the formal rigour in which Émile is used as a generalised Prototype that in my opinion must be understood genderless.

2 In what follows, I will make use of my own translations from the original in French, here: [The first word among them was not 'aimez-moi' [love me] but 'aidez moi' [help me].] (Rousseau, Jean-Jacques, *Essai sur l'origine des langues* (Paris: Gallimard, 1995), 408).

3 [For us, to exist is to feel; and our sensitivity is incontestably prior to our reason. Whatever the cause of our existence might be, it has provided for our preservation by giving us feelings in conformity to our nature; and one could not deny that at least those are innate. With

When referring more specifically to the sentiment, Rousseau expresses within the category of *amour de soi* a feeling in the original sense as well as it expresses a specific self-relation in terms of loving oneself which can primarily be understood as a basic instinct of self-preservation, whereas the self that is referred to here must be understood as a self without yet specified identity, without the me in the I in terms of an awareness of an ego, since this kind of extended and human self-consciousness only develops in relation to one's own kind. *"Le premier sentiment de l'homme fut celui de son existence ; son premier soin celui de sa conservation."*[4] This kind of *amour de soi* therewith forms *"une loi constitutive de l'existence de l'individu, c'est le désir d'exister, principe antérieur à la raison, antérieur à toute réflexion."*[5] Especially when picturing the natural man as a solitary being, Rousseau almost radicalises the term of self-preservation in comparison to Hobbes, while with respect to Rousseau's moral conclusions concerning the natural man he rather diametrically opposes Hobbes' theory of human's original state. Considering that it must be understood very prosaic – meaning self-preservative and not yet genuinely social in an empathic sense – when the first sentiment of loving oneself according to self-preservation soon is transformed into loving those who are close to us.[6]

Alongside this basic passion, Rousseau posits yet another one that directs us to attend to and relieve the suffering of other beings as long as it does not conflict with our self-preservation, namely *pitié*. This form of basic sympathy or compassion may later on turn out to not only serve as a sort of corrective for when the *amour de soi* transforms to or gets accompanied by the self absorbing *amour-propre*, but may also be the basic source of developing a compassion that not only passively avoids doing harm to others, but also actively fulfils the needs of what Rousseau identifies as virtue.[7] While *amour de soi* does not

---

    regard to the individual these feelings are love of oneself, fear of pain and of death, and the desire for well-being.] (Rousseau, Jean-Jacques, *Lettres Morales* (Paris: Gallimard, 1969), 94).

4 [Man's first sentiment was that of his existence, his first care that of his preservation.] (Rousseau, Jean-Jacques, *Discours sur l'origine et les fondemens de l'inegalité parmi les hommes* (Hamburg: Meiner, 1995), 192).

5 [A constitutive law of existence, it's the wish to exist, a principle, which is preceding reason as well as reflection.] (Rousseau, Jean-Jacques, *Émile ou De l'éducation*, (Paris: Gallimard, 1969), 491); Bjørsnøs, Annlaug, "Le processus d'individuation dans La Nouvelle Héloïse de Jean-Jacques Rousseau", *Romansk Forum*, vol. 16, no. 2 (2002): 4.

6 Rousseau, *Émile ou De l'éducation*, 491. As quoted above, the individual is instinctively attracted to what creates well-being and rejects what does harm to him. Rousseau emphasises that it is only the intension that makes instinct become a sentiment. This idea of sentiment therewith seems to belong already to a category of reflection, which is already based on another level than the original feeling of mere existence.

7 Rousseau, *Discours sur l'origine et les fondemens de l'inegalité parmi les hommes*, 71–72.

yet necessarily points to the meaning of inter-subjectivity, the latter *amour-propre* does. That given, the latter as we will see has the potential to become the most serious opponent to empathy, while it also marks and defines empathy's genuine condition and realisation, since compassion unfolds it's full range merely in the context of a social realm that only the reflective category of *amour-propre* is allowed to utilise.

The first and most simple – meaning pre-rational – principles that move the soul as depicted by Rousseau can therewith be identified as (1) *amour de soi*,[8] which passionately takes care of the own wellbeing, and (2) compassion, which – even if still in a non reflected way – kind of intuitively carries out the self-preservation with the least damage to others.[9] Only in a second step, the (here still pre-rational) compassion develops due to the faculty of imagination and reason to an active moral entity. In this regard, it makes sense that several recipients interpreted this evolvement as a two-staged principle of pity or compassion.[10] Analogously Rousseau differentiates between a reason of sentiment and an intellectual reason:

> Comme tout ce qui entre dans l'entendement humain y vient par les sens, la première raison de l'homme est une raison sensitive ; c'est elle qui sert de base à la raison intellectuelle.[11]

While Rousseau does not project empathy in its more complex sense back to the state of brute, animalistic existence, he nevertheless gives its rudimentary form a genuine place in humans origins.[12] It is helpful to hint here to a terminological specification that will later on mark a significant turning point for what being human really means according to Rousseau. This is the very differentiation between compassion or pity and the later moral compassion, which

---

8   *Ibid.*, 169. The latter citation marks the first reference in his work where Rousseau makes a terminological differentiation between *amour de soi* and *amour-propre*. In Émile this will play a central role while it is eventually depict in the first Dialogue as a differentiation of *amour* and *haine par excellence*.
9   *Ibid.*, 177.
10   vid. Müller, Reimar, *Anthropologie und Geschichte* (Berlin: Akademie, 1997), 129.
11   [Since man perceives everything he understands only through his senses, the first reason of man is a sensual reason; the latter is the basis for intellectual reason.] (Rousseau. *Émile ou De l'éducation*, 370).
12   vid. Goldschmidt, Victor, *Anthropologie et politique. Les principes du système de Rousseau* (Paris: Librairie Philosophique Vrin, 1983), 336–338.

is based on a more complex version of empathy. While these distinctions can be controversial, especially when referring to a theory that is not in the strict sense systematic, it is even more necessary to narrow down the terminology according to what the context allows.

The pity Rousseau addresses in the first place is, as said, a rather pre-rational affect. It is the repugnance of seeing others or one's own kind suffering. When empathy is, roughly speaking, defined as the capacity to put oneself in someone else's position – i.e. to feel alike – then this first repugnance of seeing somebody suffering can already be seen as a very poor, but nonetheless, crucial form of empathy. However, it has not yet arrived at the responsive state of compassion.

When Rousseau sees the good of the natural man have originating already in the brute, limited beginnings, it becomes obvious how far away his description is from the widely spread romanticism of the *bon sauvage* and the glorification of the primitive in the 17th and 18th century. Even though there are good reasons to call him the precursor and representative of the epitome of a new sentimentality, the qualitative classification of the natural state he depicts show that he is not nostalgically devoted to a vain idyll. Nevertheless, he contrasts the predominant logocentrism of his time with a strong emphasis on the sentiment:

> Car nous sentons nécessairement avant que de connoitre, et comme nous n'apprenons point à vouloir nôtre bien personnel et à fuir notre mal, mais tenons cette volonté de la nature, de même l'amour du bon et la haine mauvais nous sont aussi naturels que nôtre propre éxistence.[13]

This clear differentiation of emotional and rational drive may also serve as an indication for his understanding of a pre-rational, not yet reflected and in that sense even amoral empathy which can be addressed as a receptiveness and a minimalistic understanding of the other as a possibility of commitment and implementation. Still, the constitution of the human in the natural state captures so far only the potential of human's possible social structures. Making the sentiment the primacy before ratio he does not only refer to a vague passionateness, but to emotional affection that he explicitly links to moral

---

13   [For we necessarily feel before knowing, and since we do not learn to wish for our personal good and to flee from our harm, but obtain that will from nature, in the same way love of the good and hatred of the bad are as natural to us as our own existence.] (Rousseau, *Lettres Moral*, 1109).

impressions and opposes it in his cultural critical understanding to rational cognitive operations:

> Mais dans ce siècle où l'on s'efforce de matérialiser toutes les opérations de l'âme et d'ôter toute moralité aux sentiments humaines, je suis trompé si la nouvelle philosophie ne devient aussi funeste au bon goût qu'à la vertu.[14]

Besides all cultural and academic criticism, the process of civilisation however demands basing the rules and laws that spring from nature not only on the sentiment but also on reason and reasoning to establish them as laws in the sense of norms[15] or to enhance the empathic affect in terms of a reflective declaration of intent or obligation. Conversely, society or social life is the basis upon which to actually derive such rational conclusion. That means that what defines the content of rational agency forms itself according to the natural sentiment only in the inter-subjective context. What is shown with the emphasis of the sentiment is the conviction that the emotional component has with respect to the moral orientation a key role that is prior to *ratio*, while it's effectively normative content is formed by the latter through mutual inter-subjective, cooperative and empathic bonds. The social context is nevertheless variable and, concerning *amour-propre*, relative; this also means that it can be as corruptive as it can be (self-)enhancing. However, regarding the diagnosis of his society Rousseau tends to see its influence very pessimistically. That is also his angle when denunciating the civilised human in writing:

> L'homme sensuel est l'homme de la nature ; l'homme réfléchi est celui de l'opinion ; c'est celui-ci qui est dangereux. L'autre ne peut jamais l'être quand même il tomberoit dans l'excès.[16]

This notion of the sentiment in general and the basic empathy in terms of pity might be understood as a genuine moral inclination and that the development of this potential becomes characteristic for being human. Simple

---

14 [But in this century, when every effort is made to materialize all the operations of the soul and to deprive human feelings of all morality, I am mistaken if the new philosophy does not become as fatal to good taste as to virtue.] (Rousseau, *Essai sur l'origine des langues*, 419).
15 Rousseau, *Discours sur l'origine et les fondemens de l'inegalité parmi les hommes*, 73.
16 [The sensual man is the natural man, the reflective man is the one of opinion and this one is dangerous. The first could never be dangerous even if he would fall victim of excess.]

words therefore mean nothing according to Rousseau, because *"si l'impression n'en pénètre jusqu'à son cœur, elle est nulle."*[17] As soon as reflexivity is involved though, the paradigms change drastically – yet, undecided if for the better or worse. It marks the moment when pure sensation transcends into a judgement, respectively when sensations become terms and shift from the sensual sphere into matters of the mind.[18] While primarily the empathy Rousseau accounts for the natural state is acted out in a negative way – repugnance at seeing somebody suffer – it is nonetheless a primal motivation for deriving later on, through a reflexive process of abstraction and (self-)objectification, active behavioural manuals or norms. Nevertheless, the sentiment alone will not be sufficient to spell out norms in a concrete, legitimated way. This calls for the moment when reflexivity derives actual ideas and, in a further active step, judgements from our passive sensual perception. It therefore becomes plausible why Rousseau puts so much emphasize on the first period, the negative education, to avoid prejudice and mere imitation to let the pupil form genuine, unbiased ideas.[19]

In fact, Rousseau does not develop a system of affects with this, nor is he spelling out a scientific moral psychology of sentiments and reason; still he drafts a psychology of a natural mentality and potentiality.[20] In that sense the *amour de soi* turns out to be the starting point for the complex intertwining of reason, imagination and empathy. Especially when later the *amour-propre* comes into play, it is necessary to emphasise that according to Rousseau this still native feeling towards oneself and the self-preservation prescribes no genuine and, in particular, no moral devaluation of the other. The inborn *amour de soi* though points to the essence of feeling and to the specific self-relation. It is therewith a departure not only in its negative function concerning the avoidance of pain etc., but also in a positive sense as an impetus to a more complex, active drive. *"L'amour des hommes d'rivé de l'amour de soi est le principe de la justice humaine."*[21] This is called upon later with the development of *amour-propre*, although we shall leave it undecided for now if *amour-propre*

(Rousseau, Jean-Jacques, *Rousseau juge de Jean-Jacques : Dialogues* (Paris: Gallimard, 1959), 808).

17   [If their impression does not pierce to the heart, it is null.] (*Ibid.*, 808).
18   *vid.* Rousseau, *Émile ou De l'éducation*, 380–430.
19   *Ibid.*, 458–481.
20   *vid.* Rang, Martin, *Rousseaus Lehre vom Menschen* (Göttingen: Vanderhoeck&Ruprecht, 1959), 120.
21   [Out of *amour de soi* is love for humanity deduced as the basis for human justice.] (Rousseau, *Émile ou De l'éducation*, 523).

develops out of *amour de soi* or if it is a completely new developed passion in terms of perfectibility. Let us accept for now that *amour-propre* is in its essence (though being a passion and according to Rousseau all passions derive from *amour de soi*) qualitatively different from the later. While *amour-propre* can partly be seen as a means for self-preservation – namely the social survival[22] in terms of recognition – *amour-propre* as a relative feeling aims at extending oneself and furthermore often seduces to make oneself the centre:

> Il ne faut pas confondre l'amour-propre et l'amour de soi-même, deux passions très différentes par leur nature et par leurs effets. L'amour de soi-même est un sentiment naturel qui porte tout animal à veiller à sa propre conservation, et qui, dirigé dans l'homme par la raison et modifié par la pitié, produit l'humanité et la vertu, amour-propre n'est qu'un sentiment relatif, factice, et né dans la société, qui porte chaque individu à faire plus de cas de soi que de tout autre, qui inspire aux hommes tous les maux qu'ils se font mutuellement, et qui est la véritable source de l'honneur.[23]

Without responding to all the difficulties and problems that are bound to *amour-propre* or that come along with it, it confronts us in its negative or inflamed condition as a major threat to empathy. When this reflective capacity comes into play, humans start to compare or vice versa, with the comparison humans start to reflect and become judgmental.[24] This, in its essence, comparative and therefore relative capacity, crucially affects or even corrupts our judgment and validation as it has or puts the I as a reference point to all relational constructions – whether in terms of subjectivity or even worse in terms of competition – and forms an ego that easily becomes a victim of vanity and vain glory. Unfolding only in a social context, *amour-propre* also becomes therewith a pitfall to all

---

22   Neuhouser, Frederick, "Rousseau und das menschliche Verlangen nach Anerkennung", in *Deutsche Zeitschrift für Philosophie*, vol. 56 (2008): 903.

23   [You must not confuse *amour-propre* and *amour de soi*. According to their nature and their effect, they are two very different passions. *Amour de soi* is a natural feeling. It demands every animal to take care of its own preservation. In us humans, it is directed by reason and tempered by pity and leads to humanity and virtue. *Amour-propre* is only a relative, artificial feeling, originated in society. It seduces every being to consider himself more than anybody else. It infiltrates the human with all evils they can do to each other. It is the very root of honour.] (Rousseau, *Discours sur l'origine et les fondemens de l'inegalité parmi les hommes*, 169).

24   *vid.* Rousseau, *Essai sur l'origine des langues*, 396.

human potential. The dangers *amour-propre* can be inflamed of are plenty and reach from alienation over self-estrangement to inner conflict and misery.[25] The main problem I want to focus on in this contribution is the controversial part amour-propre contains as an antagonist, catalyst as well as the pylon of empathy and in a further step moral integrity and normativity.

While Rousseau, as we have seen above, considers pity in its not yet reflected state as a purely natural passion, it evolves through the process of socialisation only due to *amour-propre* and its reflexive component as well as imagination and rationality to a normative factor in the moral sense.

> Celui qui n'a jamais refléchi ne peut être ni clement ni juste ni pitoyable : il ne peut pas non plus être méchant et vindicatif. Celui qui n'imagine rien ne sent que lui-même ; il est seul au milieu du genre humain.[26]

The natural form of pity or compassion must therefore be understood as a corrective for the later *amour-propre* and in combination with imagination as a basic source of insight to equality.[27] With its relational condition, *amour-propre* embeds to realise contexts that on the one hand allow to the development of identity, while on the other hand entailing self-objectification. With respect to the empathetic development, it eventually allows an interpretation of the other from first-, second-, and third-person perspective that will be crucial to alternate the self-other distinction in terms of an altruistic identification and to conclude to an equality that transcends differences to the equality of sensitivity respectively a qualitative similarity.

In contrast to *amour de soi*, *amour-propre* is never satisfied and has the potential to take on a strongly competitive drive that puts (hu-)man beings out of themselves.[28] While both forms of this love consist in a certain love of oneself, they are directed very differently or seek even different goods. While one is, as written above, occupied with a basic, physical self-preservation, the other already mirrors a more complex structure, as through and by it the social realm opens up through comparison.[29] The latter leads to a relational position of the

---

25 vid. Neuhouser, Frederick, *Rousseau's Theodicy of Self-love: Evil, Rationality, and the Drive for Recognition* (New York: Oxford University Press, 2008), 70.
26 [He who has never reflected cannot be clement, or just, or pitying – no more than he can be wicked and vindictive. He who imagines nothing feels only himself; he is alone in the midst of mankind.] (Rousseau, *Essai sur l'origine des langues*, 395–396).
27 Rousseau, *Discours sur l'origine et les fondemens de l'inegalité parmi les hommes*, 171.
28 Rousseau, *Émile ou De l'éducation*, 491–492.
29 Rousseau, *Discours sur l'origine et les fondemens de l'inegalité parmi les hommes*, 204.

self that is due to inflamed *amour-propre* very prone to end up in a highly competitive way, which perpetuates self-estrangement and a society that is built up on all kippers and curtains.[30]

> Les hommes, livrés à l'amour-propre et à son triste cortége ne connoissent plus le charme et l'effet de l'imagination. Ils pervertissent l'usage de cette faculté consolatrice, et au lieu de s'en servir pour adoucir le sentiment de leurs maux ils ne s'en servent que pour l'irriter. Plus occupés des objets qui les blessent que de ceux qui les flatent, ils voyent par tout quelque sujet de peine, ils gardent toujours quelque souvenir attristant ; et quand ensuite ils méditent dans la solitude sur ce qui les a le plus affectés ; leurs cœurs ulcerés remplissent leur imagination de mille objets funestes. Les concurrences, les preferences, les jalousies, les rivalités, les offenses, les vengeances, les mecontentemens de toute espéce, l'ambition, les désirs, les projets, les moyens, les obstacles remplissent de pensées inquiétantes les heures de leurs courts loisirs.[31]

Reflexion or, more in general, imagination can therefore lead to a self-consciousness which does not only undermine the natural *pitié* and *commisération* but conditions also a sort of cleverness with that the individual superordinates himself over the fitness of the social order according to selfish, tactical considerations.[32] In a seemingly disordered society, imagination that conditions pity, is by means of rational calculation abused to distance oneself from the other, to ignore the other and to consider and enforce only one's very selfish interests. This is also how the relation between amour-propre, imagination and pity was storied in the discourse of many recipients and commentators.[33]

---

30   Rousseau, *Émile ou De l'éducation*, 534.
31   [Men who are devoted to *amour-propre* and its sad entourage don't know anymore the impulse and effect of imagination. They confuse the use of this comforting capacity and instead of making use of it to ease their maladies, they use it only to stire them up. More occupied with the objects that hurt them than with those who please them, they see only objects of misery, keep always sort of a doleful memory; and when they think then lonely what left the biggest impression on them, they fill their eroded hearts with thousand adverse things. Competition, preference, jealousy, rivalry, insult, revenge, dissatisfaction of all sorts, ambition, desires, attempts, means, obstacles fill the rare hours of rest with calming ideas.] (Rousseau, *Rousseau juge de Jean-Jacques : Dialogues*, 815).
32   *vid.* Rousseau, *Discours sur l'origine et les fondemens de l'inegalité parmi les hommes*, 221–225.
33   See Roger Masters, David Marshall, Jacques Derrida and Jean Starobinski to name but a few.

This summarises briefly the negative aspects of *amour-propre* concerning pity and how the competitive drive as well as the dismissive cleverness that can accompany its evolution, which can result in being at least ignorant towards the suffering of the other or sees even the own advantages in the disadvantage of the other. It can go even so far that *amour-propre* becomes perverted in the sense of degrading the other to uplift oneself.[34] But since one does not want to forfeit social recognition, the degradation or the dismissal of the other is not expressed openly. It ends in a dilemma, a pathological inner condition that derives from the conflict of interests between social demands and one's own desires.

> Quand enfin tous les intérêts particuliers agités s'entrechoquent, quand l'amour de soi mis en fermentation devient amour-propre, que l'opinion, rendant l'univers entier nécessaire à chaque homme, les rend tous ennemis nés les uns des autres et fait que nul ne trouve son bien que dans le mal d'autrui, alors la conscience, plus foible que les passions exaltées, est étouffée par elles, et ne reste plus dans la bouche des hommes qu'un mot fait pour se tromper mutuellement. Chacun feint alors de vouloir sacrifier ses intérêts à ceux du public, et tous mentent.[35]

Amour-propre and all faculties that evolve or even develop alongside with it, like imagination and reflection, can therefore serve negative effects like fragmentation, alienation and discrimination, as well being the source and tool to cultivate the most human affects and intrinsic understanding, like identification, respect, reason and morals.

With Émile, Rousseau tries to give an example – not a manual, but an exemplary case – of how to avoid developing *amour-propre* in a way that deprives us from becoming human, and to rather cultivate it to serve the principles of best humanist ideals. Rousseau's approach here is that if we reflected us into this dilemma, we must also reflect ourselves out of it – not diminishing thereby that we only

---

34 *vid.* Rousseau, *Rousseau juge de Jean-Jacques : Dialogues*, 806.
35 [When all the agitated particular interests finally collide, when love of self put into fermentation changes into *amour-propre*, when opinion, making the whole universe necessary to each man, makes them all one another's born enemies and determines that none finds his own good except in someone else's ill, then conscience, weaker than the excited passions, is stifled by them, and is no longer in men's mouths except as a word made to deceive each other. Each one then pretends to wish to sacrifice his interests to those of the public, and they are all lying.] (Rousseau, *Lettre à Beaumont* (Paris: Gallimard, 1969), 937).

reached a certain objectivity, by being a subject which cannot be understood only through particular subjective interests that form a greater whole, but by individuals who understand themselves through their participation and creation within in a (universal) collective "and associating themselves with others as members of a larger social organization who think of their social membership as essential, not merely accidental, to who they are."[36] On an emotional and empathetic level, this reflects a sort of functional causality. Referring to the self-other distinction, a causal construct (such as a 'shared manifold')[37] is deployed below the threshold of introspective awareness through the other which allows taking perspective in a rational as well as emphatic-emotional way.

2   Pitié and Compassion

Bringing this back now to Rousseau's human genealogy and applying it to rudimentary capacities like *amour de soi*, pity and compassion, the tendency of instinct, is according to Rousseau, in the beginning indifferent. One desires without knowing what.[38] The spontaneous and not yet reflected self-confirmation of the natural human operates as an instinct that aims for self-preservation according to *amour de soi*. Ansell-Pearson explains the innocence of the good in the natural state in the way that: "[i]t does not arise from a comparison with others, but it is a purely physical sensation accompanied by a spontaneous feeling of compassion."[39] The later social form of pity will then, according to Rousseau, carry further, more complex traits. When the self is configured by the means of mediation with and through the other, the social pity transforms into a more complex empathy that includes the dimension of the extension of the self and a responsive sentiment of compassion. It is imagination that goads to abstraction and reflection. When in that sense the self-love of *amour de soi* is transcended to love one's own kind; that the self expands to humanity, the selfish aspect of *amour-propre* is transformed into a virtue and can form a morally binding, explicit norm.[40] The capacity to put oneself in someone else's

---

36   *vid.* Neuhouser, Frederick, "Jean-Jacques Rousseau and the Origins of Autonomy", in *Inquiry*, vol. 54, no. 5 (2011): 480.

37   *vid.* Gallese, Vittorio, *The Shared Manifold Hypothesis: Embodied Simulation and its Role in Empathy and Social Cognition* (Cambridge: Cambridge University Press, 2007).

38   *vid.* Rousseau, *Émile ou De l'éducation*, 493–502.

39   Ansell-Pearson, Keith, *Nietzsche contra Rousseau* (Cambridge: Cambridge University Press, 1991), 66.

40   *vid.* Rousseau, *Émile ou De l'éducation*, 547.

position springs from the cognitive potential of imagination and accounts together with extending the self-love of *amour de soi*, pity and on a broader scale empathy, as well as the reflective ability of *amour-propre*, to identify with the other or to differentiate oneself from the other. Using *amour de soi* and the perspective of extending oneself as a source of empathy, serves even another psycho-social component:

> Moins l'objet de nos soins tient immédiatement à nous-même, moins l'illusion de l'intérêt particulier est à craindre ; plus on généralise cet intérêt, plus il déviant équitable, et l'amour du genre humain n'est autre chose en nous que l'amour de la justice. Voulons-nous donc qu'Émile aime la vérité, voulons-nous qu'il la connoisse ? Dans les affaires tenons-le toujours loin de lui. Plus ses soins seront consacrés au bonheur d'autrui, plus ils seront éclairés et sages, et moins il se trompera sur ce qui est bien ou mal.[41]

In this regard, empathy accounts for transcending the everywhere fragmented person that cannot be a complete, whole human being anymore, to engage in a life with integrity: to feel whole again. Empathy therefore becomes a sort of antidote. It functions as an on-going, isomorphic and communicable process of distinguishing, sustaining, and strengthening the structure of the self. The independence and autonomy the tutor tries to foster in Émile therefore aims at a certain impartiality that has to balance out two extreme ends to arrive at a rational altruism, based on critically reflected autonomy: the emotional contagion and an unbiased ideal to transcend the tension of simply taking over the opinions of the respective social environment on the one hand and autarkic isolation as a radical social estrangement as the other extreme of the spectrum.

Considering this, it becomes clear how all-important the child's natural innocence is for Rousseau's theory, since the moral judgements and formation of the consciousness is based on these very first notions and ideas. Keeping the child uncorrupted by social dogmas, emotional blackmailing or socio-political

---

41   [The less our preservation is focused on our selves, the less we have to be afraid to be mislead by our self-interest. The more one generalises this interest, the more just it becomes and our love for humanity becomes but love for justice. If Émile is supposed to love and recognise truth, he must be occupied as little as possible with himself. The more he is occupied to contribute to the happiness of others, the more enlightened and intelligent he becomes and the less he will be confused about good and evil.] (Rousseau, *Émile ou De l'éducation*, 547).

prejudices is the foundation for an undetermined judgement according to a rationality that evolved from the natural sentiment.

> Le voir sans le sentir n'est pas le savoir, et comme je l'ai dit cent fois, l'enfant n'imaginant point ce que sentent les autres ne connoit de maux que les siens ; mais quand le prémier développement des sens allume en lui le feu de l'imagination, il commence à se sentir dans ses semblables, à s'émouvoir de leurs plaintes et à souffrir de leurs douleurs. [...] Ainsi nul ne devient sensible que quand son imagination s'anime et commence à le transporter hors de lui.[42]

Society creates new possibilities as well as manifold different needs and demands to adapt flexibly or according to perfectibility to the transforming environment or circumstances. The capacity to reflect that evolves alongside is not only provoking a focus on similarity and identification but also on differences and demarcation:

> C'est la raison qui engendre l'amour-propre, et c'est la réflexion qui le fortifie ; c'est elle qui replie l'homme sur lui-même ; c'est elle qui le sépare de tout ce qui le gêne et l'afflige.[43]

With the progression of reflexion that is conditioned by comparison as well as fostered by it, a whole new entity gains foothold in the social fabric. It's assessment though comes to an ambivalent conclusion – as ambivalent as the relational core of *amour-propre* in general, since introspection and extraversion are conditioned in a relational way and take on an irreversible dimension of evaluation, across both an ethical and aesthetic dimension. Thus this structure of judging easily leads to corruption or perversion of the moral perspective and attitude.

> Enfin tel est en nous l'empire de l'imagination et telle en est l'influence, que d'elle naissent non seulement les vertus et les vices, mais les biens et

---

[42] Thesseing without the feeling is not knowing, and how I said a hundred times, the child does not imagine what others feel nor knows the pain they feel; [but if the first sensual triggers inflame his imagination, he begins to feel along with his kind; their laments move him and he suffers their pain [...] One only becomes sensitive, when imagination is stirred and starts to put us out of ourselves.] (Rousseau, *Émile ou De l'éducation*, 505–507).

[43] [It is reason that generates *amour-propre*, and it is reflection that strengthens it; it is reflection that withdraws man into himself; it is reason that separates him from all that bothers and afflict] (Rousseau, *Discours sur l'origine et les fondemens de l'inegalité parmi les hommes*, 175).

> les maux de la vie humaine, et que c'est principalement la maniére dont on s'y livre qui rend les hommes bons ou méchans, heureux ou malheureux ici bas.[44]

At this point according to Rousseau the conscious identification with the other sets in, which allows – and Rousseau does not differentiate here between human and animal – to realise the common and the similarity of feeling beings. Are the correct terms and ideas imparted, the child finds himself in every being.

> C'est à dire en d'autres termes d'exciter en lui la bonté, l'humanité, la commisération, la bienfaisance, toutes les passions attirantes et douces qui plaisent naturellement aux hommes, et d'empêcher de naitre l'envie, la convoitise, la haine, toutes les passions repoussantes et cruelles qui rendent, pour ainsi dire, la sensibilité non seulement nulle, mais négative et font le tourment de celui qui les éprouve.[45]

The education and channelling of imagination therefore has a major influence on how to make use of the natural potential – in that specific case regarding empathy. Thus, imagination turns out to be a crucial factor for empathic behaviour, since this emotional-cognitive feature marks the basis to abstract. This then allows for objectification of oneself, which can indicate to fragment and to distance oneself as well as to put oneself in somebody's situation and to identify with the other in an empathic sense. When accompanied by evaluative *amour-propre*, it can lead to fraternity as well as to social combustion, which in Rousseau's eyes makes it even more essential to form precise ideas and terms – containing the reference of the development of language and the formation of terms and ideas as quoted in the beginning.

---

44 [Briefly, the power of imagination and its influence on us is so big that it springs from there not only virtue and vice but also goods and evils of human life and it's primary the way one gives in to it, that makes humans righteous or bad, happy or unhappy.] (Rousseau, *Rousseau juge de Jean-Jacques : Dialogues*, 815–817).

45 [In other words, to awake in him the benignity, the humanness, the mercy, the benevolence and all appealing and gentle passions humans are attracted to by nature; but neglect envy, greediness, hate and all repellent and cruel passions that not only annul sensitivity, but make it a negative parameter that tortures the one who feels it.] (Rousseau, *Émile ou De l'éducation*, 506).

> Les affections sociales ne se dévelopent en nous qu'avec nos lumiéres. La pitié, bien que naturelle au cœur de l'homme resteroit éternellement inactive sans l'imagination qui la met en jeu. Comment nous laissons-nous émouvoir à la pitié ? En nous transportant hors de nous-mêmes ; en nous identifiant avec l'être souffrant. Nous ne souffrons qu'autant que nous jugeons qu'il souffre ; ce n'est pas dans nous c'est dans lui que nous souffrons. Qu'on songe combien ce transport suppose de connoissances acquises ![46]

In his educational program, the first period is therefore limited to getting familiar and used to necessities and constraint to foster only limited needs, decency and humbleness. While this first period of education (which mainly focuses on the physical realm) is realised in a relatively straightforward manner, education becomes more and more complex with the aging Émile and the entering of psychological and social components.

> Tant que sa sensibilité reste bornée à son individu il n'y a rien de moral dans ses actions ; ce n'est que quand elle commence à s'étendre hors de lui qu'il prend d'abord les sentimens et ensuite les notions du bien et du mal qui le constituent véritablement homme et partie intégrante de son espéce.[47]

Authors like O'Hagan or Cohen interpret Rousseau's pedagogical project to be ordered according to three moments: the one of necessity, the one of possibility or option and the one of morality.[48] What develops according to this is with reference to Cohen a triadic development of the human moral:

> In the first, we direct our compassion on those who suffer, focusing on forms of suffering to which we are susceptible ourselves. Next, we are

---

46 [Social affections develop in us only with our enlightenment. Pity, although natural to the heart of man, would remain eternally inactive without the imagination that puts it into play. How do we let ourselves to pity? By transporting ourselves outside of ourselves; by identifying ourselves with the suffering being. We suffer only as much as we judge he suffers; it is not in ourselves, it is in him that we suffer. Consider how much this transport presupposes acquired knowledge!] (Rousseau, *Essai sur l'origine des langues*, 395).

47 [As long as the sensitivity is limited to the individual, his acts have no moral character. Only if it moves beyond, he starts to feel and gets an idea of good and bad which makes him truly human and an inseparable part of his species.] (Rousseau, *Émile ou De l'éducation*, 501).

48 *vid.* O'Hagan, Timothy, *Rousseau* (London and New York: Routledge, 1999), 28.

to consider people in society, and study how they – particularly the more powerful – mask their suffering and weakness: frailty, we then understand, is part of our human condition. Finally, we confront our own weakness, and see ourselves as objects of compassion, not merely as its subjects. At each stage, the confirmation of the sense of equality generalizes and reinforces compassion, ensuring that it takes the common good as its object.[49]

Therefore, Cohen concludes that insofar as our (primitive) affects are bound to our (social) obligations, both are directed to match the common good. Émile is prepared to appreciate the useful goods[50] so that prestige objects, also from a moral perspective, do not compromise him, but rather make him pity those who believe they need them.[51] Moreover, the potential of natural compassion is fostered in a way that it makes him empathic to the sentiments of others while consciousness according to the development of reason matures to form a moral normativity that remains except of basic, universal values, relatively open.

> La voix de la conscience ne peut pas plus être étouffée dans le cœur humain que celle de la raison dans l'entendement, et l'insensibilité morale est tout aussi peu naturelle que la folie.[52]

We see here an explicit link between a genuine emphatic condition of the human and the more complex socially generated development of consciousness. While Rousseau presupposes a certain inborn consciousness,[53] in terms of

---

49 Cohen, Joshua, *Rousseau A Free Community of Equals* (Oxford: Oxford University Press, 2010), 126.
50 This can indeed be understood as a far-reaching impulse against that even reflects in Karl Marx discussion of commodity fetishism and the brutal act of force of power, the organised and concentrated execution of the society to develop and enforce capital. See also Marx, Karl and Engels, Friedrich, "Die sogenannte ursprüngliche Akkumulation", in *Karl Marx-Friedrich Engels Werke, Band 23: Das Kapital. Kritik der politischen Ökonomie*, Erster Band, Buch I, Kapitel 24 (Berlin: Dietz Verlag, 1962), 741–791.
51 vid. Perkins, Merle L., *Jean-Jacques Rousseau on the Individual and Society* (Lexington: University Press of Kentucky, 1974).
52 [The voice of consciousness can't be suffocated in the human heart as well as reason can't be without knowledge and a moral insensitivity is as unnatural as madness.] (Rousseau, *Rousseau juge de Jean-Jacques : Dialogues*, 972).
53 vid. Rousseau, *Émile ou De l'éducation*, 334.

feeling as genuine law of consciousness, it develops only in the inter-subjective and cooperative sphere to a rationally prescribing insight of legitimacy and normativity.

On the one hand empathy is a form of receptivity to the other; on the other hand it is also a form of understanding that provides cooperative behaviour to go beyond mere pragmatically, tactical strategy and therewith evolves to a canonical obligation of pro-social behaviour that shapes an ethical dimension. The understanding addressed here refers to putting oneself in the place of the other conceptually, while receptivity here captures the experientially openness to the affects, sensations, emotions that the other experiences. Thus, empathy is a capacity that allows access to a broader understanding of the self and the other as well as providing a foundational structure as such.

When before the basic sentiment was mentioned as the source for moral insights, it marks the social-critical emphasis of Rousseau in which he sees the nascence of the *esprit de commerce* accompanied by the moral dysfunction and so holds the commercial society responsible for the loss of moral resources and affectionate bonds. Hannah Arendt considers this to be the "Rebellion des Herzens gegen die eigene gesellschaftliche Existenz",[54] with which Rousseau brings the subjectivity of emotions in position against the dominating socio-political condition, which make the human a slave of the social claims, standards and criterions. Virtue as defined by Rousseau in *his Discourse on Political Economy*, is the conformity of the particular will with the *volonté générale*. The virtue that evolves in the process of social interaction (when amour-propre is cultivated according to humanist terms) is a crucial feature for overcoming the mechanism of estrangement and remains a central attribute of the human as a unit that has transcended or mastered the inner conflict and therefore can obey to the law given by himself to become what he is.

The aim is to enhance an autonomous mindset that allows Émile (as a universal prototype and not as a male archetype)[55] to be capable of making a living that is as far as possible free of pre-conditioning and limits the needs so that competition gains the least foothold that is possible. Applying this to the educational project means: *"Il s'agit moins de lui apprendre une vérité que de lui montrer comment il faut s'y prendre pour découvrir toujours la vérité."*[56]

---

54 Arendt, Hannah, *Vita activa oder Vom tätigen Leben* (München/Zürich: Piper, 2002), 49.

55 *vid.* "Mes exemples, bons peut-être pour un sujet, seront mauvais pour mille autres." [My examples, good for maybe someone, will be bad for a thousand other] (Rousseau, *Émile ou De l'éducation*, 465).

56 [It's not about conveying truth to him, but much more to show him how to always find truth.] (*Ibid.*, 484).

Rousseau wants to support an autonomous being, who has his social bonds and its impact intrinsically imprinted for the sake of overcoming fear and weakness to consciously be aware of how an altruistic choice is at the same time a choice for the other and a choice for oneself. This tries to balance the possible conflict between the individual and society, independence and the utilisation of the human potential through cooperation and interaction as well as the oft misleading juxtaposition of ratio and sentiment. Rousseau's theory gives a rich impulse about how those apparent antagonists must be understood as mutually dependent and inseparable. This consolidation is a claim that our society today still has not resolved, which makes it even more pressing to exhaust this idea in depth in order to benefit if maybe not solve the dilemma of the human condition, or at very least, with reference to Rousseau, aiming for the modest intent:

> J'ai commencé quelques raisonnements, j'ai hasardé quelques conjectures, moins dans l'espoir de résoudre la question, que dans l'intention de éclaircir et de la réduire à son véritable état.[57]

Bibliography

Ansell-Pearson, Keith, *Nietzsche contra Rousseau* (Cambridge: Cambridge University Press, 1991).

Arendt, Hannah, *Vita activa oder Vom tätigen Leben* (München/Zürich: Piper, 2002).

Bjørsnøs, Annlaug, "Le processus d'individuation dans La Nouvelle Héloïse de Jean-Jacques Rousseau", in *Romansk Forum*, vol. 16, no.2 (2002): 289–296.

Cohen, Joshua, *Rousseau A Free Community of Equals* (Oxford: Oxford University Press, 2010).

Gallese, Vittorio, *The Shared Manifold Hypothesis: Embodied Simulation and ist Role in Empathy and Social Cognition* (Cambridge: Cambridge University Press, 2007).

Goldschmidt, Victor, *Anthropologie et politique. Les principes du système de Rousseau* (Paris: Librairie Philosophique Vrin, 1983).

Marx, Karl and Engels, Friedrich, "Die sogenannte ursprüngliche Akkumulation", in *Karl Marx-Friedrich Engels Werke, Band 23: Das Kapital. Kritik der politischen Ökonomie*, Erster Band, Buch 1, Kapitel 24 (Berlin: Dietz Verlag, 1962), 741–791.

---

57   [I thought about some things. I dared some assumptions, not so much with the hope to answer the question, but rather with the intention to illuminate it and to bring it back to the true the face of affairs.] (Rousseau, *Discours sur l'origine et les fondemens de l'inegalité parmi les hommes*, 66).

Müller, Reimar, *Anthropologie und Geschichte* (Berlin: Akademie, 1997).

Neuhouser, Frederick, "Rousseau und das menschliche Verlangen nach Anerkennung", in *Deutsche Zeitschrift für Philosophie*, vol. 56, no. 6 (2008): 899–922.

Neuhouser, Frederick, *Rousseau's Theodicy of Self-love: Evil, Rationality, and the Drive for Recognition* (Oxford: Oxford University Press, 2008).

Neuhouser, Frederick, "Jean-Jacques Rousseau and the Origins of Autonomy", in *Inquiry*, vol. 54, no. 5 (2011): 478–493.

O'Hagan, Timothy, *Rousseau* (London and New York: Routledge, 1999).

Perkins, Merle L., *Jean-Jacques Rousseau on the Individual and Society* (Lexington: University Press of Kentucky, 1974).

Rang, Martin, *Rousseaus Lehre vom Menschen* (Göttingen: Vanderhoeck & Ruprecht, 1959).

Rousseau, Jean-Jacques, *Rousseau juge de Jean-Jacques: Dialogues* (Paris: Gallimard, 1959).

Rousseau, Jean-Jacques, *Émile ou De l'éducation* (Paris: Gallimard, 1969).

Rousseau, Jean-Jacques, *Lettre à Beaumont* (Paris: Gallimard, 1969).

Rousseau, Jean-Jacques, *Lettres Morales* (Paris: Gallimard, 1969).

Rousseau, Jean-Jacques, *Essai sur l'origine des langues* (Paris: Gallimard, 1995).

Rousseau, Jean-Jacques, *Discours sur l'origine et les fondemens de l'inegalité parmi les hommes* (Hamburg: Meiner, 1995).

CHAPTER 6

Empathy in Education: the Successful Teacher

Giovanna Costantini

Abstract

If empathy means to put oneself in someone else's shoes, it plays a great role in education. Teachers are supposed to be empathic because they have to understand the needs and the emotions of his/her pupils in order to make them successful in terms of learning and autonomy. Their ability consists on creating a positive atmosphere inside the classroom thanks to their attitude; this helps the students to cooperate thus enhancing the process of learning. From a survey conducted in seven classes of students between 11 and 14 years old, in which the teenagers were asked to answer some questions related to what empathy was for them, how important it was between mates and with teachers, and what they would have done to improve it, it has emerged that empathy is necessary in class, either between mates or with teachers; students have given some personal definitions about empathy and some advices to the teachers in order to improve their attitude, among others for example, to be more open-minded and talk to the students more often. Several people think that empathy is a natural ability, but, as the Australian comedian, Tim Minchin declared, empathy is intuitive, but is also something you can work on, intellectually. That is why professionals should work on how to acquire practiced skills. This chapter gives some advices to the teachers in order to strengthen their abilities as empathic and successful teachers. One of the approaches considered in this analysis is the flipped classroom, where pupils have the opportunity to prepare and to present lessons thanks to the support of the teacher and of the technological instruments. In this context, empathy plays a decisive role because students are really asked to put themselves in the teachers' shoes, either in terms of emotions or in terms of skills.

Keywords

education – empathy – survey – class – pupils – students – skills – flipped classroom

1 Some Hints on Empathy

The word 'empathy' comes from the Greek word 'empatheia' which means 'inaffection and páthos'. Nevertheless, it literally means taking part to others' emotions by understanding their feelings. The mother of one of the theories is Edith Stein, the philosopher and author of the book *On the Problem of Empathy*.[1] She intends empathy as the 'grasping' of realizing, in a non-original way, about a lived experience as alien, that is an extraordinary intuition which has as its object the psychic experience of others. For example, you can experience a feeling, like the joy, through a living other than itself. It is a representation of the other's experience, it is non-original but it is surely a way to feel what the other is feeling. The otherness is seen as a diversity that must be accepted in its entirety, even if through an empathic effort. According to Stein, empathizing with other people's psychic life is a necessary step for the individual's own mental construction. In this statement it is clear that openness to community life is necessary. Each fact is not enough in itself because only a constant dialogue between people is necessary even not to see precluded of a greater knowledge of themselves. If a child is suffering, I do not need to suffer with him but I have to figure out what to try to help him. Empathy has a social value, which is used to cultivate relationships between individuals; it is also a positive relationship away from all prejudices of any kind.

Daniel Goleman, author of the book *Working with Emotional Intelligence*, defines empathy as the awareness of others' feelings, needs and concerns.[2] In his book, he states that empathy means being able to read the emotions and he gives a list of useful instructions for parents, friends, teachers and any social actor in order to use appropriately the emotional self-awareness, the emotional control, the way of addressing the emotions in a productive way, and the relationship management. He keeps stating that empathy leads to benevolence, altruism and compassion. According to him, seeing things from others' point of view breaks the stereotypes and prejudices and therefore feeds the tolerance and the acceptance of differences.[3] There are more definitions of 'empathy'. Here you can find a congruous number to get the idea of the various perspectives of observation: "Empathy, the power of entering into another's

---

[1] Rega, Andrea, "Edith Stein, Il Problema dell'empatia", in *Rivista Formazione Lavoro Persona*, Anno III, no. 8 (2013): 282.
[2] Goleman, Daniel, *Intelligenza Emotiva* (Milano: RCS Libri, 2015), 395.
[3] Goleman, *Intelligenza Emotiva*, 456.

personality and imaginatively experiencing his experiences."[4] "I call him religious who understands the suffering of others'.[5] 'Empathy is intuitive, but also something you can work on, intellectually."[6] This last statement is important to understand that, even if a professional hasn't good empathic skills, he/she can work on it in order to acquire the practiced skills necessary to his/her job. Trying to empathize through a constant and planned work is definitely a good workout to succeed sooner or later.

2   Empathy in Education

The ability to organize a highly communicative and empathic didactics has never been much considered in recruitment of teachers and it is unlikely to happen in the close future. So we may say that it is an essential element for a teaching of excellence that an empathic teacher has a great success with their students, but we are convinced as well that the general recruiting system is not able to select the teachers considering their empathic dimension. It is important to empathize with the own students to better understand their reality and in order to make choices for them as a true cultural reference leader, choices that are not influenced only by the own point of view, which is too often limited. Through the empathic dimension, it is possible to have the absolute control of the group class that recognizes the cultural leadership of the teacher and, consequently, cooperates to learn any discipline, without suffering the time spent in class.

School is not only the place where you learn, but it is also the environment in which we let our emotions and our experience come in. Learning, discovering, building new knowledge and skills are rich activities of emotional life. Relating with peers, collaborating or comparing, discussing, doing and untying friendship and ties, living intense relationships with adults, all this happens at school and it is rich of emotional life, even if sometimes dangerous and painful. Alongside structured and formal paths, it is important to enrich and 'flavour of affection' daily activities through informal

---

4   *Chambers English Dictionary*, ed., in *SkillsYouNeed* (blog), Lampeter. Viewed on the 21st August 2016. http://www.skillsyouneed.com/ips/empathy.html
5   Gandhi, Mahatma, in *SkillsYouNeed* (blog), Lampeter. Viewed on the 21st August 2016. http://www.skillsyouneed.com/ips/empathy.html
6   Minchin, Tim, "Occasional Address", *Tim Minchin.com* (blog), Melbourne: September 25th, 2013. Viewed on the 21st August 2016. http://www.timminchin.com/2013/09/25/occasional-address/

routes, keeping in mind the three main levels of emotional life: emotions, moods and feelings.[7]

The process of teaching-learning is full of emotions. Attention and listening are the first strategies. It means to feel the emotional tones of the students when they try to learn, to feel their anxiety, their sense of helplessness or of satisfaction and joy, their anger at the failures, their jealousy and envy. For all these reasons, some of the skills that cannot be missed in a teacher are: the active listening skill, the understanding of the group dynamics and the willingness to get involved. The teacher has to reveal his human face, by encouraging the students to open up through the empathic listening and inspiring them on their path of discovery and self-knowledge. So, teachers must understand, process and express themselves.[8] At the meantime, the teacher's attitude may not fall in the separation of his/her educational assertiveness, his/her authority, his ability in the group class holding in a context of rules and commitments. His/her role is also to spread culture and to let the students acquire the skills and the abilities planned in the curriculum project of the own discipline. The pupils must be trained to the emotional life as well as to the life of commitment, work and discipline in order to be a good man of the future.

3   The Survey

The survey was conducted in seven classes of students between 11 and 14 years old where. After reading and discussing about the meaning of empathy, the teenagers were asked to answer the following questions:
- What is empathy for you? (Open answer);
- How important is empathy between mates? (Open answer);
- How important is empathy between teachers and pupils? (Open answer);
- How important is empathy with the teacher on the learning of the subject that you are studying? (Tick one number from 1 to 5 where):
  1 is equal to 'not at all important'
  2 is equal to 'unimportant'
  3 is equal to 'important enough'
  4 is equal to 'important'

---

7   Badiali, Massimiliano, *Affetti ed Empatia nella Relazione Educativa* (Dissertation. Firenze: Università degli Studi di Firenze, 2003).
8   Ianes, Dario and Demo, Heidrun, "Intelligenza Emotiva", in *Funzioniobiettivo.it* (blog), Vol. 7 (Forlì: 2008). Viewed on 21st August 2016. http://www.funzioniobiettivo.it/glossadid/intelligenza_emotiva.htm

5 is equal to 'very important';
'I don't know'.
- How much the relationship of trust that you have with your teacher entice you to study? (Tick one number from 1 to 5, see above);
- How important is it for you that the teacher is able to put himself in your shoes and understand your needs? (Tick one number from 1 to 5, see above);
- How empathetic is your teacher? (Tick one number from 1 to 5 where):
  1 is equal to 'not at all empathetic'
  2 is equal to 'unempathetic'
  3 is equal to 'empathetic enough'
  4 is equal to 'empathetic'
  5 is equal to 'very empathetic';
  'I don't know'.
- What do you advice your teacher to be more empathetic? (Open answer).

From a sample of 117 pupils, the results were the following:
- As for the question 'What is empathy for you?', 29 students answered 'to figure out what a friend/a person is feeling'; 3 students answered 'affection, helping a person'; 32 students answered 'share the emotions and put yourself in another's shoes'; 18 students answered 'to have a good relationship with other people'; 3 students answered 'confidence'; 1 student answered 'to deepen the students' problems'; 3 students answered 'to be in tune with a person'; 12 students answered 'the ability to listen and understand others'; 8 students answered 'to have an intellectual connection between people'; 5 students answered 'opening to others'; 1 student answered 'to understand each other'; 2 students understood 'to be helped/understood'.
- As for the question 'How important is empathy between mates?', 5 students answered 'very important'; 93 students answered 'important'; 10 students answered 'important enough'; 6 students answered 'unimportant'; 3 students answered 'not at all important'.
- As for the question 'How important is empathy between teachers and pupils?', 88 students answered 'very important'; 17 students answered 'important enough'; 9 students answered 'unimportant'; 2 students answered 'not at all important', 1 students answered 'I don't know'.
- As for the answer 'How much the relationship of trust that you have with your teacher entice you to study?', 7 students answered 'not at all important', 12 students answered 'unimportant'; 27 students answered 'important enough'; 45 students answered 'important'; 24 students answered 'very important', 2 students didn't answer.
- As for the question 'How important is it for you that your teacher is able to put himself/herself in your shoes and understand your needs?', 3 students

answered 'not at all important'; 5 students answered 'unimportant'; 13 students answered 'important enough'; 27 students answered 'important'; 67 students answered 'very important'; 1 student answered 'I don't know'; 1 student didn't answer.
- As for the answer 'How empathetic is your teacher?', 5 students answered ' unempathetic'; 26 students answered 'empathetic enough'; 43 students answered 'empathetic'; 41 students answered 'very empathetic'; 1 student answered ' I don't know'; 1 student didn't answer.
- As for the question 'What do you advice your teacher to be more empathetic?', 7 students answered 'be more open and talk often with us'; 3 students answered 'not to blame'; 1 student answered 'having no preferences'; 2 students answered 'do not offend'; 3 students answered 'do not put pressure'; 17 students answered ' to be more sympathetic'; 16 students answered 'to give less homework'; 2 students answered 'to work more with the technology'; 2 students answered 'to put at ease the pupils during tests'; 7 students answered 'to amuse more the pupils'; 1 students answered 'to give better marks'; 5 students answered 'to be more young-looking in the ways and ideas'; 3 students answered 'to make the lesson more interesting'; 1 student answered 'to listen more'; 1 student answered 'to plan group works'; 1 student answered 'to give more confidence'; 7 students answered 'to be as it is'; 8 students answered 'to be more helpful'; 1 student answered 'to support in the study'; 3 students answered 'to be more gentle and calm'; 26 students didn't answer.

From the survey, it has emerged that empathy is necessary in class, either between mates or with teachers; students have given some personal definitions about empathy and some advices to the teachers in order to improve their attitude, among others for example, to be more open-minded and talk to the students more often or to be more sympathetic.

4 The Empathy Project

Several people think that empathy is a natural ability, but as the Australian comedian Tim Minchin declared, empathy is intuitive, but is also something you can work on, intellectually.[9] That is why professionals should work on how to acquire practiced skills. From the premise of not claiming to be a perfect teacher, based on the analysis made in my classrooms and starting from the

---

9 Minchin, "Occasional Address".

students' need, during the school year 2015–16, I decided to plan a program based on empathy and the needs and concerns of my pupils. The project I planned was an attempt to improve the relations with my pupils, the relationships between peers, the motivation to learning and to behave properly in most situations. I have to admit that the project has proved rewarding for each component and it was quite successful. At the end of the project, I think the message was received by the majority of the group. Any teacher interested in improving this aspect may take inspiration and adapt it to his/her contest class.

The project entitled 'Project on Empathy' was conducted in seven classes of pupils between 11 and 14 years old but mainly focused on the third classes of lower secondary school (13–14 years old). These teenagers are living a time of great transformation because they are moving from the condition of being children to the one of adults, undergoing physical, emotional and psychological changes. This moment of rebellion leads the adolescents to criticize and challenge the adults, parents and teachers, and disclosing their weaknesses and lacks. An empathic teacher has to be intuitive and he should read between the lines, capture the emotional spies and the nonverbal signals in order to understand the pupil's mood.

The project had a double aspect because it worked in parallel on two fronts and two different approaches: the flipped classroom and the analysis of the role of the teacher. After an introduction to feelings, emotions, and the discussion about empathy with the questionnaire mentioned in chapter 3, in the middle of a teaching unit on American history, we read a famous poem written by the American author Walt Whitman – "O Captain! My Captain!"– dedicated to Abram Lincoln's death. We analysed and discussed about this poem and I asked the pupils who was their captain/guide, after telling them who was mine during my life experience. Most of them declared that their captain was one of their parents, a friend or an idol. The interesting fact of that moment was the authenticity and the freedom of that exchange. After that, we watched some sequences of the film "Dead Poets Society" with the aim of reflecting on the teacher figure. On that occasion, the students were divided in 4/5 groups and were asked: to comment the sequences, to find the character traits they considered important in an ideal teacher, to explain the meaning of the word 'captain' in that film. After observing the different behaviours of the two main teachers in the film, I handed them a sheet with some descriptions and examples about the difference between an authoritative teacher and an authoritarian one. Through brainstorming, discussion and writing activities, the students reflected on the figure and the role of the teacher and they tried to develop the critical thinking and the intellectual formation about this profession and his/her sometimes difficult relationship with students.

The second aspect of the project was learning about English and American history and civilization topics with the approach of the flipped classroom, where pupils had the opportunity to prepare and to present lessons thanks to the support of the teacher and of the technological instruments. This kind of work was possible thanks to a virtual class on a digital socio-educational platform where I uploaded photocopies, links and videos useful to the preparation of lessons. Also on this occasion, the students were divided in groups of 4/5, one for each topic, and they had to read, decode, select, process, prepare presentations in power point, and memorize their topic in order to present their work to the whole class in a clear and appropriate manner, maintaining their peers' attention high and being ready to answer any question, just if they were real teachers. In this context, empathy played a decisive role because students were really asked to put themselves in the teachers' shoes, either in terms of emotions or in terms of skills. At the end of this work, I gave the students a test in which I asked them how they felt at that kind of work, how they felt at putting themselves in their teacher's shoes, if they would repeat it and what they would change. 95% of students wrote that they enjoyed it, even if hard, they admitted to having experienced the pre presentation with a lot of anxiety for fear of making mistakes, but they definitely understood better the commitment of each teacher in preparing lessons, maintaining a high level of attention of the class, handling various requests, and being as clear as possible so that everyone was able to understand. They also added that they would definitely repeat it without changing anything.

These two parallel activities ended with the vision of the play "My Captain" performed at the theatre at the end of the school year. A local theatre performed the story of the film "Dead Poets Society" in a compelling and engaging way. During the performance, the students felt emotionally involved and understood even better the value of the role of a teacher and the influence he/she may have towards his/her students' education.

5   Conclusions

This experience proved to be formative and educational because I had the opportunity to learn more about my students and more about myself. When I started my career as a teacher I had as a model the one of my high school teachers, and I was just like them, authoritarian. Step by step, I realized that this method didn't work, especially in the difficult cases. Through experience and constant education, I learned to open myself with my students, joking with them and being demanding at the same time. I understood that the teacher must stand equidistant towards authoritarianism and permissiveness, and choose to be authoritative guide and then travel the route of dialogue, of exchange and of communicative reciprocity. The teacher is an authoritative guidance if it is recognized by the students as a person who possesses certain skills, and when his/her superiority intervenes through guidance, orientation and regulatory functions.

This chapter doesn't want to be a model to follow because any relationship between teacher and pupils is unique. It is definitely a point to start from in order to face such a complex subject that holds empathy at its centre. Certainly, the discussion of the role of the teacher helped the students to better understand the difficulties he/she has to face every day and to be more collaborative, on the other hand, I learned that being an affective teacher means to value subjectivity and otherness of students since there is no humanity without the full and unconditional recognition of the other's value in its unique and peculiar character. There is still a lot to learn but we will find out just living.

Bibliography

Badiali, Massimiliano, *Affetti ed Empatia nella Relazione Educativa* (Dissertation. Firenze: Università degli Studi di Firenze, 2003).

Chambers English Dictionary ed., in *SkillsYouNeed* (blog), Lampeter. Viewed on 21st August 2016. http://www.skillsyouneed.com/ips/empathy.html

Ghandi, Mahatma, in *SkillsYouNeed* (blog), Lampeter. Viewed on 21st August 2016. http://www.skillsyouneed.com/ips/empathy.html

Goleman, Daniel, *Intelligenza Emotiva* (Milano: RCS Libri, 2015).

Ianes, Dario and Demo, Heidrun, "Intelligenza Emotiva", in *Funzioniobiettivo.it* (blog), Vol. 7 (Forlì: 2008). Viewed on 21st August 2016. http://www.funzioniobiettivo.it/glossadid/intelligenza_emotiva.htm

Minchin, Tom. "Occasional Address", in *Tim Minchin.com* (blog), Melbourne, 25th September 2013. Viewed on 21 August 2016. http://www.timminchin.com/2013/09/25/occasional-address/

Rego, Andrea, "Edith Stein, Il Problema dell'empatia", *Rivista Formazione Lavoro Persona*, Anno III, no. 8 (2013): 282.

CHAPTER 7

Anti-Utilitarian Empathy: an Ethical and Epistemological Journey

Irina Ionita

Abstract

If time is money and the human being an endless range of the *homo œconomicus* figure who maximizes profit/pleasure by minimizing losses/pain, isn't empathy eminently anti-utilitarian? Isn't the effort to connect with the Other, by putting oneself in the place of the Other in order to understand their perspective from their point of view, a risk of minimizing profit/pleasure by maximizing losses/pain? And isn't *that* a promising prospect? Stemming from this questioning, the paper tells the story of an interdisciplinary doctoral research in development studies on the nomadic concept of empathy. Beyond inter- or trans-disciplinary, empathy becomes an *undisciplined* concept, which not only navigates from a discipline to the next, but also questions the ethics and epistemology of every step of the way by taking the researcher into unexpected conceptual, geographical and geopolitical territories. In this case, it moves conceptually from anti-utilitarianism to decoloniality; geographically, from Geneva to Quebec and Ontario; and geopolitically, from a Western perspective to Indigenous loci of enunciation. Through three hypostases, empathy raises some interesting ethical and methodological questions in the realm of social sciences. While trying to answer the initial question of the pertinence of an anti-utilitarian type of empathy by exploring what seemed to be from afar an original case study, the concept took the researcher to Canada, to the Iroquois nations and their notion of responsibility towards the 7th generation into the future. However, when confronted with the complex colonial dimension of the relationship with the Indigenous peoples, the concept became a heuristic tool for the researcher who had to redefine her own capacity to empathize with her interlocutors, which in turn redefined her entire project. Undisciplined, empathy finally became an ethical decolonial practice, helping the researcher build unexpected bridges between several schools of thought and perceive a reciprocal, respectful and responsible dialogue.

Keywords

empathy – social sciences – anti-utilitarianism – ethics – epistemology – indigenous epistemes – decoloniality – Canada

1 Empathy as Concept and Phenomenon: through an Anti-Utilitarian Lens

When I chose to work on the concept of empathy, I had an inkling there that it would be a constant challenge to it. Not only it seems to be a slippery concept, nomad, contested and constantly reevaluated across disciplines, but also, in everyday life, empathy seems to be one of those familiar words anyone can relate to, instantly and dare I say 'instinctively.' *Empathy is: walking in another person's shoes; always positive; sympathy; compassion; care. Everyone is empathetic. No one is empathetic.* Yet, I've also had the intuition that empathy could offer insightful theory on the ways we relate to others (and more broadly to the 'cultural' Other), precisely because it is an elusive concept that requires striving and thorough analysis. In reality, empathy took me into unforeseen territories and went way beyond my expectations; a detailed recount of my doctoral research and its unexpected turns has been published in 2015 in French.[1]

The initial central point of my doctoral research was an interdisciplinary reconceptualization of empathy (defined at this stage as the capacity to put oneself in the place of another person) in an anti-utilitarian perspective, inspired by the work of sociologist Marcel Mauss on the gift and the interdisciplinary work of MAUSS, evocative abbreviation of the French group *Mouvement Anti-Utilitariste en Sciences Sociales*. Alain Caillé, co-founder of the MAUSS, develops the argument that the 'axiom of interest' has become the main paradigm in social sciences today, reinforced by a strong rationalization in the Western world.[2] Through a specific historical lens, developed since the Enlightenment period, the concept of a calculating and self-interested reason has come to be considered a universal and natural characteristic of humankind. The main preoccupation of Caillé and his colleagues is that rationalization has thus been

---

[1] Ionita, Irina, *Un itinéraire de recherche en terrain autochtone au Canada: L'empathie dans tous ses états* (Paris: L'Harmattan, 2015).
[2] Caillé, Alain, *Critique de la raison utilitaire* (Paris: Ed. La Découverte, 1989).

reduced to an exclusively economic rationale. Consequently, the concept of interest has been subsumed to self-interest, as epitomized by the fiction of an omnipresent *homo œconomicus* who is exclusively preoccupied by the maximization of his profits and the minimization of his losses. In contrast, anyone who seems to act selflessly, as defined in utilitarian terms, is considered irrational.

In order to find alternative forms of interest outside the economic realm, the anti-utilitarian movement proposes a 'paradigm of the gift'[3] inspired by Marcel Mauss. In Mauss's seminal work,[4] a gift necessarily calls for an ulterior counter-gift, defined by an inescapably repetitive movement of giving, receiving and later giving back, which is simultaneously interested *and* disinterested. The Maussian gift is highly ambivalent in this sense because it represents *at the same time* the clear interest in creating and maintaining social ties and the free will to do so in a movement towards the other which is stripped of economic and material interest. This opens new horizons to other rational forms of interest which cannot be reduced to self-interest and economic rationale.

My argument was that the empathic process could be such an alternative form. This prompted me to look into several salient aspects of empathy, based on Carl Rogers' definition of empathy as the capacity to perceive "the internal frame of reference of another with accuracy [...] as if one were the person, but without ever losing the 'as if' condition."[5] Indeed, using a transdisciplinary framework, broadened from psychotherapy and psychoanalysis to anthropology and phenomenology, empathy appeared as a potentially different form of interest in the 'cultural' Other.

Contrary to the common belief, one can argue that the capacity to empathize is not intrinsically positive or even moral. It depends on the ethical use one makes of it,[6] which may explain in part the difficulty to agree on a working definition. For this reason, I articulated an analytical distinction between the concept of empathy (as a generic and morally neutral ability) and the phenomenon of empathy (as different actualizations of empathy in context). Anti-utilitarian empathy becomes thus a phenomenon of empathy, in a particular

---

3 Caillé, Alain, "Notes sur le concept d'utilitarisme. L'antinomie de la raison utilitaire normative et le paradigme du don", in *Revue du MAUSS*, vol. 14, no. 4 (1991): 101–117.
4 Mauss, Marcel, *Essai sur le don* (Paris: Quadrige/PUF, 2007).
5 Rogers, Carl, "A theory of therapy, personality, and interpersonal relationships, as developed in the client-centered framework", in *Psychology: A study of science. Volume 3: Formulation of the person and the social context*, edited by S. Koch (New York: McGraw-Hill, 1959), 210–211.
6 Hollan, Douglas and Throop, Jason, *The Anthropology of Empathy: Experiencing the Lives of Others in Pacific Societies* (New York-Oxford: Berghahn Books, 2011).

moral context where one is both free to relate to others and socially required to do so in order to maintain the social link. In the light of Mauss' gift and Rogers' definition, I identified the main characteristics of anti-utilitarian empathy which helped me better understand its functioning.

Anti-utilitarian empathy calls in my opinion for a sustained psychological and intellectual effort of decentring, ambivalence and responsibility, which requires a fair amount of time to unfold. To empathize with another person, one needs to suspend judgement temporarily, in order to be able to grasp the internal frame of reference of the other in their own terms. As opposed to other similar concepts, like sympathy, empathy is based on the platinum rule *do unto others as they wish you to do unto them*, in other words one should treat others as *they* wish to be treated. From a Rogerian perspective, this means the empathic process is ambivalent because it requires one to both become the other and remain one self, understand the other's point of view while acknowledging that one cannot dismiss one's own perspective yet suspending one's frame of reference. Furthermore, from an anti-utilitarian perspective, empathizing becomes both a free choice and a social requirement within a shared community and space – whether one initially identifies or sympathizes with the other or not. The moral context dictates a certain responsibility towards the other to try and understand their reasoning and engage in dialogue, but also towards the whole community in order to maintain a liveable and peaceful social environment. Finally and for all these reasons, the empathic effort requires a particular personal commitment to the other(s) and takes a lot of time that not only cannot be compressed, but also and more importantly comes in contradiction with the allegedly prevailing utilitarian logic of self-interest.

In order to put these theoretical hypotheses to the test, I was interested in situations where empathy was made difficult by spatial or temporal distance or by any perceived differences between two entities. I was pondering how anti-utilitarian empathy would unfold if there was little identification with or understanding of the Other. That is how I came to be interested in the Iroquois Confederacy, a group of six Native American nations living mainly in southern Ontario and Quebec and northern New York State. Often present at the United Nations in Geneva, Switzerland, the Iroquois representatives have regularly used rhetorics of present accountability to the future generations,[7] up to the seventh generation yet to come. The will, be it concrete or virtual, to take into account and in the present the potential interests of an entity who would only

---

7   Six Nations, *A Basic Call to Consciousness: The Hau de no sau nee Address to the Western World, Geneva, Switzerland, Autumn 1977* (New York: Mohawk Nation, Akwesasne Notes, 1978).

be born seven generations into the future, seemed to be an exciting starting point for my research on empathy. My fieldwork in Ontario and Quebec started with these questions in mind.

2 Empathy as Heuristic Tool: the Successful Failure of the Field

Fieldwork is a complicated process and we are taught that the best way to deal with it is … to deal with it. One day at a time. Anticipate the unexpected without knowing what to expect.

Given the complex history of the relations between Indigenous communities – in this case, the Iroquois nations – and non-Indigenous scholars, and the unresolved tensions between mainstream society and Indigenous communities in Quebec and Ontario, I knew even before I took the plane from Geneva that it would be complicated to negotiate my research. My initial preparation to fieldwork was to put it in the sociohistorical context and immerse myself in the literature available in Switzerland, which was anything but abundant.

Once in Canada, the first unexpected and painful experience was to actually sense the pervading animosity existing at all levels when Indigenous issues were in question,[8] from the generally negative (mis)representation of the Indigenous population in the media to the general Indigenous mistrust towards academic research.[9] Yet, unexpectedness did not come so much from my ignorance of the situation, as from the tangible reality one can only grasp *on site*. The ocean of distance separating my original location from the Canadian context did not allow me to fully capture the extent of the intricate relations and idiosyncratic sensitivities. My difficulty to enter the field (contact and meet people, explain my project, negotiate my presence) was only the tip of the iceberg. Distrust, refusal to engage in dialogue and lack of interest were the main reactions to my first attempts to engage with my interlocutors. Whatever the subject or the method, tensions between Iroquois communities and mainstream Academy predated my arrival and tinted my attempts to conduct a relatively 'neutral' research.

Fortunately, the second unexpected but fruitful experience was to discover the impressive amount of literature produced by new generations of Indigenous scholars. From different origins (Wendat, Mohawk, Sioux, Plains Cree,

---

8   Biolsi, Thomas and Zimmerman, Larry J., *Indians and Anthropologists: Vine Deloria, Jr. and the Critique of Anthropology* (Tucson: University of Arizona Press, 1997).

9   Deloria, Vine Jr., *Custer Died for Your Sins: An Indian Manifesto* (Norman: The University of Oklahoma Press, 1988).

Pueblo, Maori, Sami, etc.) and disciplinary locations (law, education, history, social work, political science or anthropology), these intellectuals were talking back, challenging both the content and the form of previous academic assumptions about Indigenous matters. Bitter disputes over land, rights and culture were not only political, legal and historical, but also and more importantly epistemological, as diverging conceptual matrices were constantly colliding. Isabelle Schulte-Tenckhoff offers an enlightening anthropological interpretation of the legal colonial relationship to land treaties in Canada – what she calls 'the founding dilemma'[10] of the Neo-European states – and the difficulty to understand Indigenous rights. The mere presence of Indigenous intellectuals and activists was giving a relatively new twist to the confrontation, taking it to an epistemological and even ontological realm: the production and validation of knowledge was profoundly political.[11] From an Indigenous point of view, knowledge has been evolving within a space filled with colonial wounds, transgenerational trauma, unresolved arguments, contested histories, original misunderstandings determining their whole existence up to the present day. In this context, academic research had become 'one of the dirtiest words in the indigenous world's vocabulary.'[12] In order to make sense to the Indigenous communities, research needed to be decolonized first. The dirty word needed to be replaced by the healing terms of relationality: to conduct research with Indigenous peoples, scholars were required to show respect, reciprocity and responsibility as defined in Indigenous terms. Therefore, what mattered to the Indigenous communities and scholars did not necessarily coincide with an academic agenda,[13] neither in content nor in time[14] and personal effort (such as completing a PhD, producing a monograph or publishing articles). Old questions of legitimacy and voice,[15] who spoke for

---

10   Schulte-Tenckhoff, Isabelle, "Treaties, peoplehood and self-determination: understanding the language of indigenous rights", in *Indigenous Rights in the Age of the UN Declaration*, edited by Pulitano, Elvira (Cambridge, UK: Cambridge University Press, 2012), 64–86.
11   Alfred, Taiaiake, *Peace, Power, Righteousness: An Indigenous Manifesto* (Ontario: Oxford University Press, 1999).
12   Smith Tuhiwai, Linda, *Decolonizing Methodologies: Research and Indigenous Peoples* (London: Zed Books, 1999), 1.
13   Simpson, Audra, "On Ethnographic Refusal: Indigeneity, 'Voice' and Colonial Citizenship", in *Junctures*, no. 9 (2007): 67–80.
14   Kovach, Margaret, *Indigenous Methodologies: Characteristics, Conversations, and Contexts* (Toronto : University of Toronto Press, 2009).
15   Alcoff, Linda, "The Problem of Speaking for Others", in *Cultural Critique*, no. 20 (1991–1992): 5–32.

whom[16] and who spoke to whom, who was heard and what was silenced, were anything but solved in this configuration of power.

In light of these challenges, the last unexpected aspect of my fieldwork was to realize that theoretical empathy had gradually shifted into a heuristic tool. The reality of the field pushed me to question the established rules of the academic world I was myself a part of, to pay more rigorous attention to the meanings attached to situations and words, starting with the basic word 'empathy.' Faced with refusal and distrust, was I empathetic towards the people I was hoping to work with on ... empathy? What was I really negotiating: my way to extract information from a resistant Other in order to complete my research whatever the cost? What was I giving, receiving or giving back? In reality, what predated my arrival was not only social tension in a colonial context, it was a complicated secular movement of the Maussian gift. *From an Indigenous point of view*, Indigenous peoples had given an initial gift[17] – in terms of lands, knowledge, skills, even lives – to the European colonisers, who had only taken and rarely given back. I was therefore involved in a movement that forced me to review my entire approach. Negotiation actually became self-negotiation to find out how far I was willing to go without betraying the very concept I had been working on and the ethical space within which it had been defined.

The methodological characteristic of working *on* and *with* anti-utilitarian empathy urged me to take into account in my own research the epistemological claims of the Indigenous community, in and outside the academic world. As a heuristic tool, empathy allowed me then to identify a triple bind in my research with Indigenous peoples: I was simultaneously and inescapably accountable to the academic world (in terms of methodology, deadlines, protocols), to the people and communities I was interested in (in order to listen respectfully and responsibly to them *in their own terms*) and to myself (as a reflexive researcher and a coherent social being). These accountabilities were not perforce compatible, yet they were intrinsically related and I had to accept that I could not elude any of them. Conducting a responsible and, in the final analysis, a successful research on empathy, meant that I needed to put empathy into practice in order to engage in an intelligible and respectful dialogue with the Indigenous interlocutors. As uncomfortable as it was, this finally led to a paradigmatic shift in my theoretical framework which helped me measure the importance of the colonial dimension of my research.

---

16   Cordova, Viola, *How It Is : The Native American Philosophy of V.F. Cordova* (Tucson: The University of Arizona Press, 2007).

17   Kuokkanen, Rauna, *Reshaping the University: Responsibility, Indigenous Epistemes and the Logic of the Gift* (Vancouver: UBC Press, 2007).

3   Empathy as Ethical Practice: a Decolonial Perspective

Therefore, empathy became an ethical practice in the last part of my doctoral journey, allowing me to consider Indigenous epistemes as valid knowledge and as *sui generis* epistemologies. To do so, I drew on the work of sociologist Boaventura de Sousa Santos on the 'epistemologies of the South,'[18] as well as on the theoretical material of decoloniality, a promising and manifold intellectual movement stemming from Latin America. Beyond inter- and transdisciplinarity in social sciences, a protean group of Latin American scholars has been offering in the recent years an undisciplined interpretation of the present power relations in the Americas. Most of this prolific literature has been mainly written in Spanish, but it has been gradually available in English and some authors use both languages, like semiologist Walter Mignolo, philosopher Nelson Maldonado-Torres, anthropologist Arturo Escobar, etc. One of their main arguments is that the project of modernity was built on coloniality, an intricate web of colonial actions that have been lastingly defining every aspect of the American life – and beyond the Americas – since the first European arrival in the 15th century. The self-declared European superiority has been progressively built on the material, cultural, intellectual, spiritual exploitation of Indigenous peoples. European colonizers have thus created new social categories in which Indigenous peoples were considered inferior by their very nature, allowing their knowledge, survival strategies and mere existence to be legitimately silenced or ignored. But in a decolonial perspective, Indigenous voices are heard again or, in most cases, for the first time and these voices claim to be listened to in their own terms and from their own perspective. Finally, Indigenous strategies, methodologies and epistemologies can become valid in their own right.

In this new light, the ethical practice of anti-utilitarian empathy allowed me to consider my Indigenous interlocutors as being much more than just defiant informants who would refuse to play by the established academic rules. If I wanted them to trust me and talk to me, I had to suspend judgement, stop talking and first listen, *really listen* to what they had to say. Yet, taking their epistemological claims seriously did not mean accepting them uncritically. On the contrary, in order to criticize them, one would need to understand first their internal logic, their genealogy and frame of reference. Empathy as an ethical decolonial practice became thus a way of accepting the Indigenous gift,

---

18   De Sousa Santos, Boaventura, *Epistemologies of the South: Justice against Epistemicide* (Boulder/London: Paradigm Publishers, 2014).

allowing it to transform research in a respectful dialogue between equally valid propositions and only then, potentially, in a healing process of the colonial wound.

Bibliography

Alcoff, Linda, "The Problem of Speaking for Others", in *Cultural Critique*, no. 20 (1991–1992): 5–32.

Alfred, Taiaiake, *Peace, Power, Righteousness: An Indigenous Manifesto* (Ontario: Oxford University Press, 1999).

Biolsi, Thomas and Zimmerman, Larry J., *Indians and Anthropologists: Vine Deloria, Jr. and the Critique of Anthropology* (Tucson: University of Arizona Press, 1997).

Caillé, Alain, *Critique de la raison utilitaire* (Paris: Ed. La Découverte, 1989).

Caillé, Alain, "Notes sur le concept d'utilitarisme. L'antinomie de la raison utilitaire normative et le paradigme du don", in *Revue du MAUSS*, vol. 14, no. 4 (1991): 101–117.

Cordova, Viola, *How It Is : The Native American Philosophy of V.F. Cordova* (Tucson: The University of Arizona Press, 2007).

De Sousa Santos, Boaventura, *Epistemologies of the South: Justice against Epistemicide* (Boulder/London: Paradigm Publishers, 2014).

Deloria, Vine Jr., *Custer Died for Your Sins: An Indian Manifesto* (Norman: The University of Oklahoma Press, 1988).

Hollan, Douglas and Throop, Jason, *The Anthropology of Empathy: Experiencing the Lives of Others in Pacific Societies* (New York-Oxford: Berghahn Books, 2011).

Ionita, Irina, *Un itinéraire de recherche en terrain autochtone au Canada: L'empathie dans tous ses états* (Paris: L'Harmattan, 2015).

Kovach, Margaret, *Indigenous Methodologies : Characteristics, Conversations, and Contexts* (Toronto: University of Toronto Press, 2009).

Kuokkanen, Rauna, *Reshaping the University: Responsibility, Indigenous Epistemes and the Logic of the Gift* (Vancouver: UBC Press, 2007).

Mauss, Marcel, *Essai sur le don* (Paris: Quadrige/PUF, 2007).

Rogers, Carl, "A theory of therapy, personality, and interpersonal relationships, as developed in the client-centered framework", in *Psychology: A study of science. Volume 3: Formulation of the Person and the Social Context*, edited by Koch, S. (New York: McGraw-Hill, 1959), 184–256.

Schulte-Tenckhoff, Isabelle, "Treaties, Peoplehood and Self-determination: Understanding the Language of Indigenous Rights", in *Indigenous Rights in the Age of the UN Declaration*, edited by Pulitano, Elvira (Cambridge, UK: Cambridge University Press, 2012), 64–86.

Simpson, Audra, "On Ethnographic Refusal: Indigeneity, 'Voice' and Colonial Citizenship", in *Junctures*, no. 9 (2007): 67–80.

Six Nations, *A Basic Call to Consciousness: The Hau de no sau nee Address to the Western World, Geneva, Switzerland, Autumn 1977* (New York: Mohawk Nation, Akwesasne Notes, 1978).

Tuhiwai Smith, Linda, *Decolonizing Methodologies: Research and Indigenous Peoples* (London: Zed Books, 1999).

CHAPTER 8

Empathetic Art in a Paediatric Oncology Clinic

Judy Rollins

Abstract

Today there is an emergent movement in hospitals led by artists dedicated to creating unique work designed specifically to promote positive outcomes for patients, family, visitors, and staff. The style of this contemporary 'purpose built' art may be abstract, realistic, fanciful, ambiguous, or on occasion, threatening. Research to date is scant and primarily anecdotal, yet findings indicate that patients use these artists' work in very specific ways and find such artwork helpful in coping with healthcare settings and experiences. The purpose of this international study, the author's Scholar project at The Institute for Integrative Health, is to identify this type of art in hospitals, and to examine the perceptions of the individuals who create, choose, or use this art; the principles that guide their creation and selection process; and evidence of the impact on individuals exposed to the art. An early finding of this research is the work of Boston artist Joan Drescher. Drescher was commissioned to create a series of murals for the oncology waiting area and treatment rooms at the Floating Hospital for Children in Boston. The 'Symbols of Courage' murals depict the journey that children and families travel, from feeling well before diagnosis, to not feeling well and diagnosis, through the entire treatment protocol. She hung her sketches in the doctors' conference room to give children, their families, and staff the opportunity to review them and verify themes. Children have used Drescher's images to communicate feelings about their illness or hospitalization. When they look at the murals, children say they feel that someone understands where they are. Parents sense being seen and heard, saying that at last someone knows what they are going through. Hospital staff report having a better understanding of what patients and families undergo.

Keywords

artwork – artists – empathy – healthcare environment – cancer – children – hospital

1   Hospital Art

Over the centuries, art has been exhibited in hospitals for a variety of reasons, such as to honor a patron or religious figure, depict daily activities of the hospital, offer prayer, or reflect the hospital's power and prestige. Only in recent history has there been a deliberate focus on hospital art's ability to affect the well-being of patients and others, and to improve the healthcare experience.

Art program directors use a variety of criteria for selecting art for hospitals. Thus, vast differences in art are seen amongst hospitals. Some hospitals feature artwork similar to what would be found in contemporary art galleries; others display art based on research findings. Ulrich and Gilpin advise decision makers to base choices on whether the artwork improves patient outcomes, "not whether it receives praise from art critics and artists or approaches museum standards for quality".[1] McCullough cautions that it is considered risky if the quality of the aesthetics in the healthcare environment is not based on research findings and other evidence.[2]

In America, for the past two decades, guidance for the selection of art for hospitals has suggested realistic art that depicts soothing and comforting images such as tranquil waters, green vegetation, flowers, open spaces, and compassionate faces. These recommendations are based on research findings supported by two major theories—evolutionary and emotional congruence.[3] Based on these findings, curators have been cautioned to avoid art with uncertain meaning or risk upsetting viewers already in a stressful state. Yet some hospitals in the U.S. exhibit ambiguous or abstract art and cite anecdotal evidence of its appropriateness for healthcare settings.[4] Researchers in other English speaking countries acknowledge similar thoughts on this topic.[5]

Considerable disagreement exists about the purpose of art in hospitals and whether it is intended to challenge and provoke in addition to soothing and comforting. Although the majority of hospital artwork is created for public consumption and then selected for a particular site in the hospital, there is

---

1   Ulrich, Roger and Gilpin, Laura, "Healing Arts: Nutrition for the Soul", in *Putting Patients First: Designing and Practicing Patient-Centered Care,* edited by S. Frampton, L. Gilpin and P. Charmel (San Francisco: Jossey-Bass, 2003), 120.
2   McCullough, Cynthia, *Evidence-Based Design for Healthcare Facilities* (Indianapolis: Sigma Theta Tau International, 2010), 3.
3   Ulrich and Gilpin, "Healing Arts", 120.
4   Rollins, Judy, "Arousing Curiosity: When Hospital Art Transcends", in *Health Environments Research & Design Journal,* no. 4 (2011): 72–94.
5   Lankston, Louise, *et al.*, "Visual Art in Hospitals: Case Studies and Review of the Evidence", in *Journal of the Royal Society of Medicine,* no. 103 (2010): 490–499.

an emergent movement led by artists dedicated to creating unique work designed specifically to promote positive outcomes for patients, family, visitors, and staff. The style of this contemporary bespoke or 'purpose built' art may be abstract, realistic, fanciful, ambiguous, or on occasion, threatening. Research to date is slim and primarily anecdotal, yet findings indicate that patients use these artists' work in very specific ways and find such artwork helpful in coping with healthcare settings and experiences.[6]

What is the impact of this 'purpose built' commissioned artwork on patients, families, visitors, and staff in healthcare settings? This international study seeks to identify examples of this kind of art and explore the perceptions of the individuals who make, select, or use this art; the principles that guide its creation and selection; and evidence regarding outcomes for individuals exposed to the art.

2   Empathetic Art

Even though the study is in its early stages, certain themes of pupose built art are already emerging. For example, there is 'meditative art', 'inspirational art', 'interactive art', 'remembrance art', 'messaging art', and 'culture art'.

For this researcher, perhaps one of the most intriguing and exciting themes to emerge is 'empathetic art'. Empathetic art is not to be confused with 'empathy art', a term from the art therapy profession. For art therapists, empathy art or response art refers to post session artwork some art therapists create to respond to material that arises in their therapy work. It is a place to contain difficult material, express and examine their experiences, and share their experiences with others.[7] The concept used here is also different from art that generates empathy from the viewer and helps the viewer connect to others, cultures, and causes.

In this paper, empathetic art is art that the artist creates to empathize with the viewer. Something about the work captures the viewer's attention, arouses his or her curiosity, drawing the viewer in. While engaged in viewing the art, the viewer may feel that the artist has some understanding of the viewer's experience.

---

6   Rollins, "Arousing Curiosity: When Hospital Art Transcends", 74.
7   Fish, Barbara, "Response Art: The Art of the Art Therapist", in *Art Therapy: Journal of the American Art Therapy Association*, no. 29 (2012): 138–143.

3   'Symbols of Courage' Murals

Joan Drescher's work illustrates the concept of empathetic art. In 2006, she was commissioned to create a series of six murals for the oncology waiting area and treatment rooms at the Floating Hospital for Children in Boston. The 'Symbols of Courage' murals illustrate the journey that children and families travel, from before diagnosis when feeling well, to not feeling well and diagnosis, through the complete treatment protocol.[8] Using symbols and images, she began the process of storytelling, which came naturally to Drescher as an author and illustrator of children's books. She was tasked to paint the dark shadows as well as the rays of hope. Said Drescher,

> The clinic was a place where pain and joy lived side by side. Here, it didn't matter what you looked like on the outside, because it would probably change soon anyway—what mattered was how you felt on the inside.[9]

To really get to know her subject well, Drescher felt she needed to become intimate with it. She spent the summer observing the ebb and flow of the clinic. Sitting in the corner of the clinic, she drew and spoke with the children. She also brought along drawing materials for the children, and some of them drew pictures of her. She displayed her sketches in the doctors' conference room so that children, their families, and staff could review them and verify the themes. They suggested additional images, such as the oncology chief's favorite necktie.

The first mural in the series is "Kite Flying" (see Figure 8.1). This depicts the time before diagnosis when children are happy and healthy. A mother is playing with her child, children are playing together, and one child seems to be simply enjoying herself alone being outdoors on a nice day.

In the second mural, "Not Feeling Well" Drescher shows children sad, worried, and inactive (see Figure 8.2). Amongst the gloom, she has also added comforting images such a kittten, dog, stuffed teddy bear, and, as in the first image, a mother is present.

The next image depicts the clinic where children receive their treatment (see Figure 8.3). Children can be seen receiving chemotherapy, engaging in medical play, as well as doing enjoyable things such as making art.

---

8 Drescher, Joan, "Symbols of Hope and Healing: Using Art with Families and Children", in *Journal of Pedagogy, Pluralism, and Practice*, no. 12 (2007): 5.
9 Drescher, "Symbols of Hope", 5.

FIGURE 8.1 Kite Flying
© 2006, JOAN DRESCHER. USED WITH PERMISSION.

FIGURE 8.2 Not Feeling Well
© 2006, JOAN DRESCHER. USED WITH PERMISSION.

EMPATHETIC ART IN A PAEDIATRIC ONCOLOGY CLINIC 97

FIGURE 8.3   The Clinic
© 2006, JOAN DRESCHER. USED WITH PERMISSION.

Figure 8.4 is "The Goldfish Tank" with a small, frail boy receiving chemotherapy. Drescher remarked that he seemed transfixed by the fish in the tank:

> As I began to draw him, my paper became host to an amazing transformation. I painted him riding on the back of a goldfish, while attacking cancer cells with his hypodermic needle. Each cell was magically turned into a goldfish. I had climbed inside the mind of an eight-year-old patient.[10]

---

10   *Ibid.*

FIGURE 8.4 The Goldfish Tank
© 2006, JOAN DRESCHER. USED WITH PERMISSION.

Children with cancer may undergo a lengthy course of treatment, but along the way they often see evidence of healing. Figure 8.5 features a mandala with healing symbols. Chemotherapy is depicted as a stream of healing hearts. A child celebrates reaching his birthday.

What was to be the final mural in the Symbols of Courage series is presented in Figure 8.6. The disease is in remission. The child resumes school and other activities, hair grows back, and life begins to return to normal.

During her time at the clinic, Drescher was especially touched by a teenage girl named Chandy. Chandy loved art and poetry, and wrote a beautiful poem about a wonderful white unicorn shortly before she died. Drescher then created a seventh mural to celebrate Chandy and all the other children like her, who expressed their courage through art and poetry (see Figure 8.7).

Children with cancer have used Drescher's images to communicate feelings about their ilness or hospitalization. When looking at the murals, children say they feel that someone understands where they are. Parents sense being seen and heard, saying that at last someone knows what they are going through. Hospital staff report having a better understanding of what patients and families undergo.

EMPATHETIC ART IN A PAEDIATRIC ONCOLOGY CLINIC 99

FIGURE 8.5 Healing Mandala
© 2006, JOAN DRESCHER. USED WITH PERMISSION.

On another note, some family members have told clinic staff that at times the images, while empathetic, were an ever present reminder of their child and family's current situation. Seeing them at every clinic appointment sometimes made them sad. Thus, location of empathetic art can be an important consideration.

4   Empathy and the Artist

According to Bellet and Maloney, empathy is the capacity to understand or feel what another being (a human or non-human animal) is experiencing from

FIGURE 8.6   Coming Home Again
© 2006, JOAN DRESCHER. USED WITH PERMISSION.

within the other being's frame of reference, i.e., the capacity to place oneself in another's position.[11] Researchers typically cite three types of empathy: cognitive, emotional or affective, and somatic.[12] Cognitive empathy is the capacity to understand another's emotions. Emotional or affective empathy is the capacity to respond with an appropriate emotion to another's mental state. The third type, somatic empathy, is a physical reaction in the somatic nervous system.[13]

---

11   Bellet, Paul and Maloney, Michael, "The Importance of Empathy as an Interviewing Skill in Medicine", in *Journal of the American Medical Association*, no. 266 (1991): 1831–1832.
12   Rogers, Kimberley, *et al.*, "Who Cares? Revisiting Empathy in Asperger Syndrome", in *Journal of Autism and Developmental Disorders*, no. 37 (2007): 709–715.
13   Rothschild, Babette and Rand, Marjorie, *Help for the Helper: The Psychophysiology of Compassion Fatigue and Vicarious Trauma* (New York: Norton, 2006).

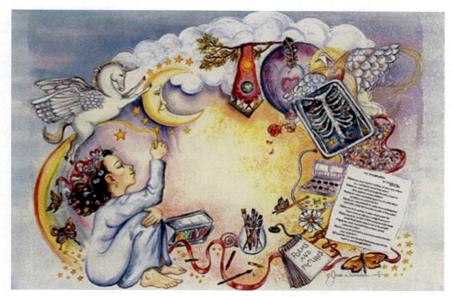

FIGURE 8.7   Chandy
© 2006, JOAN DRESCHER. USED WITH PERMISSION.

Of these three types of empathy, empathetic art appears to represent a pairing of cognitive and affective empathy. Artists use their capacity to understand another's situation and in turn express this understanding emotionally through creative emotional expression.

It is proposed that when art is placed in an area of a healthcare setting where people who view the piece identify with the emotions the artist expressed, they feel understood, comforted, and no longer alone. Such comfort can reduce distress.[14]

Do artists have a higher capacity for being empathetic? One of the gifts of being highly sensitive is greater empathy.[15] Being a highly sensitive person is a trait of 15% to 20% of people; however, Elaine Aron, author of *The Highly Sensitive Person*, says it seems to be much more common among artists.[16]

---

14   Miceli, Maria; Mancini, Alessandra and Menna, Palma, "The Art of Comforting", in *New Ideas in Psychology*, no. 27 (2009): 343–361.
15   Borhcard, Therese, "5 Gifts of Being Highly Sensitive", in *Psych Central* (blog), March 29, 2010. Viewed on the 16th October 2018. http://psychcentral.com/blog/archives/2010/03/28/5-gifts-of-being-highly-sensitive/.
16   Aron, Elaine, *The Highly Sensitive Person* (New York: Citadel Press, 1998), ix.

5 Other Examples of Empathetic Art

Other artists create artwork that seems intent on being empathetic. For example, Quentin Blake, British cartoonist, illustrator, and children's writer, in describing his process for creating "Mothers and Babies Underwater" for the maternity hospital of the Centre Hospitalier Universitaire in Anger, France, mentioned needing to imagine himself in the situation of giving birth. His hope was that the images would provide reassurance to mothers in labor that birth is going to happen:

> These swimmers are absolutely unclothed, surrounded by trails of seaweed in decorative Rococo swirls. In former times young women appeared nude in paintings with the excuse that they were classical—they were nymphs and goddesses and suchlike. These Angers mothers and babies are real, but the places where the pictures appear are private and, although real, they appear in a parallel world where their swimming expresses and celebrates, I hope, their new-found liberty after the pains of labour.[17]

William Wegman's photograph "Trio" can be considered empathetic art (see Figure 8.8). Wegman is an American artist best known for creating series of compositions involving dogs, primarily his own Weimaraners. The photograph appears in the waiting area of Georgetown Lombardi Comprehensive Cancer Center, Washington, DC. Julia Langley, Director of Lombardi's Arts and Humanities Program, said she selected the piece for the entrance to the waiting area because she believed people would identify with the dogs sitting and waiting. The image's message is 'we empathize with you for we are waiting, too.'

6 Discussion

Commissioning artwork is becoming a fairly common practice when building new hospitals or renovating or expanding older ones. Increasingly, those who commission or select art are recognizing that art can do more than improve the aesthetics of the healthcare environment. As with other decisions in healthcare settings, the choice of art should be based on evidence of efficacy.

To date, much of the evidence supporting the use of this kind of art with intent is anecdotal. Although showing empathy is a highly relevant social

---

17   Blake, Quentin, *Quentin Blake: As Large as Life* (Warwickshire: Compton Verney, 2011), 17.

FIGURE 8.8 Trio
© 2016, WILLIAM WEGMAN. USED WITH PERMISSION.

interaction pattern, the focus on measurement has almost exclusively been studied with a focus on the sender, neglecting the effects on the recipient.[18]

For a meaningful understanding of empathetic art, research is needed that looks not only at the recipient of the empathy (i.e., patients, families, visitors, staff), but also the artists who create it and the arts program curators or administrators who select it. Research should also address whether certain art might be used successfully as temporary exhibits in addition to or rather than permanent installations (defined by most curators as five years). Printed or recorded commentary may increase understanding.

Viewers might be asked to draw 'what the art makes you think about and what it makes you feel', a method used successfully by Ho and colleagues.[19] This directive is based on Moon's concept of response art, which involves creating

---

18   Seehausen, Maria, *et al.*, "Effects of Empathic Social Responses on the Emotions of the Recipients", in *Brain and Cognition*, no. 103 (2016): 50–61.

19   Ho, Rainbow T., *et al.*, "Art Viewing Directives in Hospital Settings Effect on Mood", in *Health Environments Research & Design Journal*, no. 8 (2015): 30–43.

art about a person or situation to gain understanding about oneself, another, or a situation.[20] The process of drawing is thought to deepen one's observation and ability to notice the emotional effect of the art. Further, drawing can help sustain the viewer's interest, and the novelty of drawing may encourage curiosity as to what the artwork means to the viewer.[21]

Empathetic art has the potential to play a powerful role in humanizing hospitals and other healthcare settings. Evidence of its effectiveness is a major step in increasing understanding and use of this 'art with intent'.

Bibliography

Aron, Elaine, *The Highly Sensitive Person* (New York: Citadel Press, 1998).

Bellet, Paul and Maloney, Michael, "The Importance of Empathy as an Interviewing Skill in Medicine", in *Journal of the American Medical Association*, no. 266 (1991): 1831–1832.

Blake, Quentin, *Quentin Blake: As Large as Life* (Warwickshire: Compton Verney, 2011).

Borhcard, Therese, "5 Gifts of Being Highly Sensitive", in *Psych Central* (blog). 29 March 2010. Viewed on 16th October 2018. http://psychcentral.com/blog/archives/2010/03/28/5-gifts-of-being-highly-sensitive/.

Drescher, Joan, "Symbols of Hope and Healing: Using Art with Families and Children", in *Journal of Pedagogy, Pluralism, and Practice*, no. 12 (2007): 1–11.

Fish, Barbara, "Response Art: The Art of the Art Therapist", in *Art Therapy: Journal of the American Art Therapy Association*, no. 29 (2012): 138–143.

Ho, Rainbow T.; Potash, Jordan S; Fang, F. and Rollins, Judy, "Art Viewing Directives in Hospital Settings Effect on Mood", in *Health Environments Research & Design Journal*, no. 8 (2015): 30–43.

Lankston, Louise; Cusack, Pearce; Fremantle, Chris, and Isles, Chris, "Visual Art in Hospitals: Case Studies and Review of the Evidence", in *Journal of the Royal Society of Medicine*, no. 103 (2010): 490–499.

McCullough, Cynthia, *Evidence-based Design for Healthcare Facilities* (Indianapolis: Sigma Theta Tau International, 2010).

Miceli, Maria; Mancini, Alessandra, and Menna, Palma, "The Art of Comforting", in *New Ideas in Psychology*, no. 27 (2009): 343–361.

---

20 Moon, Bruce, *Existential Art Therapy: The Canvas Mirror* (Springfield-IL: Charles C. Thomas, 2009), 125.

21 Ho, *et al.*, "Art Viewing", 30–43.

Moon, Bruce, *Existential Art Therapy: The Canvas Mirror* (Springfield-IL: Charles C. Thomas, 2009).

Rogers, Kimberley; Dziobek, Isabel; Hassenstab, Jason; Wolf, Oliver T., and Convit, Antonio, "Who Cares? Revisiting Empathy in Asperger Syndrome", in *Journal of Autism and Developmental Disorders*, no. 37 (2007): 709–715.

Rollins, Judy, "Arousing Curiosity: When Hospital Art Transcends", in *Health Environments Research & Design Journal*, vol. 4, no. 3 (2011): 72–94.

Rothschild, Babette, and Rand, Marjorie, *Help for the Helper: The Psychophysiology of Compassion Fatigue and Vicarious Trauma* (New York: Norton, 2006).

Seehausen, Maria; Kazzer, Philipp; Bajbouj, Malek; Heekeren, H. R.; Jacobs, Arthur, M.; Klann-Delius, Gisela; Menninghaus, Winfried, and Prehn, K., "Effects of Empathic Social Responses on the Emotions of the Recipients", in *Brain and Cognition*, no. 103 (2016): 50–61.

Ulrich, Roger, and Gilpin, Laura, "Healing Arts: Nutrition for the Soul", in *Putting Patients First: Designing and Practicing Patient-centered Care,* edited by S. Frampton, L. Gilpin and P. Charmel (San Francisco: Jossey-Bass, 2003), 117–146.

CHAPTER 9

Practicable Empathy in Acting: Empathic Projection in Sophocles' *Ajax*

Christopher J. Staley

Abstract

A holistic understanding of theatrical empathy must comprise at minimum a three-pronged account of simulative enactment between multiple perspectives and situational selves. These three phases of emergent empathy include: from actor to character; from actor/character to audience; and then from the audience to themselves and each other. This activation may result in an infra-collective potentiation for emotional experience in audience members which often metatheatrically foregrounds audience membership itself. Put in simpler terms, dramas are designed to provoke affective group responses *in audiences* based on the conventional and collective witnessing of actors performing dramatic actions *in front of audiences*. Individual audience members can easily become aware of their place in a collective experience through affective entrainment with real agents ostensibly blending themselves into and out of fictional characters and circumstances. This paper explores said three-part process, demonstrating the ways in which Sophocles' *Ajax* can be understood as a platform not only for thematic empathy within the plot, but also structural metatheatrical empathy within its dramatic technics. Such thematic and metatheatrical phenomena may be more keenly engendered through the actor's technical performance of dramatic action. Throughout, I mean to highlight the utility and efficacy of acting as a skillset and practice uniquely suited to enhancing the capacity for empathy in artists and audiences alike. Thus this paper will parse the three steps of theatrical empathy – as interactive and practicable exercises which might facilitate the emergence of empathy – by analyzing the ways in which actors and audiences jointly conceive empathic projection, per George Lakoff and Mark Turner's terminology. I argue that aside from the play's thematic relevance as an example par excellence of theatre of war, Sophocles' *Ajax* is innately suited for therapeutic and remedial functionalization due to its humbling frames of multiple 'selves' for the characters, actors, and audiences.

Keywords

acting – drama – theatrical empathy – empathic projection – collective experience – humility – Sophocles' *Ajax*

Sophocles' *Ajax* is an exemplary text with which to explore the practicability of theatrical empathy to develop humility in both ancient and contemporary audiences. Given the play's functional usage as a remedial and therapeutic tool to elicit emotional connection, this paper analyzes an applicative understanding of *Ajax* within the growing discourse of cognitive theatre studies and cognitive performance historiography.[1] Such a study should not reduce the ineffable quality of theatrical/dramatic empathy to moral prescription (i.e. is this good for you?) but rather highlight how practitioners and scholars of theatre and performance theory are uniquely situated to study and exercise the praxis of empathy (i.e. how might this work for you?). I propose rereading *Ajax* as prototypical of empathic projection in drama because it uniquely models metatheatricality in its structure and themes.[2] In so doing, I offer a three-pronged account for the holistic study of theatrical empathy by affirming the necessity of audience collectivity to the actor's process through the joint 'handshake' of metatheatrical conventions. Actors empathize with characters in the rehearsal and improvisation of dramatic action; actor/characters are perceptibly 'coupled' with audience members who gather in socio-cultural contexts in which they come to witness the play; ultimately, this serves the creation of a collective awareness through which audiences reflect – and reflect on – their own empathetic responses to actors, fellow audience members, and the conventions themselves. Put in simpler if reductive terms, acting involves three minimal

---

1 This paper originally began as a performance and paper titled "Demonstrating the Actor's Process: Empathic Projection in Sophocles' *Ajax*" for the University of Pittsburgh Classics Department Conference on *Empathy, Sympathy, and Compassion: The Dynamics of Other-Oriented Emotions*. My thanks to Dr. Christina Hoenig and Dr. Jacques Bromberg for their invitation and the impulse for this work. It should be noted that Dr. Peter Meineck provided the keynote address at this conference, and as will become clear, his humbling presentation and expansive written work have significantly impacted the direction of my present study.
2 While I do engage the play as performance, I do not analyze any specific productions per se. All line references to the text are from Herbert Golder and Richard Pevear's translation in *The Complete Sophocles*, vol 2, edited by Peter Burian and Alan Shapiro (New York: Oxford University Press, 2010).

levels of empathic connection: the actor/character performance, the audience reception, and the reflexive nature of their relationship.

Why is *Ajax* proto-typical of this model? For those unfamiliar with the play, a selective synopsis may be helpful. The play begins *in media res* following Achilles' death. Ajax perceives disgrace from Agamemnon and Menelaus after losing their judgment in a funeral contest for Achilles' arms. Despite Ajax's brute strength, Odysseus wins due to intellectual prowess. Ajax accuses corruption against the brother-generals and pledges revenge. Intervening, the goddess Athena grips Ajax in hallucination which causes him to torture and kill animals whilst thinking them to be Odysseus and the sons of Atreus. The play opens after this gruesome episode, where we encounter Odysseus seeking out Ajax's bloody trail. Before Odysseus peers in upon the *scene* at the tent, Athena suspends the action, enacting a uniquely theatrical optic device: Ajax can see Athena but not Odysseus, who himself can see both figures. (The staging of this famous prologue is at the crux of my argument and will be explored more fully below.) Odysseus sympathetically witnesses Ajax's ravings and leaves until the end of the play. As Ajax returns to a more lucid state, he is wracked with guilt and shame. Perceiving a lack of options, he plots – literally – towards a gruesome onstage suicide despite fervent protests by his lover, Tekmessa, and a chorus of his fellow sailors.[3] This first 'act' sets up the conditions by which more explicit models of theatrical empathy are presented for the audience in the second half. Seeking burial for his brother, Teucer is stalled in fulfilling the funerary rituals by the Atreidae who demand Ajax's corpse remain unburied. The rest of the play consists of argumentation for and against the rites/rights of burial. When Odysseus returns, he demonstrates mental flexibility and unimpeachable intellect such that Ajax receives burial by enabling the Atreidae to leave without shame or defeat.

Within this overt exhibition and supplication for spectatorial empathy, the play primes thematic constructs that, I argue, are crucial for its presumed remedial effectiveness. Most notably, the play continually trades in themes of self-representation (i.e. big vs. small selves), humility in perspective, self-control, and mindful compassion, all in the face of unspeakable horror and trauma. We see ostensibly 'big men' railing with pride or diminishing themselves in shame, and supposed 'small men' assert the ability to act and 'talk big.' *Ajax* structures this tangle of actor/characters who at times display trait/

---

3 Golder and Pevear, *Ajax*, 44, line 504. See their introduction for analysis of the tragic question 'What now?' or 'What should I do now?' (*Ibid.*, 3–24); also Doerries, Bryan, *The Theater of War: What Ancient Greek Tragedies Can Teach Us Today* (New York: Alfred A. Knopf, 2015), 68.

state qualities of humility, virtue, and mindfulness along with pride, shame, and mindless egoism. How did audiences make sense of this moral and theatrical knottiness, and how could this be helpful for a citizenry suffering from trauma and war? I offer that the vivid conventions of metatheatricality in the play not only schematize how to 'read' for empathy, but subsequently model how to enhance the capacity for it in a war-ravaged polis primed by and for the intertextual mythology of their Homeric tradition.

Jon Hesk explains the longstanding possibility for a metatheatrical analysis in *Ajax* saying "this kind of criticism sees Athena as a playwright or director who orchestrates a tragic spectacle in order to make an impression on her audiences both inside and outside the tragedy."[4] In performance, the actor playing Athena demands the actor playing Odysseus to "see this sickness with [his] own eyes and proclaim it aloud to all the Greeks."[5] She hides actor/Odysseus in plain sight such that he may witness the insane spectacle of actor/Ajax reeling in his own layers of fictional double-blindness. This is not just to show Athena's power, but it creates Athena as an actor/director whereby the audience witnesses an actor/character witnessing another actor/character. Hesk delineates this recursive model mostly by building off of Thomas Falkner's excellent analyses of metatheatre within Sophoclean tragedy, notably *Ajax* and *Philoctetes*.[6] The extendibility of Falkner's analysis is that through metatheatre we are able to contextualize the particularity of the tragic event in such a way that audience's generalize the material with their own prior, particular experiences. Despite Falkner's arguments otherwise, Hesk says "the case for significant metatheatrical meaning in Sophoclean tragedy ha[d] not yet been made to [his] satisfaction."[7] I contend that evidence from cognitive studies and applied performance theory *does* coalesce affirmatively in the years following this evaluation.

Moreover, Hesk contradicts himself in what may be an overly cautious if tactical misreading of Thomas Falkner's argument. To start he says, "Odysseus' capacity for pity and sympathy can also be connected to our opening scene's invocation of the cognitive and emotional experience of watching tragedy."[8] This appreciation of the cognitive and affective experience of tragedy is rather prescient given the relative pace of cognitive science advancements, yet he

---

4 Hesk, Jon, *Sophocles: Ajax* (London: Duckworth, 2003), 46–47.
5 Golder and Pevear, *Ajax*, 29, lines 79–85.
6 Falkner, Thomas M., "Containing Tragedy: Rhetoric and Self-Representation in Sophocles' *Philoctetes*", in *Classical Antiquity*, vol. 17, no. 1 (1998): 25–58.
7 Hesk, *Sophocles: Ajax*, 46–47.
8 *Ibid.*

avoids endorsing a metatheatrical model. It is unclear if Hesk also interprets metatheatre in line with Falkner's usage of Jorge Luis Borges's idea of *dédoublement,* or is solely reporting these opinions when he defines metatheatre as an "infinite regress [...] Such effects encourage audiences to think about the way in which their real lives involve the play of roles."[9] So far so good. This helpfully outlines metatheatre's 'zooming effect' which creates the ideal conditions for spectators to cogitate on their own circumstances and roles whereby they telescope inside and outside the boundaries of the conventional shared theater space.

But Hesk continues with this line of logic, "They promote the feeling that lives are shaped by forces and powers which are discomfortingly hidden but perhaps follow some design."[10] I am reticent to agree with a definition of metatheatre which inherently distributes the locus of agency outside of the individual; also, I do not leverage nor interpret Falkner's analysis in this way. Falkner highlights the multiplicity of subject positions that – kaleidoscopically – can be generated by the coalescing singularity of the shared event. He writes, "the audience is here offered a subject position which serves as a signpost for its response and a standard against which it may monitor its reading."[11] While supposed feelings of a 'hidden design' may be an effect in certain groups and circumstances, so too may metatheatre generate conditions by which individual agency is enhanced through one's subscription and participation into coalition membership rather than reduced to the idea of peeling back reality to find the rhetorical man behind the curtains. As Rhonda Blair says of theatre and thus metatheatre, "What the actor is doing becomes simply – and complexly – that: what the *actor* is *doing.*"[12] In this way, metatheatrical reflection is both simply and complexly pedestrian, and need not necessarily invoke disabling superstition. Audiences might simply end up at the theatre to think about why they go to the theatre. Falkner explicitly ends his analysis saying that metatheatre does indeed *enable* a democratic individuality, concluding that "we are the better equipped to accept, resist, or reject the arguments [metatheatrical rhetoric] makes and the *subject position* it offers."[13] This

---

9   *Ibid.* Also see Falkner on Borges and *dédoublement,* in "Containing Tragedy", 29.
10 Hesk, *Sophocles: Ajax,* 46–47.
11 Falkner, "Containing Tragedy", 49.
12 Blair, Rhonda, *The Actor, Image, and Action: Acting and Cognitive Neuroscience* (New York: Routledge, 2008), 82–83. Emphasis in original. For alternate readings of Blair's well-turned phrase, *vid.* Worthen, W.B., *Shakespeare Performance Studies* (Cambridge: Cambridge University Press, 2014), 120.
13 Falkner, "Containing Tragedy", 55–56. My emphasis.

alternative, *pace* Hesk and his milestone study, resonates with how cognitive science has come to bear affirmatively on Falkner's assertions of metatheatrical reflection by co-locating performance's joint-agency between both the actor and the spectator.

Spectatorial perspective-taking is achieved through linguistic frames as well as embodied performance technics, both of which contribute to a complex model of theatrical empathy that builds upon theatre's inherent multi-perspectivism and the ability to enact versions of ourselves into infinite scenarios and roles. This idea of enaction aligns with breakthroughs in cognitive theatre studies and cognitive performance historiography, overlapping fields which often gravitate upon the notion of theatrical empathy across cultures and periods, or 'theatrical emotion', to use Bruce McConachie's definition. The utility of such a blanket phrase like theatrical emotion is that it "implicitly distinguishes between the theatrical level of a production [...] and the dramatic or fictional level, which (as we have seen) requires actor/characters interacting within a subjunctive world." Most importantly for present purposes is that "theatrical emotions could also include a spectator's emotional response to the other auditors watching the production."[14] Put another way, per Amy Cook, "To be a spectator or a reader is to be an individual. To be a part of an audience is to be part of a whole."[15] Rhonda Blair and Peter Meineck both have theorized these joint models of acting and spectating as all building on '4E Cognition', positing what aptly if redundantly would be a fifth 'E' following Embodied, Embedded, Extended and Enacted models – Empathic Cognition.[16]

There is the immediate flag to raise concerning possibly misunderstanding the neural mechanisms underlying empathy as conflated with what I propose as a practicable exercise giving rise to empathic projection in acting. Empathic projection is not something one *does* nor performs, but rather "from the perspective of current cognitive science, empathy is generally defined as mind reading – the attempt by one person to understand the intentions, emotions

---

14   McConachie, Bruce, *Theatre and Mind* (New York: Palgrave Macmillan, 2013), 63. See also McConachie, Bruce, "Introduction: Spectating as Sandbox Play", in *Affective Performance and Cognitive Science: Body, Brain, and Being*, edited by Nicola Shaughnessy (London: Bloomsbury, 2013), 183–199.
15   Cook, Amy, *Shakespearean Neuroplay: Reinvigorating the Study of Dramatic Texts and Performance Through Cognitive Science* (New York: Palgrave Macmillan, 2010), 1.
16   Blair, Rhonda and Cook, Amy, *Theatre, Performance, and Cognition: Languages, Bodies, and Ecologies* (New York: Bloomsbury, 2016); Meineck, Peter, *Theatrocracy: Greek Drama, Cognition, and the Imperative for Theatre*, (London: Taylor & Francis, 2017).

and beliefs of another."[17] While one might colloquially empathize with another or attempt 'to mind read', this is largely an automatic unconscious process, and not a willful and volitional application of one's emotive faculties. In conscious terms, it is more so the ability to reflectively/reflexively attend to one's circumstances and role amidst others such that the possibility for empathic projection may emerge.

In addition to various conversations within the field regarding definitions and methods, W.B. Worthen cautions against the risk of essentialism for cognitive theatre scholars who – he argues – derive empirical study of 'real life' or experimental lab methods in applications onto theatre, such as theories of empathy based solely on mirror neuronal simulation, for example. He also questions research data and examples which may trend towards skewing limited models of Western character-based theatre at the occlusion of other more immersive forms. While I find Worthen's own critique of the field obscures the largely cautious and disciplined work of the cognitive theatre scholars he cites, his reminder is vital, that "theatrical empathy takes place in a highly conventionalized environment, one that [...] must work to differentiate its constitutive behaviors from those that take place onstage."[18] As McConachie (mentioned above) parses the theatrical, textual, dramatic levels, so Worthen delineates: "not only are these dramatic situations unique, the skill that creates them in the theatre is unique, and uniquely visible as well."[19] Worthen's own 'signal' through the 'noise' is useful here to remember that theatrical conventions impact our cognitive schemas as much as we shape theatre's supposed structural properties by the standards and metrics we use – or purport to use – in research and analysis.

Largely anteceding these fields and influencing said debates have been cognitive linguists and philosophers George Lakoff and Mark Johnson, whose seminal *Philosophy in the Flesh: The Embodied Mind and Its Challenge to Western Thought* marked a signal moment for the 'cognitive turn' and in turn theatre/performance scholars and artists. Lakoff and Johnson define empathic projection as:

> the capacity to take up the perspective of another person, that is, to see things as that person sees them and to feel what that person feels. It is conceptualized metaphorically as the capacity to project your consciousness

---

17 McConachie, "Spectating as Sandbox Play", 188–192.
18 Worthen, *Shakespeare Performance Studies*, 111.
19 *Ibid.*

into other people, so that you can experience *what* they experience, the *way* they experience it. This is metaphorical because we cannot literally inhabit another person's consciousness.[20]

Embodiment through conceptual metaphor is not an end-result symptom of linguistic narrativizing. Instead, our physicalizing and metaphorizing of information is itself our means of meaning-making across modal domains through situated interactions with the environment.

One metaphor particularly salient for acting is the idea of the body as a container, which pervasively registers in training and theory as a conceptualization of the body's interiority, or the differentiation between inner thought and outer expressivity, or acting techniques that start from the 'outside in' or the 'inside out'.[21] Related is the Jamesian metaphor of multiple selves, and of an essential self, which is pervasively though incorrectly thought to actually exist. This idea of an immutable inner self can pop up in the cliché of 'finding oneself in the role' or finding the 'real character.' We can see this idea of essential selves in a number of ways within the *Ajax:* the idea that his syntactically-assumed pure mind could be poisoned; the oscillation of friends into enemies and back again as with Hector/Ajax or Odysseus/Teucer; the idea that a man's nature might be of many turns or could turn into something new. While the subject-self metaphor is often constituted by and through the figuration of an essential being (whether a soul, persona, one's innate nature, etc.), cognitive science and performance theory give the lie to the idea of an unchanging constancy to identity. There is no little homunculus just as there is no *real* self that actors (or audiences) either reveal or find within the character, or themselves. It is always a metaphoric performance.

Empathy and morality are co-articulated within this embodied logic, but this does not mean that we cannot and do not parse them situationally in life and onstage. Importantly,

> *absolute empathy* is simply feeling as someone else feels, with no strings attached. But very few people would ever espouse this as moral doctrine, since we recognize that other people sometimes have values that are inappropriate or even immoral. Most of the time, we project onto other people not just our capacity to feel as they feel, but also our own value

---

20   Lakoff, George and Johnson, Mark, *Philosophy in the Flesh: The Embodied Mind and its Challenge to Western Thought* (New York: Basic Books, 1999), 309.
21   Cook, *Shakespearean Neuroplay, passim.*

system. This is *egocentric empathy*, which is a way of trying to reach out to other people while preserving your own values.[22]

Lakoff and Johnson list empathic projection as one of several central metaphors constituting or qualifying the subject-self system. They list two cases of such projection: advisory projection occurs when a person projects their own values onto another's situation; empathic projection is different in that one experiences another's circumstances *from the other's perspective* and with their value system. As acting theorist Rick Kemp notes, the ability to shape performance and reception along these differential projections is fundamental to the actor's skillsets.[23] In this light, Falkner's reading of the Sophoclean functionality on Athenian audiences already traces this system as a joint-creation of two or more parties: "a subject position in the form of a character who so engages in our own sympathies carries powerful incentives for the audience to collaborate in the process of construction."[24] If reception cannot be divorced from performance, and if advisory and empathic projection involve inherent duality in subject and circumstance (i.e. 'If I were you ...'), how does this joint agency relate to acting under the dramaturgical conventions surrounding *Ajax*?

Both the exercise of acting and the exercise of witnessing acting are co-extensive instrumental skillsets, each demonstrably enhancing plasticity of empathy and theory of mind in empirical studies.[25] Theatre is an especially conducive tool, operating as a kind of 'gymnasium for the soul'. While this phrase may seem florid, tracing its component etymology suggests helpful connections for the ancient Greek ethos surrounding dramatic performance and athletic performance. The Greek roots of *gymnasium* mean both 'exercise' and 'naked'; it of course also implies a place for physical action, like a theater. Both are places where the activity and the vulnerability of the body are displayed in the service of organismic wellbeing. Combined with the idea of a place where one might alter, enlarge, or enhance the paradoxically im/mutable self, both are understood as places where we strive for and project different versions of ourselves, with a focus on self-representations related to strength, size, flexibility, pride, etc. As Neal Utterback reminds, it is important

---

22   Lakoff and Johnson, *Philosophy in the Flesh*, 309–310.
23   Kemp, Rick, *Embodied Acting: What Neuroscience Tells Us About Performance* (New York: Routledge, 2012). For an excellent reading of the differences between advisory and empathic projection for actors, see Chapters 4 and 5.
24   Falkner, "Containing Tragedy", 49–50.
25   Goldstein, Thalia R. and Winner, Ellen, "Enhancing Empathy and Theory of Mind", in *Journal of Cognition and Development*, vol. 13, no. 1 (2012): 19–37.

to remember that ancient Greek drama emerged out of the same cultural crucible as that of sports, Olympiads, and funerary competitions, like of course, *Ajax*. As with athletes, actors are competing agonists in competition. Rather than thinking of real conflict, however, Utterback reminds that competitive play derives from *competere*, meaning to 'come together' and 'to seek.' The expectation was that only by coming together in competition could individuals seek their best, by engaging one another in con-tests in front of others.[26] His study on the 'pre-theatrical individual' in light of acting training and emotional sensitivity/resilience begs the question, what becomes of the syntactically posited post-theatrical individual?

From a cognitive perspective, it is no new idea that Greek drama was a functional art form used to foster group cohesion and to redress individual trauma and stigma within a war-ravaged polis. So too, a growing body of literature and evidence establishes the practical utility of these dramas to provide forums for discussion and healing in contemporary audiences. An early groundbreaking example is Jonathan Shay's *Achilles in Vietnam: Combat Trauma and the Undoing of Character.*[27] Shay writes from a physician's vantage, working with combat veterans in clinical settings. Much of the resonance he unearthed between Homer's cultural milieu and today's regards how individuals and societies engage in 'communalizing' trauma through various processes of 'griefwork.' Intersecting medical humanities, Shay's work provokes a rich discourse of questions for doctors and scholars of PTSD, military stress, suicidality, and their clinical interventions. Indeed, beginning with his "Author's Caution to Veterans, Their Families, and Their Friends", Shay's text is a stark reminder of the triggerability of PTSD even and especially in our scholarly writings about millennia-old narratives. Shay's second chapter is of especial importance regarding healthy and unhealthy manifestations for the diminishment of self-representation into big/small selves. Ultimately, per the subtitle, one of the central thrusts of the book is to understand the undoing of real and/or fictional *character* through trauma and its re-presentations.

---

26 Utterback, Neal, "The Olympic Actor: Improving Actor Training and Performance Through Sports Psychology", in *Theatre, Performance, and Cognition: Languages, Bodies, and Ecologies,* edited by Rhonda Blair and Amy Cook (New York: Bloomsbury, 2016), 63–76. See additional chapters by Utterback and McConachie in Shaughnessy, *Affective Performance and Cognitive Science.* Relevantly, McConachie throughout discusses collective spectatorship and 'SEEKING' (sic) as a primary emotion.

27 Shay, Jonathan, *Achilles in Vietnam: Combat Trauma and the Undoing of Character* (New York: Scribner, 1994).

Solidly preceding Cognitive Theatre Studies as a discipline writ large, Shay reminds, "restraint is always in part the cognitive attention to multiple possibilities in a situation; when all restraint is lost, the cognitive universe is simplified to a single focus."[28] What acting and spectating allow for is the ability to take on – or at least consider – multiple viewpoints and perspectives available in any situation. Not only is there the seemingly dyadic protagonist and antagonist, but within any and all audiences, each space is assembled in a network of participatory individuality by each member constituting that space of viewership. Shay keenly notes that "unhealed severe trauma from any source [...] destroys the unnoticed substructure of democracy, the cognitive and social capacities that enable a group of people to freely construct a cohesive narrative of their own future."[29] His work derived on "how narrative heals *personality changes*, how narrative enables the survivor to rebuild the *ruins of character*."[30] While Shay's definition of character is mostly pedestrian insofar as it encompasses one's mettle, attributes, fortitude, etc., it clearly evokes the narratological dimension of character formation within temporal arts such as theatre, drama therapy, and/or the temporality of reading texts like the *Iliad*. In this vein, Bryan Doerries of Theatre of War attests he was "hoping to answer Shay's challenge to create a vehicle that would help Americans to come together to share the burden of the pollution of war."[31]

At the forefront of this practical evolution, Peter Meineck specializes in the application of cognitive science in theatre, especially performances from antiquity. His hands-on engagement with Aquila Theatre and the Warrior Chorus has been foundational, and his most recent *Theatrocracy: Greek Drama, Cognition, and the Imperative for Theatre* is by far one of the most holistic applications of cognitive science to ancient and contemporary performance and reception. Meineck addresses the predictive neuro-biology of our cognitive schemas as it interacts with the proprieties and properties (i.e. affordances) of cultural artifacts. Ultimately, the "experience of Greek drama contributed to the cognitive regime of Athenian democracy and attempted to offer alternative views of prescient themes in contemporary life."[32] Scaffolding his chapters serially through Aristotle's six dramatic elements of the *Poetics*, Meineck largely leans on theories of predictive processing and interaction theory in order to argue:

---

28   Shay, *Achilles in Vietnam*, 86.
29   Ibid., 182.
30   Ibid., 187. My emphases.
31   Doerries, *The Theater of War*, 76–77.
32   Meineck, *Theatrocracy*, 217.

that [Greek drama] offered a dissociative absorbing experience that increased empathy, not in the sense of "feeling with" the characters presented but in being emotionally provoked to *project* one's own feelings, which were perhaps repressed by the social norms of the prevailing culture ...[33]

Meineck's theories strongly link the latest neuroscience and prevailing accounts of antiquity to begin to understand what clinical and folk psychologists as well as theatre practitioners have long known but have yet to encapsulate: that ancient Greek drama did and can have powerful effects on its participants, both as actors and audiences.

A meta-review of this evidence, I believe, begets a three-part approach to theatrical empathy as the minimal means by which to account for the ecological complexity alive in any performance. My goal is not to essentialize from these findings nor to completely instrumentalize our still nascent understanding of cognitive empathy into a programmatic model. Rather, it is to emphasize that under no circumstances can the ecological network of the actor-character-audience be disentangled when analyzing the theatrical event, and certainly theatrical empathy. Thus, while it is a three-part process, the processual nature should not reinscribe the very binaries that cognitive theatre studies have effectively and productively destabilized over the last few decades since the 'cognitive turn.'[34] These three parts are not prescriptive, linear distillations of the theatrical event; rather, they are a way to encapsulate the process of acting and spectating together as simultaneous and co-emergent.

The first step, actor to character, subsumes an actor's preparation with her role(s), which involves rehearsed as well as improvisatory performance. The second step, from actor/character to audience, involves the biological coupling required between spectators and actors. Thirdly, spectators may become aware (through their own biological coupling) of fellow audience members' reactions, creating a complex interplay of witnessing a fiction while witnessing others witnessing the same fiction; here too, spectators may judge whether their own experience is the same or different than that of their colleagues. Empathic projection recurs within this regression whereby one can telescope in and out of the multiple framing devices with ease as audiences can oscillate

---

33   *Ibid.* Emphasis added.
34   Said constructed binaries, as Cook notes in her study of metatheatre in *Hamlet*, involve the paradoxical nature of theatre and performance studies in which the object studied is itself the lens by which it is objectifies and studies itself. She writes, "the text uses [this] perspective as a way of compelling intellection and empathy" (Cook, *Shakespearean Neuroplay*, 21).

between the actor's craft and the technicality of the performance versus blending in and out of absorption within the fictional world.

Interestingly, Falkner's reading of Sophoclean meta-theatricality builds off of James Phelan's own tri-partite breakdown of narrative fiction. This 'triple-vision' between *mimetic, synthetic,* and *thematic* layers is helpful insofar as it also regenerates oscillation between each level:

> At one moment, we may find ourselves attending primarily at the mimetic level of the text, absorbed in its story and characters; at another stepping back, more conscious of the 'constructedness' of the text and the medium of its presentation, appreciating just how it is achieving its effects; at another, focused on some more abstract issue to which the text seems to point.[35]

In an eloquent justification, Falkner adds that meta-theatrical presence – authorial, performative, or otherwise – need not be explicit and overt for its influence to be felt. Especially considering the extra degree of intertextuality in the Greek tradition, "the difference among spectators [is] one not of kind but of degree."[36]

A three-part delineation of theatrical empathy is certainly a limited model, insofar as it posits theatre as a character-based medium, thus prioritizing character-driven action over what ought to be horizontally-privileged actants within the performance event such as scenic landscapes and design elements of sound, light, costume, etc.[37] Indeed, McConachie, picking up with neurobiologist Evan Thompson, starts with four stages; the fourth consists of the ideal impulse toward altruistic action.[38] My three-part categorization is less a realistic account than it is a winnowing heuristic to understand the dynamic complexity of empathy in action. Acting is a collaborative endeavor occurring within an ever-shifting web of cultural proprieties regarding audience relations. While such collective sensibility may be thought of as an a priori infra-collective framing (i.e. top-down), the ascription and per-formation of membership must also be considered and studied as a supra-individual phenomenon (i.e. bottom-up). Put another way, as the convention of gathering for the performance itself generates such a top-down frame, it also relays a feed-forward/feed-back loop whereby individuals are (to varying degrees) aware of

---

35 Falkner, "Containing Tragedy", 31.
36 *Ibid.*, 32.
37 Worthen, *Shakespeare Performance Studies,* 118.
38 McConachie, "Spectating as Sandbox Play", 190–199.

their own perspectives, the perspectives of other people, and their collective perspective as each dynamically emerges *in the presence of others*.

Reconnecting to Lakoff and Johnson's expansive definition, empathic projection is deeply connected to a spirituality of immanence. Their text ends with a compelling if radical proposition of inherent morality through an ecological embodiment of sacredness:

> It is through empathic projection that we come to know our environment, understand how we are a part of it and how it is a part of us. This is the bodily mechanism by which we can participate in nature, not just as hikers or climbers or swimmers but as part of nature itself, part of a larger all-encompassing whole. A mindful embodied spirituality is thus an ecological spirituality.[39]

We see this embodied, ecological, certainly pantheistic spirituality played out in Ajax's powerful death knells. However limited, he does display an ability to acknowledge Tekmessa's pain and to feel pity for her and Eurysaces: "Yes, the thought of leaving her a widow [...] and my son an orphan moves me to pity."[40] There are multiple times where Ajax not only addresses but re-invests in his connection to the environment, saluting personifications of 'river streams of Scamander' to 'Helios' to 'Death.' In his final words, he calls out to "the Holy Ground of Salamis [...] famous Athens and [his] one people [...] rivers, streams, and the wide plain of Troy." He says that they "have all sustained [him]."[41] In the face of death, Ajax still finds a way to empathize with his loved ones and with a spiritual worldliness around him.

It is at this point that I find Lakoff and Johnson's final extension of empathic projection newly opens criticism and discussion to the effectiveness and affective-ness of experiencing *Ajax*: "Here is a metaphor for God in which empathic projection onto anything or anyone is contact with God. This is an embodied spirituality based in empathy with all things."[42] Such a morality or religiosity, they offer, is not imposed from a higher authority, but instead derives, like any other metaphorical construct, from the universal nature of embodiment. Their notion of moral pluralism and intra-multiplicity in perspective resonates with the findings that Falkner, Meineck, McConachie, and others have put forward: that the capacity for perspective-taking derives

---

39   Lakoff and Johnson, *Philosophy in the Flesh*, 566–568.
40   Golder and Pevear, *Ajax*, 51, lines 721–724.
41   *Ibid.*, 58, lines 953–963.
42   Lakoff and Johnson, *Philosophy in the Flesh*, 556–568.

from a process of interactive prediction whereby our neural 'selves' constantly compare and contrast changing situational and cultural representations of 'selfness'; this too is constantly updated and simulated with confluent and dissonant information that we re-present in our interaction with other people. These selves involve past selves, future selves, 'small selves', and ultimately the mortal self. As many of these scholars attest, the narratological dimension of trauma gives access to temporal 'control' over the situation whereby one may helpfully re-play situations over again for analysis. The alternate is to 'lose control' over the temporality of said traumatic memories, becoming stuck in triggered loops such as with PTSD. Quoted above, Meineck theorizes the former process as one of healthful absorption and dissociation whereby dramatic empathy can occur. I offer that metatheatre operates as a vehicle for such thematic reflection to become salient and possible, much like metacognition and perspective-taking are engendered as vehicles for mindful 'selftalk.'[43]

Given this targeted application of the play to traumatized audiences terrorized by reminders of mortality and violence, the question is how this three-part model might overlay onto functional working models for theatrical empathy in applied settings, and how it aligns with other cognitive research. As Doerries remarks, "And if there's one thing I've since learned from listening to audiences all over the world respond to Greek tragedy, it's that people who have come into contact with death [...] seem to have little trouble relating to these ancient plays."[44] Similarly, Shay and Meineck have both articulated different descriptions of their work as generative towards an "empathetic image of death."[45] Death is central to the performance event at the root of *Ajax,* both preceding, driving, and following the action. Indeed, Ajax "*becomes* himself – by ceasing to be."[46] Not only is the play steeped in the brutality of war, but for at least half, a corpse is presented and/or discussed onstage. In this final section, I ask what a cognitive view of mortality can illuminate for performance and for empathy. As *embodied* beings, the universal sequel of living embodiment inevitably turns to disembodiment. How, if at all, have cognitive theatre studies – dedicated to the study of the embodied mind – addressed this?

Despite the disciplinary overlaps, it is remarkable that none of the work mentioned above has incorporated research findings into the cognition of mortality. Research from Terror Management Theory, a paradigm of social psychology developed by Sheldon Solomon, Jeff Greenberg, and Tom Pysczyncski,

---

43   Utterback, "The Olympic Actor", 73–76.
44   Doerries, *The Theater of War,* 6–7.
45   Meineck, *Theatrocracy,* 215.
46   Golder and Pevear, *Ajax,* 14. Emphasis in original.

holds that reminders of death engender unique psychological responses broadly construed as worldview defense and self-esteem striving.[47] In laboratory and real-world settings, reminders of death have been shown to elicit polarizing attitudes and behavioral responses that often correspond with a rigidity in worldview defense, based on individual belief systems and meaning-making strategies. While outside the bounds of this paper to explicate TMT as a functional model in social psychology and its overall relevance to the 'appeal of tragedy', a few topline findings from this robust body of literature can buttress existing assertions regarding *Ajax* and its cognitive mechanics, evoking consideration of alternative perspectives and future directions of research.[48]

For example, in a study entitled "Awe, the Diminished Self, and Collective Engagement: Universals and Cultural Variations in the Small Self", researchers Yang Bai et al. theorized awe as a collective emotion that enables individuals to integrate into social collectives.[49] This collective engagement of the individual's "diminished self", or small self, likely mitigates and buttresses the polarizing effects of mortality salience through a process of self-humbling such that we might maintain a healthier psychosocial stance towards the collective. The 'small self hypothesis' follows that awe functions to diminish self-representation which enables individuals to re-orient toward others, and to re-enter into social collectives. Their overall findings indicate that this resultant shift from awe towards collaboration facilitates key functions such as identity formation, action orientation, and group cohesion. Each of these demands and adaptive skillsets are ontologically central to any theatrical enterprise. It is not *just* an evolutionary fact of working together to achieve a common goal, but rather a deeply theatrical question of how we generate the reflexivity to question our roles within the group orientation. In light of these findings, further study of *Ajax* ought to consider the cognitive and psycholinguistic impact of a lexicon linking *Megas* (*big/great*) with *Smikros* (small) and their scaling variations. Hesk notes that the choral 'dependency' on Ajax plays out as "their

---

47   Greenberg, Jeff; Pyszczynski, Tom and Solomon, Sheldon, "The Causes and Consequences of a Need for Self-Esteem: A Terror Management Theory", in *Public Self and Private Self*, edited by R. F. Baumeister, (New York-NY: Springer-Verlag, 1986), 189–212.

48   Goldenberg, Jamie L., *et al.*, "The Appeal of Tragedy: A Terror Management Perspective", in *Media Psychology*, no. 1 (1999): 313–329.

49   Bai, Yang, *et al.*, "Awe, the Diminished Self, and Collective Engagement: Universals and Cultural Variations in the Small Self", in *Attitudes and Social Cognition*, vol. 113, no. 2 (2017): 185–209. My thanks to Sheldon Solomon for his cautious reminder in generalizing mortality salience effects to theatre and performance, and for sharing this constellation of TMT studies on mindfulness, humility, and the small self.

repeated attribution of 'bigness' to Ajax (and their own sense of smallness) introduces a network of imagery which runs through the play."[50] If we read the chorus traditionally as representative of the audience/polis, this is especially pertinent given that "the issue of who is 'big' and what 'bigness' consists of is contested *in the post-death scenes.*"[51]

Ajax could be said to be about the eponymous hero's failure of empathy and humility and the subsequent humiliation that sequesters him, ultimately leading to suicide. Alternately, the play can be said to depict models of humble perspective-taking by Odysseus and Teucer, versus the desire to humiliate and punish by the Atreids, in how to handle Ajax's corpse. In this regard, the play oscillates between alternating definitions of humiliation within state-behavior and trait-orientation of acting humble in the face of unspeakable, awesome gore. By alternating ideas of humiliation, I mean between the more negatively valenced usage now thought of versus the obsolete idea of positive, self-humiliation. Currently, humiliation invokes shame, guilt, embarrassment, and negative diminishment of self-appraisal; humbling, on the other hand, involves contracting one's ego to acknowledge the overall ecology we are all part of. Anachronistically, Sophocles' *Ajax* is a story about the performance of proper (if obsolete) humiliation versus its current association. As Pelin Kesebir notes experimentally, the ability to adopt a humble *eco-centric* mindset instead of an *ego-centric* mindset is modeled as a means to enact such prosocial tendencies and behaviors in a world in which death is made salient often theatrically and spectacularly.[52] Odysseus – this version of him at least – displays proper humility not just to Athena, but to his fellow soldiers and to a broader humanity, engaging in an eco-centric stance whereby he allows us to witness and to also act out his storied 'intellectual virtue.'

In light of these findings, Odysseus' intellectual virtue can itself be thought of as a possible elicitor of awe, much as scholars above have pointed to the appreciation of technical skill in rhetoric, playwriting, and acting. Diminishing the sense of self is not strictly a function of awe, nor is it always a positive change for the individual psyche; diminished representations can also occur during feelings of shame for example. The study by Bai *et al.* used the size/ratio of *change* as its metric for diminishment in self-representation, something akin but distinctly separate from the reversal in self-representation characteristic of *peripeteia* and hubristic falls from grace. It is important to note

---

50   Hesk, *Sophocles: Ajax*, 48.
51   Hesk, *Sophocles: Ajax*, 198. Emphasis added.
52   Kesebir, Pelin, "A Quiet Ego Quiets Death Anxiety: Humility as an Existential Anxiety Buffer", in *Personality Processes and Individual Differences*, vol. 106, no. 4 (2014): 610–623.

the degree to which culture does and does not mediate the phenomenon, especially around conceptions of individualistic and collectivist cultures. If in fact the "imagery and rhetoric of 'bigness versus smallness' informs the entire tragedy's debate over what a good man looks like", then such a proposed ideal humiliation can be thought of in cognitive terms as this diminishment of self-representation.[53] There is an irony to the action and ability of the small self here: the operative function is to contract one's own self-ideation so as to have a more accurate representation of the global picture: as one decenters and diminishes their own vertical representation in lieu of a more horizontal multiplicity in perspective, it can be thought of as a social contraction in order for social connections to then re-develop. Thus, we contract in order to socialize, mobilize, and connect.

Ajax uniquely questions this model by doubly framing the roles of actors, characters, and audiences. As this paper demonstrates, any holistic study of theatrical empathy should embrace the thorough complexity of the performance event by investigating the bio-psycho-social cognition operating at multiplex levels: from the actor to the character; from the blended actor/character to the audience perceiving them; and from the audience to their self-reflexive sense of theatrical convention. Enhancing empathy through ancient Greek drama is not just helping people to get along better together. Rather, it holds the potential for individuals to enter a fluid mental space of humility, flexibility, and mindfulness, one in which to better themselves by witnessing new alternative possibilities in the face of the stark realities in war, trauma, and mortality overall. The exercise of perspective-taking through acting is essential in enacting these opportunities to re-version ourselves as individuals and societies. It enables us to ask the fundamental question, what kind of people do we want to be?

Bibliography

Bai, Yang; Maruskin, Laura A.; Chen, Serena; Gordon, Amie M.; Stellar, Jennifer E.; McNeil, Galen D.; Peng, Kaiping and Keltner, Dacher, "Awe, the Diminished Self, and Collective Engagement: Universals and Cultural Variations in the Small Self", in *Attitudes and Social Cognition*, vol. 113, no. 2 (2017): 185–209.

Blair, Rhonda, *The Actor, Image, and Action: Acting and Cognitive Neuroscience* (New York: Routledge, 2008).

---

53   Hesk, *Sophocles: Ajax*, 28.

Blair, Rhonda and Cook, Amy, *Theatre, Performance, and Cognition: Languages, Bodies, and Ecologies* (New York: Bloomsbury, 2016).

Cook, Amy, *Shakespearean Neuroplay: Reinvigorating the Study of Dramatic Texts and Performance Through Cognitive Science* (New York: Palgrave Macmillan, 2010).

Doerries, Bryan, *The Theater of War: What Ancient Greek Tragedies Can Teach Us Today* (New York: Alfred A. Knopf, 2015).

Falkner, Thomas M., "Containing Tragedy: Rhetoric and Self-Representation in Sophocles' *Philoctetes*", in *Classical Antiquity*, vol. 17, no. 1 (1998): 25–58.

Greenberg, Jeff; Pyszczynski, Tom, and Solomon, Sheldon, "The Causes and Consequences of a Need for Self Esteem: A Terror Management Theory", in *Public Self and Private Self*, edited by R.F. Baumeister (New York-NY: Springer-Verlag, 1986), 189–212.

Goldenberg, Jamie L.; Pyszczynski, Tom; Johnson, Kern D.; Greenberg, Jeff, and Solomon, Sheldon, "The Appeal of Tragedy: A Terror Management Perspective", in *Media Psychology*, no. 1 (1999): 313–329.

Golder, Herbert, and Pevear, Richard, "*Ajax*", in *The Complete Sophocles*, vol 2, edited by Peter Burian and Alan Shapiro (New York: Oxford University Press, 2010), 26–94.

Goldstein, Thalia R., and Winner, Ellen, "Enhancing Empathy and Theory of Mind", in *Journal of Cognition and Development*, vol. 13, no. 1 (2012): 19–37.

Hesk, Jon, *Sophocles: Ajax* (London: Duckworth, 2003).

Kemp, Rick, *Embodied Acting: What Neuroscience Tells Us About Performance* (New York: Routledge, 2012).

Kesebir, Pelin, "A Quiet Ego Quiets Death Anxiety: Humility as an Existential Anxiety Buffer", in *Personality Processes and Individual Differences*, vol. 106, no. 4 (2014): 610–623.

Lakoff, George, and Johnson, Mark, *Philosophy in the Flesh: The Embodied Mind and its Challenge to Western Thought* (New York: Basic Books, 1999).

McConachie, Bruce, *Theatre & Mind* (New York: Palgrave Macmillan, 2013).

Meineck, Peter, *Theatrocracy: Greek Drama, Cognition, and the Imperative for Theatre* (London: Taylor & Francis, 2017).

Shay, Jonathan, *Achilles in Vietnam: Combat Trauma and the Undoing of Character* (New York: Scribner, 1994).

Shaughnessy, Nicola, *Affective Performance and Cognitive Science: Body, Brain, and Being* (London: Bloomsbury, 2013).

Worthen, W.B., *Shakespeare Performance Studies* (Cambridge: Cambridge University Press, 2014).

CHAPTER 10

Empathy in Experimental Narratives

Barış Mete

Abstract

Empathy in narrative fiction is broadly defined as the capability of readers to share the feelings or the experiences of characters. It is already indisputable that all forms of character identification in fictional narratives essentially require empathy. In other words, readers have empathy with fictional characters whose experiences they personally share. In addition to this, readers have empathy especially with protagonists for they spend most of their time dealing with them during the course of reading. What should specifically be underlined here, moreover, is the fact that empathy not only emerges but also fully develops between readers and characters mostly in narratives that have traditional characteristics in terms of their plot structures and character development. Non-traditional narratives either interrupt or exactly block the possibilities of the rise of shared feelings between readers and characters by reason of a number of elements. As empathy in fictional narratives necessarily builds on the spoken descriptions of the events by the narrator, any divergence from traditional roles of the narrator – especially the role of the narrator as a truthful and reliable entity for the reader – could possibly affect the nature of interactions between readers and characters. Instead of empathy, it might then be the disagreement and the disunity that would better define what readers feel in such situations. The British novelists John Robert Fowles' *The Collector* (1963) and Jean Iris Murdoch's *The Black Prince* (1973) are two fictional narratives where readers become unable to have empathy with the protagonists as a result of the experimental narrative structures of the novels.

Keywords

empathy – narrative – experimental narrative – reader – narrator – protagonist – character

1 Empathy as a Narrative Device

As it has widely been in use in English language today, empathy as a term has originally derived from the German word, 'Einfühlung.'[1] This German word could most sensibly be translated into English as 'feeling into.'[2] Empathy, therefore, is apparently sharing of feelings and emotions of other human beings – as well as other animate entities. In terms of its history of usage in the English-speaking cultures, it is particularly asserted by Vernon Lee that the term empathy

> derived from a verb to feel oneself into something ("sich in Etwas ein fühlen") was in current use even before Lotze and Vischer applied it to aesthetics, and some years before Lipps (1897) and Wundt (1903) adopted it into psychological terminology.[3]

More precisely, as part of fictional narratives, Suzanne Keen claims that empathy "can be provoked by witnessing another's emotional state, by hearing about another's condition, or even by reading."[4] It is, as specially underlined here in this interpretation, exactly the process of reading through which readers are provided with the unique opportunity of hearing – as first-hand experience – how characters (fictional entities) are feeling in particular situations.

This part of the discussion could perhaps start with the particular assertion that researchers are more familiar with empathy in other fields of study, for example in psychology, than empathy in literature (empathy in narrative fiction). The reader, therefore, can easily discover a number of works that exactly detail the essential nature of empathy in human relations. In addition to this, the research that has been carried out into the significance of empathy in literature – more precisely empathy in narrative fiction – has fundamentally followed the footprints of studies of empathy made by researchers in other fields. This is primarily because of the fact that characters and situations in fictional narratives have been analysed mostly concluding that they somehow reflect the traces of real-world features. This is understandable, however, as long as

---

1 Lee, Vernon, *The Beautiful: An Introduction to Psychological Aesthetics* (Cambridge: Cambridge University Press, 1913), 66.
2 *Ibid.*
3 *Ibid.*
4 Keen, Suzanne, *Empathy and the Novel* (Oxford: Oxford University Press, 2007), 4.

researchers who study empathy are conducting their analyses particularly on conventional narratives. It can well be argued that only through conventional narratives, could empathy between readers and characters become comprehensible. Moreover, it should also be emphasised that it is conventional narratives where writers (or novelists in particular) are able to create the realistic illusion. What should further be stated here in this assertion is that because of the realistic illusion, readers share emotions of characters that are – in reality – entirely fictional entities.

As it is put by Amy Coplan, "There is still little consensus among scholars regarding how best to characterize the relationship between readers of fictional narratives and the characters in those narratives."[5] Therefore, conventional narratives more adequately provide readers with what they – as human beings – essentially need to have empathy with characters. Although it is actually fiction, the realistic illusion in fictional narratives successfully creates a surrogate world where readers assume that the narrative that they peruse reports actual past events really experienced by characters. Readers thus further assume that characters are real entities instead of being paper figures whose ontological status in reality is necessarily limited to the actual number of the pages. Therefore, analytical studies of empathy in fictional narratives have mostly been grounded on conventional (traditional realistic) works where readers could comfortably simulate their real-world experiences with fellow human beings. Conventional narratives offer an alternative reality where readers recreate the contemporary world. As a product of this simulation, readers have empathy with fictional characters.

Narrators in fictional narratives, but particularly the first-person narrator-protagonists, specially need the presence of readers who have empathy with them. This is because of the fact that the principal priority of narrators is to direct the narrative towards readers. In other words, this means that as long as readers read (listen to) their adventures, narrators adequately remain in their narratives not only functional but also practical entities. Empathy in fictional narratives, therefore, can be resembled to a form of partnership of readers and narrators (characters) characteristically based on mutual service. It could further be asserted that as long as fictional narratives appropriately furnish what readers ask for, there will be empathy. As it has been signified, readers have empathy as long as they are able to situate narratives and their narrators in life-like patterns.

---

5   Coplan, Amy, "Empathic Engagement with Narrative Fictions", in *The Journal of Aesthetics and Art Criticism Special Issue: Art, Mind, and Cognitive Science*, vol. 62, no. 2 (2004): 141.

2 Narrator-Protagonists

The question that should be asked now is what would possibly happen if narrators do not meet expectations of readers. This mostly occurs in experimental first-person narratives where there are especially alternative versions to the accounts of main narrators. A conventional narrative has usually a single narrator whose report of the events is acknowledged by readers as the only source of reference. That is to say, readers are almost conditioned to believe what narrators in conventional narratives tell them. That is categorically why readers have empathy with these narrators. In other words, as stated here, "In empathy [...] we feel what we believe to be the emotions of others."[6] On the other hand, if readers are provided with opportunities to make a choice in a text among the varieties of narratives, there will be no empathy since these narratives are most likely to contradict one another. If readers hesitate to believe the words of narrators, there will be no sharing of emotions. Therefore, any increase in the number of narrators in a fictional narrative would probably frustrate readers and retard empathy.

It is obvious that fictional narratives – although there are always exceptions – are filled with characters. Nevertheless, readers do not make random choices of these characters. That is to say, readers do not fully concentrate on the narratives of characters in general. Instead, they mostly pay attention to the narratives of a particular group of characters, who are protagonist. In other words, a fictional narrative conventionally depicts a number of characters whose personalities – through their appearances, behaviours and speech – readers gradually become familiar with during the course of events. However, it is observed that readers entirely establish communication only with protagonists. It can be argued that protagonists are characters with whom readers are truly in relationships in fictional narratives, which is also interpreted as "deep engagement with the interior lives of characters."[7] As a consequence of this, in traditional narratives, readers largely focus on and they have empathy particularly with protagonists.

Protagonists are, furthermore, authoritative sources of reference for readers; therefore, whatever they claim is mostly accepted as true. This means that readers can learn the great majority of events (what actually happened in the story) only from protagonists. As protagonists are the main actors and actresses of their narratives, it can further be asserted that readers hear the story – even

---

6 Keen, Suzanne, "A Theory of Narrative Empathy", in *Narrative*, vol. 14, no. 3 (2006): 208.
7 Jurecic, Ann, "Empathy and the Critic", in *College English*, vol. 74, no. 1 (2011): 11.

in third-person narratives where they are not narrators – from protagonists. Whoever the narrator is, it is the protagonists' story that readers read. Experimental first-person narratives, however, might include more than one narrator whose accounts of events possibly contradict with that of protagonists. In such a case, the following might probably occur:

a. Protagonists first lose their privilege of being the only narrators of their narratives.
b. In addition to the above issue, they lose their authority over other characters, but particularly over their readers.
c. It becomes noticeable that they try to convince their readers that they are telling them the truth.

Therefore, any alternative textual accounts in fictional narratives to the stories of protagonists dramatically challenge the reliability of these characters as narrators. In other words, "the very existence of other narratives [...] effectively challenges the main narrative perspective by providing alternative narrative consciousness."[8] If readers are provided with preferences to choose among narrators, they practically compare and contrast different accounts of the same events in narratives. This situation conclusively impairs any expectations of narrator-protagonists for empathy. In addition to this, whenever readers hesitate to trust the honesty of narrator-protagonists, they hesitate to share the feelings of these characters. This situation eventually leads to lack of empathy in fictional narratives where there is a multiplicity of narrators.

3   Discrepancy between Narratives

John Fowles' 1963 novel *The Collector* is characterised by the carefully-drawn portrayal of the psychology of its protagonist, the cold-hearted collector, who collects butterflies as well as young girls. However, Fowles' novel is especially outlined, in terms of its non-traditional narrative structure, by the presence of the novel's two distinct narrators, Frederick Clegg and Miranda Grey, whose accounts of the same events noticeably differ from one another. As a result of this discrepancy in the novel between the two accounts – that should normally be identical in any given fictional narrative – it becomes problematic for the reader to differentiate between who tells him the truth and who tells him the untruth. The reader therefore does not share most of the experiences of these

---

8 Mete, Barış, "Manipulation of the Reader's Empathy in Iris Murdoch's First-Person Narrative", in *Selçuk University the Journal of Institute of Social Sciences*, no. 38 (2017): 133–139.

narrators. It should further be underlined that the reader consequently has empathy in this fictional narrative with none of the narrators of the novel.

The first of the four chapters of *The Collector* – composing nearly one-third of the novel – is narrated by the protagonist-narrator of the novel, Frederick Clegg, who as he detailed was a clerk and who won a lottery in London in 1956 when he was twenty-one years old. As it is quite reasonable to the reader, the whole novel – the whole narrative including anything related to Miranda Grey – is actually the story of Clegg himself. Moreover, it should be accentuated that Clegg's narrative can specially be summarised as a confession of failure he makes to the reader. It is particularly a confession of how he failed to assure Miranda who as he said was a student studying art that he truly loved her. It gradually becomes discernable that the main narrative is essentially a confession to prompt the reader to have empathy with the main narrator, Frederick Clegg. It can even further be pronounced that Clegg's narrative is particularly devoted to the descriptions of his excitement of and his passion for Miranda, who he says, was totally indifferent to him and who was finally abducted and confined in a deserted house until her unexpected death.

Before anything else, what should specifically be stated here is that Clegg's narrative, as it is directly told to the reader by the main narrator himself, is largely composed of an expression of his emotions. The following speech of him, for example, details how he tells the reader he was feeling for Miranda. He describes the situation asserting,

> I can't say what it was, the very first time I saw her, I knew she was the only one. Of course I am not mad, I knew it was just a dream [...] I used to have daydreams about her, I used to think of stories where I met her, did things she admired, married her and all that.[9]

It is obvious in the above example that Clegg's narrative (his confessions) is undoubtedly an emotional appeal to the reader. In addition, Clegg's narrative largely operates as an apparatus to persuade the reader that he, as the main narrator of the text, is informing him of what actually happened. In other words, the protagonist's narrative, as it is comprehensible in the above quotation, can be summarised as an announcement trying to confirm the reader that Clegg as the narrator has been straightforward to whoever has been listening to him. It is an attempt at resolving that he has been honest with the reader. As a conclusion, the whole narrative is surely for the reader's empathy for the

---

9 Fowles, John, *The Collector* (Boston: Little, Brown and Company, 1963), 4.

protagonist, Frederick Clegg. In addition to this, another particular expression given by Clegg to the reader in his narrative significantly illustrates his psychological profile. In other words, what Clegg does is to reveal the reader his state of mind. It is clear that he seriously fantasised in terms of the proposed (dreamed) relationship between himself and Miranda Grey. As it is claimed,

> She drew pictures and I looked after my collection (in my dreams). It was always she loving me and my collection, drawing and colouring them; working together in a beautiful modern house in a big room with one of those huge glass windows [...] She all pretty with her pale blonde hair and grey eyes.[10]

Clegg specially tells the reader here in this example that he fantasised about Miranda. This is most possibly for strengthening the notion that he deeply loved her, but she did not respond him. According to what is implied by the main narrator here, it was Miranda who deliberately left him in great unhappiness; and he could only console himself with nothing but dreaming about her. Clegg insists on having had dreams about a relationship with her. His dreams, Clegg most probably believes, will establish between himself and the reader an image of him as, what should be called, the innocent narrator. Clegg dreamed – he tells the reader – that things would turn into a situation where he could discover happiness with Miranda. Clegg confesses this to the reader for he wants the reader to understand how he once felt. He says,

> I captured her and drove her off in the van to a remote house and there I kept her captive in a nice way. Gradually she came to know me and like me and the dream grew into the one about our living in a nice modern house, married, with kids and everything.[11]

Although Frederick Clegg abducted and confined Miranda Grey, which is of course absolutely unacceptable, he has never told the reader that he felt himself guilty about what he did to her. During her confinement, moreover, Miranda caught cold and died. After her death, Clegg accidentally discovers a diary secretly written by her. This diary, as Miranda's narrative, describes the same events starting from the day of her abduction from her perspective. This means that when the reader listens to what Miranda is telling in her narrative, her

---

10   *Ibid.*
11   Fowles, *The Collector*, 14.

alternative story is heard. Clegg still tells the reader that his dream was actually coming true. However, as Miranda specifies in her own narrative, it was the nightmare. She fearfully speaks,

> I write in this terrible night like silence as if I feel normal. But I'm not. I'm so sick, so frightened, so alone. The solitude is unbearable. Every time the door opens I want to rush at it and out. But I know now I must save up my escape attempts. Outwit him. Plan ahead. Survive.[12]

Despite the disturbing reality that Clegg killed Miranda, he indifferently – and coldly – claims, "I didn't want to kill her, that was the last thing I wanted;"[13] and he intentionally omits any details that would possibly frighten the reader. Clegg asserts,

> It stopped being a dream, it began to be what I pretended was really going to happen [...] so I thought of ways and means – all the things I would have to arrange and think about and how I'd do it and all. I thought, I can't ever get to know her in the ordinary way, but if she's with me, she'll see my good points, she'll understand. There was always the idea she would understand.[14]

Clegg is oddly unemotional. He heartlessly justifies to the reader what he did to Miranda. As he considers the situation merely from his point of view, he expects the reader to do the same for him. He draws an image of himself as a suffering lover which he expects the reader to have empathy with.

Even though Clegg markedly wants the reader to have empathy with him and arranges his narrative according to this particular strategy, he occasionally exposes part of the disturbing truth about the situation to the reader. It is Clegg, the main narrator of the story, who confesses to the reader that Miranda was like a prisoner of war kept by the Gestapo. Clegg states,

> I never let her see papers. I never let her have a radio or television [...] I didn't want to break her down as the Gestapo wanted to break their prisoners down. But I thought it would be better if she was cut off from the outside world, she'd have to think about me more. So in spite of many

---

12 Fowles, *The Collector*, 130.
13 Fowles, *The Collector*, 39.
14 Fowles, *The Collector*, 14.

attempts on her part to make me get her the papers and a radio I wouldn't ever let her have.[15]

It is ironic here in this example that Clegg acknowledges himself having been so merciful not to drive Miranda into insanity by absolutely isolating her from the contemporary world. Whatever he did to her in terms of the above situation, he claims, is because he wanted her to think about him. In other words, Clegg tells the reader that he did this for he loved Miranda. The following is another example of the emphasis placed by Clegg on the controversial impression that he was generous and compassionate to Miranda. Clegg's logic of argument is very strange and unusual; it is indeed absurd. He literally forced her to love him. Clegg says he told Miranda,

> I don't expect you to understand me, I don't expect you to love me like most people, I just want you to try and understand me as much as you can and like me a little if you can.[16]

There is nothing here in his behaviours to be shared by the reader. It can be claimed that it is even irritating the reader whom Clegg startlingly expects to have empathy with him. It is understandable that Clegg needs the reader and the reader's empathy. This is what conventionally happens in a fictional narrative. The problem in this specific case, however, is the existence of an alternative account to that of Clegg. It is in sharp contrast to the image of the positive atmosphere drawn by Clegg that Miranda, who as claimed elsewhere "attempts to understand her own dilemma and strives to provoke compassion and empathy in Clegg by using other artistic modes of expression, including literature and art,"[17] felt the anxiety over her life. She says in the diary,

> I know it was the right thing to do. It saved my life. If I had screamed or tried to escape he would have battered me to death. There are moments when he is possessed, quite out of his own control.[18]

Because of this, Clegg makes use of every possible occasion to demonstrate his honesty with the reader. Sometimes this situation turns into ludicrous

---

15   Fowles, *The Collector*, 41.
16   Fowles, *The Collector*, 45.
17   Philips Buchberger, Michelle, "John Fowles's Novels of the 1950s and 1960s", in *The Yearbook of English Studies: Literature of the 1950s and 1960s*, no. 42 (2012): 142.
18   Fowles, *The Collector*, 217.

illustrations. In one of these cases, he reports what he told Miranda, who called him a madman,

> And mad, I said. Do you think a madman would have treated you the way I have? I'll tell you what a madman would have done. He'd have killed you by now [...] I suppose you think I'm going for you with a carving-knife or something [...] All right, you think I'm not normal keeping you here like this. Perhaps I'm not.[19]

The above example illustrates that Clegg expects empathetic feelings from the reader for he did not kill but forgave Miranda whose "empathy for him [...] prevents her from using violence against Frederick and troubles her conscience after the single occasion on which she tries to kill him in order to escape."[20] This situation might sound quite unreasonable to the reader. It is not fair or acceptable. However, this is the particular psychological condition Clegg is in. Whatever Clegg tells the reader is mostly for the reader's empathy.

Clegg has specially illustrated himself as a decent man and has significantly underlined the idea that it was never sex that stimulated his passion for Miranda. He has frequently repeated this issue. A specific scene, however, dramatically blurs the authenticity of his account and some question marks are running through the reader's mind. After an attempt to escape, Miranda was caught by Clegg and put into the cellar lying unconscious. The following scene illuminates more clearly what Clegg has likely omitted to mention in more detail to the reader. He says,

> She was still out, on the bed. She looked a sight, the dress all off one shoulder. I don't know what it was, it got me excited, it gave me ideas, seeing her lying there right out [...] The dress was right off her shoulder, I could see the top of one stocking [...] I took off her dress and her stockings and left on certain articles, just the brassiere and the other so as not to go the whole hog. She looked a real picture lying there [...] Like she was wearing a bikini. It was my chance I had been waiting for. I got the old camera and took some photos.[21]

---

19   Fowles, *The Collector*, 72.
20   Marcus, Amit, "Narrative Ethics and Incommensurable Discourses Lyotard's *The Differend* and Fowles's *The Collector*", in *Mosaic: An Interdisciplinary Critical Journal*, vol. 41, no. 4 (2008): 87.
21   Fowles, *The Collector*, 91.

What becomes more obvious after the above scene is the possibility that Clegg has rearranged the events according to eliminate what could be likely to confuse the reader. The reader, Clegg considers, should have a clear mind to believe his story and to have empathy with him. Therefore, it is probable that Clegg has carefully omitted what he thinks can potentially violate the reader's supportive feelings about him.

On the other hand, there is another condition. Miranda's narrative, which is significantly confined to her diary which has been first found and then read by Clegg to the reader, is extremely inadequate to satisfy the reader that she is telling the truth. The diary, which had been written in the depths of despair, may not be picturing the reality. As a result, the reader is convinced of none of the narratives of the text.

4 Egotistical Narrator

In terms of their particular narrative structures, John Fowles' *The Collector* and Iris Murdoch's *The Black Prince* are similar narratives. Both of the novels notably draw narrator-protagonists whose first-hand accounts of the events are seriously confronted in the texts by the stories of alternative narrators. Fowles' *The Collector*, as it has been illustrated in the above chapter, gives the reader the opportunity to compare the narrative of the protagonist – at the same time the main narrator of the text as well – with the version of another character of the novel who witnessed the same events as the protagonist did. After hearing (reading) the two narratives, the reader, therefore, figures out that the protagonist – as well as the other narrator – has likely been hiding part of the truth from him. This specific situation, it has been discussed, decidedly eliminates any possibilities of empathy that the reader could have with the novel's narrator.

Although Murdoch's *The Black Prince*, which she first published in 1973, has a similar narrative structure to that of Fowles' *The Collector*, the novel is principally determined by the overtly displayed egotistical character of the narrator-protagonist who, throughout his narrative, grants himself not only the authority over but also the supremacy of the other characters (other narrators) of the narrative. There are a number of examples, but one of the best illustrations of this situation in the novel is Bradley Pearson's – the protagonist-narrator of *The Black Prince* who describes himself as a middle-aged writer and literary critic – foreword for the novel. As an artist Pearson asserts in his foreword that he naturally speaks the truth for he believes that not only art but also the artist have been categorically associated with truth. According to him,

> Good art speaks truth, indeed is truth, perhaps the only truth. I have endeavoured in what follows to be wisely artful and artfully wise, and to tell truth as I understand it, not only concerning the superficial and "exciting" aspects of this drama, but also concerning what lies deeper.[22]

What is discernible here is that Pearson, at the very beginning of his narrative, attempts not only to exert his authority over the reader but also to restrict him to navigate the narratives of the other narrators of the novel. The implied idea is that whatever Pearson asserts is enough, it is the truth itself. The reader never needs to listen to any other narrator of the text. It has also been suggested that "Bradley Pearson fears that friends from different parts of his life should become acquainted behind his back."[23] Apart from Pearson, however, Murdoch provides the reader in the novel with four other characters who, after reading Pearson's story, wrote their postscripts – their own accounts of what really (or possibly) happened. In other words, "In *The Black Prince* Bradley Pearson's narrative is embedded within a series of other narratives by an "editor" and other members of the cast,"[24] which is "a textual 'net' that serves seriously to call into question … the origin and meaning of the fiction."[25] Furthermore, what uniquely characterises all the postscripts is that their authors deny, in front of the reader, almost all the major assertions made by Pearson in his own narrative.

This particular situation is observable primarily in Bradley Pearson's relationship with his ex-wife, Christian Marloe. It is already interesting that Pearson briefly describes his marriage asserting "It was not a success."[26] When he goes into detail, he draws, especially for the reader, an unfavourable impression of both Christian and his marriage. Pearson says referring to Christian, for example,

> At first I saw her as a life-bringer. Then I saw her as a death-bringer. Some women are like that. There is a sort of energy which seems to reveal the world: then one day you find you are being devoured.[27]

---

22 Murdoch, Iris, *The Black Prince* (New York: Penguin Classics, 2003), 3.
23 Nicol, Bran, *Iris Murdoch: The Retrospective Fiction* (New York: Palgrave Macmillan, 2004), 69.
24 Nicol, *Iris Murdoch*, 21.
25 *Ibid.*
26 Murdoch, *The Black Prince*, 16.
27 Murdoch, *The Black Prince*, 16–17.

As it is obvious to the reader, Pearson seriously blames Christian for their failed marriage. Instead of bravely sharing the responsibility for the mistakes, Pearson simply accuses Christian of why their relationship broke down. However, in the novel, which is at the same time Pearson's narrative, the reader has an alternative. Pearson is the main narrator – in other words, the narrator-protagonist – of the text; yet he is not the only narrator of the text. The reader has the opportunity of listening to the account (the postscript) of Christian herself. One of the four postscripts, attached at the end of the novel, has been composed by her. She asserts in her narrative after reading what Pearson has written,

> I think many things are in the eye of the beholder [...] Bradley has a way of seeing everything in his own way and making it all fit together in his own picture. Perhaps we all do that, but we do not write it down in a book. He does not give a very fair picture at all of the time of our marriage [...] it is not a very true picture of the bits I know about it is all I can say.[28]

Compared to Pearson, Christian speaks to the reader in her narrative calmly. Her tone is tranquil; and she does not blame anybody in her postscript. What truly strikes the reader or what makes sense in terms of narrative empathy here, however, is the fact that Christian does not welcome in her narrative any of the claims made by Pearson. In addition to this, she underscores the egotistical character of him by referring to his easily-noticeable subjectivity. Therefore, the reader has been given an occasion of making a comparison between the two narratives. Simply because Pearson is not the only narrator of the text but there are other alternatives to him, the reader might have difficulty in trusting him.

Another illustration of the discrepancy between the accounts of the main narrator and the other narrators of the novel is the one between the stories of Bradley Pearson and Rachel Baffin. Pearson opens his narrative with the description of an emergency call he received from a close friend, Arnold Baffin. He tells the reader how Arnold telephoned and called him to his house for he thought he had killed his wife, Rachel. There was a fight between Arnold and Rachel, as Pearson says. However, his descriptions of the scene and especially of Rachel are pathetic. According to Pearson's account, Rachel had locked herself in the bedroom, and she was bleeding in tears. This is, as reported by Pearson, what Rachel pointing to her husband said:

> He has sent me to hell. He has taken my whole life from me. He has spoilt the world. I am as clever as he is. He has just blocked me off from

---

28 Murdoch, *The Black Prince*, 385.

everything. I can't work, I can't think, I can't be, because of him. His stuff crawls over everything, he takes away all my things and turns them into his things. I've never been myself or lived my own life at all. I've always been afraid of him, that's what it comes to.[29]

Similar to the situation between Bradley Pearson and Christian Marloe as two narratives of the same text and how Christian has refused the accusation made by him, Rachel calls it a 'dream.'[30] She claims that it is actually Pearson himself who she feels sorry for. Rachel in her postscript comments,

we must, I think, feel or attempt to feel pity and compassion for the author of this fantasy [...] what Pearson produces is a sort of mad adolescent dream and not the serious work of art of which he imagined himself capable and of which he so incessantly told us.[31]

Therefore, it could be relatively asserted that "we are in the position of having a play unfold before us,"[32] which is indeed "a play in which the actors knowingly take on roles, yet for which we the reader/audience willingly suspend our disbelief until the play is played out."[33]

There are other examples of divergences between Bradley Pearson's narrative and those of the other characters who have their postscripts in the novel as well. However, what probably puzzles the reader most about how he particularly feels about the experiences of the narrator is a distinctive practice of the narrator himself. Whenever Pearson, as the main narrator of the text, describes a character to the reader, he talks about that character in an unfavourable way. Furthermore, he strictly maintains the same attitude even if he is talking about his own family members. When Pearson first introduces, for example, Francis Marloe, his brother-in-law, to the reader, his portrayal of Francis includes such unkind descriptions as "copious greyish longish frizzy hair and a round face and a slightly hooked nose and big very red lips and eyes set very close together."[34] Moreover, he openly makes fun of Francis saying, "He looked [...] like a caricature of a bear. Real bears [...] have eyes rather wide

---

29 Murdoch, *The Black Prince*, 32.
30 Murdoch, *The Black Prince*, 394.
31 *Ibid.*
32 Spear, Hilda D., *Macmillan Modern Novelists: Iris Murdoch* (London: Macmillan, 1995), 78.
33 *Ibid.*
34 Murdoch, *The Black Prince*, 15.

apart [...] caricatured bears usually have close eyes, possibly to indicate bad temper or cunning."[35] On the other hand, Pearson deliberately creates the opposite image for his look. According to him, he was "thin and tall, just over six feet, fairish and not yet bald, with light fine silky rather faded straight hair."[36] Furthermore, Pearson says, "I have a bland diffident nervous sensitive face and thin lips and blue eyes. I do not wear glasses. I look considerably younger than my age."[37]

Pearson's egotism can also be traceable in his self-proclaimed identity as an artist. Pearson is a writer, yet he specially accentuates that he is an artist. Besides this, Pearson has already expressed the idea that art is truth. As a result of this emphasis, as he considers himself an artist, Pearson associates his identity with truth. Although this situation may sound absurd, Pearson's notion of truth has different connotations than the conventional meaning of the term. This is the fictional truth Pearson has been involved in as an artist. This is, in other words, Pearson's version of the truth. He particularly believes that art is superior to life; it is more dignified. According to him, for example, "characters in art can have unassailable dignity, whereas characters in life have none."[38] Moreover, Pearson argues that "life, in this respect as in others, pathetically and continually aspires to the condition of art."[39] Therefore, Pearson has not been telling the truth, he has been telling what he considers to be the truth. He does not conceal this from the reader who is supposed to have empathy with him.

5 Conclusion

What is undeniable is the fact that while readers are human beings, characters that readers have empathy with are fictional entities. Regardless of this ontological particularity, narrative empathy still characterises the true nature of the long-debated relationship between readers and characters. Readers mostly share and feel about the experiences of fabricated characters of fictional narratives. This happens as long as the activity of reading fiction situates readers in alternative worlds where they can nearly replicate

---

35 *Ibid.*
36 Murdoch, *The Black Prince*, 15–16.
37 Murdoch, *The Black Prince*, 16.
38 Murdoch, *The Black Prince*, 116.
39 *Ibid.*

their original experiences with individuals. As a result of the replication, in other words, readers build relationships with invented beings. It is also to be asserted that protagonists are indeed the characters whom readers have empathy with. Readers particularly read the narratives of protagonists where protagonists tell readers their personal experiences with other characters. In addition to this, protagonists' narratives are regarded as authentic reports of past events by readers. It is almost unthinkable that readers question the credibility of protagonists and the accuracy of their textual accounts. This is predominantly by reason of the presence of protagonists as the only narrators of their fictional narratives. Therefore, there is almost always empathy in the relationship between readers and characters in conventional narratives. However, it tends to become difficult to illustrate the essence of narrative empathy in experimental narratives where there are especially more than one narrators. If readers are addressed by other narrators in addition to protagonists in a fictional narrative, readers could have a tendency to make comparisons and contrasts between the narratives belonging to different narrators. The most probable outcome of comparisons and contrasts between the narratives is that readers question the validity of especially the protagonists' accounts. This situation possibly impairs the aptitudes of readers for empathy with characters.

Bibliography

Buchberger, Michelle Philips, "John Fowles's Novels of the 1950s and 1960s", in *The Yearbook of English Studies: Literature of the 1950s and 1960s*, no. 42 (2012): 132–150.

Coplan, Amy, "Empathic Engagement with Narrative Fictions", in *The Journal of Aesthetics and Art Criticism Special Issue: Art, Mind, and Cognitive Science*, vol. 62, no. 2 (2004): 141–152.

Fowles, John, *The Collector* (Boston: Little, Brown and Company, 1963).

Jurecic, Ann, "Empathy and the Critic", in *College English*, vol. 74, no. 1 (2011): 10–27.

Keen, Suzanne, "A Theory of Narrative Empathy", in *Narrative*, vol. 14, no. 3 (2006): 207–236.

Keen, Suzanne, *Empathy and the Novel* (Oxford: Oxford University Press, 2007).

Lee, Vernon, *The Beautiful: An Introduction to Psychological Aesthetics* (Cambridge: Cambridge University Press, 1913).

Marcus, Amit, "Narrative Ethics and Incommensurable Discourses Lyotard's *The Differend* and Fowles's *The Collector*", in *Mosaic: An Interdisciplinary Critical Journal*, vol. 41, no. 4 (2008): 77–94.

Mete, Barış, "Manipulation of the Reader's Empathy in Iris Murdoch's First-Person Narrative", in *Selçuk University the Journal of Institute of Social Sciences*, no. 38 (2017): 133–139.

Murdoch, Iris, *The Black Prince* (New York: Penguin Classics, 2003).

Nicol, Bran, *Iris Murdoch: The Retrospective Fiction* (New York: Palgrave Macmillan, 2004).

Spear, Hilda D., *Macmillan Modern Novelists: Iris Murdoch* (London: Macmillan, 1995).

CHAPTER 11

On the Bearability of Others-Being: Bartleby, Expression and Its Justification

Ricardo Gutiérrez Aguilar

Abstract

Melville's perhaps most famous character, Bartleby the Scrivener – maybe only sharing this Olympus with Ahab–, poses his crux of a problem through the difficulties of a rather succinct operation on mutual recognition: the principal character, curiously enough a lawyer, states that one has to *"construe charitably* to [ones] imagination what proves impossible to be solved by [ones] judgment". Bartleby is impervious to any attempt reason and sane judgment do in fathoming his motives. In absence of proper rational justification then, it is recommended an ancillary method, that of a *'charitable construction'* out of imagination. In this regard, there is no symmetrical relation between the efforts of the lawyer in making an individual out of what is treated merely as an object of *'passive resistance'*, and the total lack of intention in easing the operation of his understanding by Bartleby. Thus, no recognition of any kind. In the present chapter I will try to stress the possible conceptual articulation of the above-mentioned complementary method to the accustomed *rational justification* as a somehow alternative description to the very act of empathy – or *recognition–*. The first truly act of charity shall be represented under these circumstances in the fashion of an act of *moral imagination*. Probably just a subjective one. But such an act of attribution – whether self-inscriptive or not – implies a normative burden, a deontic-laden assumption in some cases, that I will try to elucidate with help of contemporary *virtue epistemology* where an expressivist account of self-knowledge could show its limits. Questions of the sort of *'what type of expressions merit for the articulation of a biography?'*, *'what type of performative force would have a narrative of the likes of it?'* and *'which mental states do have normative force?'*, will be addressed briefly in order to clarify Bartleby's *experimentum crucis*.

Keywords

moral imagination – recognition – expression – ontological charity – Bartleby

∙∙∙

> I've got no strings
> To hold me down
> To make me fret, or make me frown
> I had strings
> But now I'm free
> There are no strings on me ...[1]
>
> But how barbarous still, and more than heathenishly cruel, are we tolerating English men! For not contented to deny these prophesying enthusiasts the honour of a persecution, we have deliver'd 'em over to the cruellest contempt in the world. I am told, for certain, that they are at this very time the subject of a choice droll or puppet-shew at Bart'lemy Fair. There, doubtless, their strange voices and involuntary agitations are admirably well acted, by the motion of wires, and inspiration of pipes. For the bodies of the prophets, in their state of prophecy [...] actuated by an exterior force, have nothing natural, or resembling real life.
>
> LORD ANTHONY ASHLEY COOPER, 3rd Earl of Shaftesbury, *A Letter Concerning Enthusiasm*[2]

∴

1 Of Motion of Wires, Inspiration of Pipes and Resemblance of Life

It is astonishingly to some extent – being this perhaps one of the various mysteries that heart keeps tenderly only and just only for literature – how the alchemical variations and scents stemming from stories make us give so our spirits in. We surrender inadvertently to the spell in occasions as such, occasions in which a standing *'pallid', 'motionless', 'pitiable'* and *'forlorn' beyond any cure* young man could cast enough his meagre shadow as to overthrown the in-thunder influences of some Captain Ahab, ever in pursuit of the Big White Whale. That over there is Bartleby though, and we promptly surrender. A Scrivener. And tantamount is to tell the story of *the* Scrivener or *a* Scrivener, truth to

---

[1] *Pinocchio*, directed by Marc Lesser, Dickie Jones, Roger Carel, Christian Rub and Teddy Bills (Burbank, CA: Walt Disney Studios, 2009. DVD).
[2] Earl of Shaftesbury (Anthony Ashley Cooper), "A Letter Concerning Enthusiasm", in Earl of Shaftesbury (Anthony Ashley Cooper), *Characteristicks of men, manners, opinions, times: In three volumes*, Vol. I. I. (London: Printed by John Darby, 1711), 27–28.

be told. Ahab is Ahab and invoking his name is enough. But with Bartleby the enchantment is quite different.

Maybe all scriveners are the same scrivener. Is the set of men what is singular, the individual on the other hand is not particular. Melville's perhaps most famous character, Bartleby, void of motion upon the threshold, is in his better day an admirably well-acted resemblance of real life, not knowing from and to where do the wires and pipes lead sound and tension. Like a puppet, Bartleby is tacitly asked to play the role of the inanimate automaton. Since the very beginning of the short story: Bartleby is hold by the act itself of *copying*. Not even the prior act of *reading* is of importance. *Bartleby is a scrivener, a scrivener has to copy,* ergo *Bartleby is 'to copy'.* Then, as Ahab is always Ahab, Bartleby *should be* the illusory *life-resembling* act of copying. Life, motion, is but a delegate quality in principle, a *fantastic charity* from the narrator's point of view. And better be Bartleby what he is supposed to be! Reduced to the mere act, to the possibility of performing, he is nothing more. A *meccano* has no mysteries, all its gears exposed. Bartleby *is* luckily for the merry Wall Street people of the story *what he has to be*. Nothing more, nothing less. "Bartleby [...] is a violently comical text, and the comical is always literal."[3] As literal is that *what has to be, so be it.* Comedy rules with a left hand the litigations – and specifically the *restitution law* – between this last command and what real life resembles, for *comedy aims at representing men as worse* than they really are. A Word from Aristotle. Violently, that is radically. Bartleby – not clear if willing to – conceals himself beneath a *formula*. His literality here at large. "It means only what it says, literally. And what it says and repeats [mechanically too] is *I would prefer not to*. This is the formula of its glory."[4] *He is the formula.* His glory is apparently comically being shrunk to the size of a motto and hide in all his gaunt measures beneath it. Bartleby can no more be found. He's succeeded:

> 'I would prefer not to', said he [...] had there been anything ordinarily human about him, doubtless I should have violently dismissed him from the premises. But as it was, I should have as soon thought of turning my pale plaster-of-Paris bust of Cicero out of doors.[5]

But is this not some sort of categorical error? Can Bartleby be in any ordinary sense (not) human? Or (not) human only to any extent?

---

3   Deleuze, Gilles, "Bartleby; or, The Formula", in *Essays Critical and Clinical*, translated by Daniel W. Smith and Michael A. Greco (London-New York: Verso, 1998), 68.
4   *Ibid.*
5   McCall, Dan, "Bartleby, the Scrivener", in *Melville's Short Novels: A Norton Critical Edition* (New York-London: W.W. Norton & Co., 2002), 11.

In what follows we will argue against this long-esteemed traditional reading on Melville's short story. Bartleby's *formula* is not a weapon for a planned *mass biographical destruction*, solvent of life, desires and their companion expressions. It would be difficult to explain that hard fall with our sympathies in such a figure. In our reading, the story so told would be more likely the result of a *pragmatic contradiction*, and the literary sign for it is perplexity in all its forms. The very situation's reading suffered by the protagonist. It's this the sign to mark – *life-resembling* – the contradiction between *what it is and what has to be (and it is not)*. *What apparently is and is not (at the same time)*. In this case, a moral disappointment indeed. Being this the state of the art, it is in our purpose to try and clarify some conceptual articulations between what has been called *sound reason* and *moral imagination*. With little help of Charles Fried's *promissory logic* proposal we will ease the access to the real meaning of Bartleby's denial formula.[6] A second brief navigation into the normative weights *representations* and *expressions* imply – in the fashion of mental states – for a biographical unity now in the light of *virtue epistemology* will lastly clear the possible real moral stance Bartleby's.

> He did not look at me while I spoke, but kept his glance fixed upon my bust of Cicero, which, as I then sat, was directly behind me, some six inches above my head.[7]

2 Copying as Promise

So far it has been stated literality would make a fine candidate for a good starting point in comedy. Furthermore, possibly the best one. Parting from it, distances and distances for the shot of *'representing'* could be tended to, for *better or worse*. Adding then that it is equally suitable as rule for the tailor of gravity, does not go without saying. Explanation is a backwards-prediction, a *retrodiction*. Comedy seems to be tragedy upside-down. Unfortunately there's no space for literary drama in symmetry.

Notwithstanding, the best-known piece of *The Piazza Tales* is violently comical as it is trifled with constant calls to order, all of them destined to tune our dearest copyist. *Legal practice vocabulary* floats slightly over the prose. We are advised of obligations, commitments, expectations, assumptions,

---

6 *vid.* Fried, Charles, *Contract as Promise: A Theory of Contractual Obligation* (Oxford: Oxford University Press, 2015).
7 McCall, "Bartleby, the Scrivener", 19.

suppositions, which are alluded ceaselessly. *What has to be, so be it. What is not, is not yet.* Aiming the vast of speeches in this play directly to *what Bartleby is supposed to be,* and how *he is ought to be.* Alas, irony is but the favourite trope for comedy and thus with respect to necessity,

> this is what the attorney glimpses with dread: all his hopes of bringing Bartleby back to reason are dashed because they rest on a *logic of presuppositions* [a *fantastic charity*] according to which an employer 'expects' to be obeyed, or a kind friend listened to. ...[8]

The *logic of presuppositions* is in fact a backwards *logic of consequences*. Mechanical in its spirit so wielded. And such a logic demands by means of corollary a due *ethics of (no) consequences* or *restitution*: "[Bartleby] either you must do something, or something must be done to you."[9] And, *therefore, if* finally something is done to you, *then* you Bartleby shall – thank God!– do something. *Either way something has (ought) to be done.* Literally. And God forbid things happen otherwise. Copying is naturally a species of promise. Every sympathy bridge crumbles not just because the employer is not obeyed *when should (ought to) be,* but because *he expected to and is not,* being employer, friend and possibly humanity equally betrayed at the same time. All fraternal institutions are representing *the* institution. Thus the violent comedy. It is not just a matter of balance. *This is not a will of nothingness, something* at the very least and *some thing* which stands to (human) reason at least, *but the ever-growing nothingness of will* – concludes Deleuze.[10] As first impressions are always kind of blunt, it is not surprisingly at all that when asked for corroboration in judgment would Ginger Nut – the twelve-year-old errand-boy – sentence Bartleby's *malady* easily, with a grin: "I think, sir, he's a little *loony.*"[11] But *it is not a lesser truth that only she or he who can be reasonable can be out of all reason* ...

Yet, under irony's rule *fair is foul and foul is fair*: without rhyme or reason, the sacred bounds of community, of society, are lost in the most fundamental sense. It is a non-fulfilled promise. For even the *epistemic pact* of mutual recognition is broken upon the unfathomable voice – which is now just sound – and demeanour – which is only the deceiver *life-resembling* shape of a human being – of this Bartleby.

---

8   Deleuze, "Bartleby; or, The Formula", 73.
9   McCall, "Bartleby, the Scrivener", 29.
10 Deleuze, "Bartleby; or, The Formula", 71.
11 McCall, "Bartleby, the Scrivener", 12.

What makes it an issue about *pragmatic contradictions* and not solely the occasional less interesting *categorical error* is that we are warned by the very end of the tale that Bartleby *can* keep up with aspirations, purposes, intentions and promises – at least to himself:

> 'Bartleby, this is a friend; you will find him very useful to you.' – 'Your servant, sir, your servant,' said the grub-man [...] 'What will you have for dinner to-day?' – 'I prefer not to dine to-day,' said Bartleby turning away. *'It would disagree with me. I'm unused to dinners.'*[12]

That he comprehends the *con-sequences* of *agreement/disagreement*. That he has a *character* or will and so Deleuze is terribly wrong. It is within the *liberal tradition of contract analysis* – to which surely the attorney devotes his nightly prayers – that one speaks about freedom *of* and *from* contract.[13] Although the *pactum subiectionis* depends upon the independent acceptance – and in order to achieve this, one has to be an *individual*–, this a validity based on mutual acknowledgement between contractors. Every attribution – *ascription* – and reciprocal bound has to be granted. Mutually assented or dissented. These *'foundations'* – Charles Fried's label here – are the enforced version convention of *promise*. Contract is not the outcome of a primitive practice. Promising is on the other hand a social practice whose definite function is to create expectations where none was to be found before.[14] Nothing more, nothing less. It is an institution. But where expectations are found, it is not unusual that expectations are hoped – and sometimes look forward – to be met. Fried's proposal of a *promissory logic* precisely wanted to devote a special category to *'promise'* in *contract law*, not reducible to *restitution* or *tort law*. He rules out so that last conclusion. *Promissory logic* does not entail a *logic of instantiate consequences*: (i) *'to promise'* is a self-imposing practice. No one can promise in my place, nor in my name; (ii) *therefore, promise has some moral grounds*, for in spite its normative foundations, the difference regarding sheer obligation is its value is lost whenever I am forced to promise. There is no such type of event, if not for the mock of a promise; (iii) related to the latter, promise is the conventional instrument to utilize *trust*. Promise in the form of a linguistic artefact has its sense in the invitation to confidence, and confidence takes on account and envisions – *assumes* – future behaviour. *What has (ought) to be done and if*

---

12   *Ibid.*, 32.
13   Kimel, Dori, *From Promise to Contract: Towards a Liberal Theory of Contract* (Oxford and Portland, OR: Hart Publishing, 2003), 117–120.
14   Fried, *Contract as Promise*, 54–60.

something must be done. He or she who suffers from the break of a promise, is *used in some sense by the promissory*, who is nonetheless not necessarily lying when promising at the beginning; (iv) this convention, being linguistic, *has to be invoked.* Ostensibly.[15]

Promise-keeping is not a necessary requirement. *Logic of presuppositions* is here totally detached from the *logic of consequences.* Theory from practice.

> I *assumed* the ground that depart he must; and upon that assumption built all I had to say. The more I thought over my procedure, the more I was charmed with it. Nevertheless, next morning, upon awakening, I had my doubts – I had somehow slept off the fumes of vanity. One of the coolest and wisest hours a man has, is just after he awakes in the morning. My procedure seemed as sagacious as ever – but only in theory. How it would prove in practice – there was the rub.[16]

There was the *pragmatic contradiction.*

3 Weighing Pressures, Expressions and Its Justifications

Pensive moods entertain themselves not infrequently in solipsistic ideal juggling. *Vanity usurps in these occasions the better of charity.* "After all, that assumption *was simply my own*, and none of Bartleby's."[17] To circle the limits, to circle the boundaries of the *doctrine of assumptions*, is a task reserved for prudent and methodical men and women.[18] Men and women with a heightened sense of duty, so high as to ascertain enthusiasm in giving reasons can

---

15 A curious articulation can be introduced if considered Thomas M. Scanlon's *conative relational* approach to social practices as *blaming* analogous to *promise*: there is a *normative relationship* assumed between individuals, of *moral nature*, based in the *rational* stance of 'contractors' and subject to changes based on *expectations* and future events. *vid.* Scanlon, Thomas, M., "Interpreting Blame", in *Blame: Its Nature and Norms*, edited by Justin D. Coates and Neal A. Tognazzini (New York: Oxford University Press, 2013), 84–100; Another approach is to be found in Scanlon, Thomas, M., *Moral Dimensions: Permissibility, Meaning, Blame* (Cambridge, MA: Harvard University Press, 2006). A strongly recommended introduction into the intricacies of *blaming* in contemporary epistemology can be found in Holgado González, María Isabel, "La textura abierta del concepto de culpa moral", in *Revista Laguna* 37 (2015): 69–84.

16 McCall, "Bartleby, the Scrivener", 23.

17 *Ibid.*

18 *Ibid.*, 24.

turn *moral obligation* into *moral right* – the proverbial *pragmatic contradiction*. An assumption, a supposition, justification, are themes for property rights: *my own, your own*. This is you, this here is me. It has to have some weight further than the nude representation, some indexical of the proprietor. Or, better said, *as* representation, *a special normative charge offices by mediation of a moral burden*. One is in some sense responsible for some of his or her intellectual states and endeavours, and holds symmetrically the other responsible for his or her own. So the assumption, so the weight and burden. Such a procedure of attribution – inclusion of ancillary or essential properties, qualities, and traits in *others-being* – is an assignment for *moral imagination*. Hence, Bartleby's little tale is really a three-stage comedy. First, it is a comedy for kids. The twelve-year old Ginger Nut sees in the *luny* a person that *is* a piece of furniture. As a chair. And comedy comes from a superficial and radical level in which – balanced onto the scale, both assumptions weight the same – *he is and he is not* a chair. For a child, things are what they seem to be. Here the violent comedy. Without resistance swinging is easier. Force to be put in to transform a person in a chair, equates to the absence of force lightly assumed by imagination: because

> nothing so aggravates an earnest person as a passive resistance [of other]. If the individual so resisted be of a not inhumane temper [or a child][...] he will endeavor charitably to construe to his imagination what proves impossible to be solved by his judgement.[19]

Here a second-stage of comedy is faced. *How is it that Bartleby is not what it seems, not even what he ought to be?* The gravity – *ought to*-property – assumed by an earnest person is proportional to the added normative laden. Passive resistance is resistance self-imposed. Self-obliging charity then constructed at the expense of *moral imagination*. Justified so on a deontic basis. This is the awakening of *epistemic responsibility*. Contemporary epistemologists know about an interesting branch of their discipline that highlights the central moral role of individuals in cognitive actions. 'Virtue Epistemology' is fond of sharpening Aristotle's idea of intellectual virtues, allocated in intellectual agents as essential traits and holding *justification* issues as ones to be solved in character-constitutive terms.[20] Individuals, communities, hold and are constituted by *mental states* and *dispositions*. An *intellectual virtue* is some stable

---

19 *Ibid.*, 13.
20 Sosa, Ernest, "The Raft and the Pyramid: Coherence versus Foundations in the Theory of Knowledge", in *Midwest Studies in Philosophy* 5 (1980): 3–25.

feature which can cope with an explanation of epistemic (cognitive) success and failure. Obviously, virtue epistemologists interested in second-order virtues like *'open-mindedness'*, or *'intellectual honesty'* are enough closer to the domain of *propositional attitudes* as to not profit of their teachings: *'to believe'*, *'to assent'*, *'to dissent'*, are no less of interest as *'to wish'* or *'to expect'*. Our old friends *'to promise'*, *'to obey'* could be enlisted as well. Those in favour of this school of epistemic virtue are called *responsibility*, for knowing – or refusing to know – is an active performance. A choice.[21] Distinct epistemic charges, responsibilities, should be attributed to distinct mental acts. Intellectual events, either *motives* and *representations*, or *expressions, dispositions, intentions*, and *rules*, carry a different epistemic weight. *'I would prefer not to'*, being a broken sentence, a broken attitude, is the perfectly elusive strategy to avoid carrying any. The distance felt short in aiming is on the shooter and so is the joke. Because truth to be told, Bartleby is hidden at plain sight! That's the third level of comedy: Bartleby's implicit acceptance of *logic of consequences/preferences* in the very act of invoking it to only break it.

A second capital fragment on imagination has to be dragged to these pages as a conclusion:

> Revolving all these things, and coupling them with the recently discovered facts [...] just in proportion as the forlornness of Bartleby grew and grew to my imagination, did that same melancholy merge into fear, that pity into repulsion. So true it is, and so terrible, too, that up to a certain point the thought or sight of misery enlists our best affections; but, in certain special cases, beyond that point it does not. They err who would assert that invariably this is owing to the inherent selfishness of the human heart. *It rather proceeds from a certain hopelessness of remedying excessive and organic ill.*[22]

A lesson well learnt since the beginning by our Bartleby ...

---

21   Code, Lorraine, *Epistemic Responsibility* (Hannover: University Press of New England and Brown University Press, 1987); Zagzebski, Linda and Fairweather, Abrol, *Virtue Epistemology: Essays in Epistemic Virtue and Responsibility* (Oxford: Oxford University Press, 2001).

22   McCall, "Bartleby, the Scrivener", 18–19. A suggestive and influential study on *recognition* is with no doubt displayed in Axel Honneth's, *Reification: A New Look at an Old Idea* (*The Berkeley Tanner Lectures*) (Oxford-New York: Oxford University Press, 2008). Honneth's mentions David Finkelstein's *Expression and the Inner* (Cambridge, MA and London, England: Harvard University Press, 2003) as his inspiration (*vid.* Honneth, *Reification*, 67).

Bibliography

Code, Lorraine, *Epistemic Responsibility* (Hannover: University Press of New England and Brown University Press, 1987).

Deleuze, Gilles, "Bartleby; or, The Formula", in *Essays Critical and Clinical*, translated by Daniel W. Smith and Michael A. Greco (London-New York: Verso, 1998), 68–90.

Earl of Shaftesbury (Anthony Ashley Cooper), "A Letter Concerning Enthusiasm", in Earl of Shaftesbury (Anthony Ashley Cooper), *Characteristicks of Men, Manners, Opinions, Times: In Three Volumes*, Vol. I. I., (London: Printed by John Darby, 1711), 3–55.

Finkelstein, David H., *Expression and the Inner*, (Cambridge, MA and London, England: Harvard University Press, 2003).

Fried, Charles, *Contract as Promise: A Theory of Contractual Obligation*, (Oxford: Oxford University Press, 2015).

Holgado González, María I., "La textura abierta del concepto de culpa moral", in *Revista Laguna* 37 (2015): 69–84.

Honneth, Axel, *Reification: A New Look at an Old Idea (The Berkeley Tanner Lectures)* (Oxford-New York: Oxford University Press, 2008).

Kimel, Dori, *From Promise to Contract: Towards a Liberal Theory of Contract* (Oxford and Portland, Oregon: Hart Publishing, 2003).

McCall, Dan, "Bartleby, the Scrivener", in *Melville's Short Novels: A Norton Critical Edition* (New York-London: W.W. Norton & Co., 2002), 3–34.

Pinocchio, directed by Marc Lesser, Dickie Jones, Roger Carel, Christian Rub and Teddy Bills (Burbank, CA: Walt Disney Studios, 2009. DVD).

Scanlon, Thomas M., "Interpreting Blame", in *Blame: Its Nature and Norms*, edited by Justin D. Coates and Neal A. Tognazzini (New York: Oxford University Press, 2013), 84–100.

Scanlon, Thomas M., *Moral Dimensions: Permissibility, Meaning, Blame* (Cambridge, MA: Harvard University Press, 2006).

Sosa, Ernest, "The Raft and the Pyramid: Coherence versus Foundations in the Theory of Knowledge", in *Midwest Studies in Philosophy* 5 (1980): 3–25.

Zagzebski, Linda and Abrol Fairweather, *Virtue Epistemology: Essays in Epistemic Virtue and Responsibility* (Oxford: Oxford University Press, 2001).

CHAPTER 12

The Basis for Responsibility in Empathy: an Exploration

Paulus Pimomo

Abstract

This chapter focuses on the relational problems in empathy at the collective and individual levels in order to explore the generally neglected subject of responsibility for empathy-related behavior. The idea is that examining the relational problems at both levels would reveal probable causes and point to possible solutions. I use a fictional short story by Nigerian writer Chinua Achebe ("Dead Men's Path") to draw attention to the problems of group relations. Achebe's story deals with power relations under colonialism which, by extension, can be made to stand in for the all-too-familiar phenomenon of dominant groups trying to change, even makeover, a minority's way of life. For obstacles in individual relations I refer to a real-life event, the trial of Khmer Rouge leader Duch for war crimes, and the role played by his victim-turned-witness Francois Bizot. Bizot's empathic connection with his captor Duch is not singular in history, but it is extremely rare so I use it as a reverse example of the universal human problem of refusing to recognize the supposed 'other' in ourselves. Taken together, Achebe's story and Bizot's part in Duch's trial can help us understand what being a responsible community and a responsible individual might mean in relations that involve empathy. But any deontological exploration would require a basis for determining responsibility, so I tentatively propose the basis for empathic responsibility to be the twin obligation of a) recognizing the supposed radical 'other' in oneself (say, the torturer living inside the victim – in potential) and b) accepting human diversity, which would necessitate negotiating differences with others as a salient mode of becoming human together.[1]

---

[1] Thanks to Central Washington University, including the International Programs and Services office, for travel grants that enabled me to attend the 3rd Inter-Disciplinary.Net conference on Empathy in Oxford University. And I'm grateful to my colleagues Patsy Callaghan and George Drake for their valuable feedback on a draft of this chapter.

Keywords

relational empathy – responsibility – fictional literature – chinua achebe – khmer rouge – duch's war crimes – francois bizot – stranger within – cultural 'other'

1 Question

The question I wish to briefly explore with you is: How do we determine responsibility for empathy-related behaviour on the part of individuals and communities?

I think the open-ended outcomes that theorists have assigned to empathy make it harder to talk responsibly about empathy. What I mean by that is, empathy is understood as a human capacity that, when triggered, can motivate either prosocial or antisocial action, or even inaction. This indeterminacy of outcomes makes it difficult to account for any of them meaningfully. Secondly, if the empathic process involves both individual and societal roles, as it is generally thought to do, then assigning responsibility can be a problem. Is it the individual's or the society's responsibility? These are layered questions that can be summed up in one: What is the *basis* for determining responsibility for empathy-generated behavior of one kind or another by individuals and by society, or its absence in either?

2 Critical Context

Recent studies in empathy have taken mainly two directions, neither seeming particularly eager to talk about responsibility. One direction – empirical data-driven research in psychology, sociology, and neuroscience – continues to add significantly to our knowledge of the permutations of empathy and to our understanding of the human brain and the neural processes related to the emotions including empathy. The second direction, led by philosophers, may be described as Critical Empathy Theory (CET), and has brought greater conceptual clarity to a term with a long and checkered history. CET has successfully dislodged what it disparagingly refers to as 'theory theory's'[2] concept of empathy and debunked the traditionally held empathy-altruism hypothesis.

---

2 Coplan, Amy and Goldie, Peter, *Empathy: Philosophical and Psychological Perspectives* (Oxford: Oxford University Press, 2014), xxxii.

In this way, CET has added nuance and sophistication to the pre-theory folk notions of empathy.[3]

A caveat is in order here since ours is an interdisciplinary project. If your work is in these two areas, that is, your research depends on empirically generated data or your main concern lies with conceptual terminology, then you may be inclined to question the pertinence of a study of empathy based partly on a fictional story and partly on a rare historical event: literature is considered by both scientists and philosophers to be at least one clear remove from reality, and doubt could be raised about the usefulness of a generalization drawn from extreme events in history. But what this chapter does is raise the question of responsibility, which all approaches to empathy must eventually address even if certainty and consensus are not assured. I take a humanistic approach to explore the subject.

3   What Is and What Is Not Empathy

Empathy is a complex and contested concept, but scholars find agreement on two points about the nature of *higher-level empathy*. The first point of agreement is that empathy is *interpersonal*, which means that it takes an agent and a target to complete the empathic process, and the process occurs at multiple levels – affective, cognitive, and imaginative – which further means that a matching of 'psychological states' takes place between the two persons involved. The agent puts herself in the target's shoes so as to feel, think, and act like the target would or might. The second point of agreement is that it is *not a first-personal perspective-shifting* (to borrow Peter Goldie's term),[4] that is to say, an agent can approximate the target's perspective as closely as she may, but she cannot *become* the target. Put another way, I can put myself imaginatively in your shoes and feel and think, possibly act, like you, but I cannot *become* you. When I empathize with you, I'm matching your psychological states but not usurping your being. This may sound like common sense, and perhaps it is, but there is a critical philosophical nuance to mark here between two notions of perspective shifting: 'empathetic perspective-shifting' – the name

---

3   Coplan and Goldie's *Empathy: Philosophical and Psychological Perspectives* is an excellent latest example of what I call Critical Empathy Theory. I depend on the book for the theory section of this chapter.
4   Goldie, Peter, "Anti-Empathy", in Coplan and Goldie, *Empathy: Philosophical and Psychological Perspectives*, 302–317.

Goldie gives this ersatz empathy – is a conceptual impossibility, because human agency is radically first-personal. Goldie and others (going back to phenomenologists Edmund Husserl and Edith Stein)[5] distinguish this impossible 'empathetic perspective-shifting' from the other kind, the normative *in-your-shoes perspective-shifting*, which is what people generally mean and engage in when they talk about empathy. To sum up for my present purpose, then, higher-level empathy is an interpersonal process, but the process is not first-personal; it is an in-your-shoes perspective shifting that engages higher level human capacities, unlike in cases of spontaneous base empathy.

4   Interpersonal Perspective-Shifting and Artistic Empathy

Because my exploration of the basis for responsibility in empathy is based in part on literature, I need to point out that what I just described about higher-level empathy applies to relations between real-life human beings not to viewers and readers engaging fictional characters. Philosopher Graham McFee in "Empathy: Interpersonal vs Artistic?"[6] agrees in the main with CET's understanding of empathy as perspective-shifting, but he points out the limitations of the interpersonal and the psychological-states matching models when applied to artistic experience. First, matching psychological-states on an *interpersonal* level is out of the question in art experience since there is no live person for the viewer or reader to match directly with. Unlike in real-life empathy, in art there's only one 'brain state'[7] at work at the time of experience, only one live mind – the viewer/reader's. The audience/reader's empathic relation is not with the film maker or the author; it is an evocative connection with a *fictional* character who is not only physically non-existent but is partly a recreation of the viewer/reader's mind, and although the connection may have affective, cognitive, and imaginative elements similar to those in real-life experience, it is not the same as the interpersonal perspective shifting and matching of mental states that happen between a full-blooded agent and a full-blooded target. McFee suggests that these differences in artistic empathy require theorists to develop alternative ways of understanding empathic processes in the

---

5   Stein, Edith, *On the Problem of Empathy* [1917], translated by Waltraut Stein (The Hague: Martinus Nijhoff, 1970).
6   McFee, Graham, "Empathy: Interpersonal vs Artistic?", in Coplan and Goldie, *Empathy: Philosophical and Psychological Perspectives*, 185–208.
7   McFee, "Empathy: Interpersonal vs Artistic?", 207.

arts, perhaps along the lines of a "more humanistic picture of empathy in art appreciation."[8] But he does not go on to elaborate what that may be.

I want to follow up on McFee's suggestion and discuss a fictional short story by Nigerian writer Chinua Achebe called "Dead Men's Path." I work with CET's concept of empathy as *interpersonal perspective-shifting*, but one that operates on a different plane than happens in real life among real people. And I want to mark the difference by calling the interactions in the story *relational*, instead of interpersonal, to emphasize the point that the story is less about individuals interacting with each other than about people relating to one another as representatives of two opposing groups.

The second difference of the empathic process in literature like Achebe's story has to do with the imaginative freedom of the fictional narrative medium itself, which permits the writer to shape relational possibilities with more complexity than real-life ordinarily allows, prompting the discerning reader to imagine relational possibilities beyond those imposed on people in the real world and to think outside of the conceptual categories in which empathic relations are considered by empathy theory. The point being that literary fiction in the right writerly hands and readerly minds can be a powerful medium for structuring emotions, thoughts, and actions in a mixed realm of the real and the utopian-dystopian worlds. A fictional story copies and critiques life in order to enhance it through empathic understanding of the life-like situations it creates, often revealing sides of life that real-life is blind to. Literary fiction is to everyday life what an empathizing agent is to its target. The relation occurs as an in-your-shoes perspective shifting, but there's nothing to prevent the narrative agent from usurping its target's life, creating it anew, and (unlike in real life) acting in the first-personal mode. In short, if philosophers understand the realities of life through categorizing and conceptualizing and psychologists find meaning by mapping mental states into empirically-observable paradigms, it is the business of literature not just to transcribe realities through imaginative recreation but to offer probing, transformational critiques of conventional social reality through relational empathy.

5 Relational Group Empathy and Achebe's "Dead Men's Path"

Achebe's "Dead Men's Path" exemplifies this kind of probing literature. It is a narrative of group relations under colonialism. First, the outline of the story: An

---

8 *Ibid.*, 208.

African young man Michael Obi, who has excelled in the English colonial education system, has just been appointed Headmaster of a Mission school that needs rescuing. Obi and his wife Nancy set two goals for the school: improving the academic standards and beautifying the premises, two seminal goals of Western education going back (via Horace) to the classical Roman dictum, *docere et delectare* (to teach and to delight). But there is a problem. A path that connects the village to the burial grounds runs through the school, which Obi promptly closes because it impedes the school's mission. The village leader, who is also the priest of the Earth goddess Ani, calls on Obi and explains why the road needs to stay open. It is the sacred path that links the dead, the living, and the future generations of the village. It is their lifeline: "The whole life of this village depends on it. Our dead relatives depart by it and our ancestors visit us by it. But most important, it is the path of children coming in to be born."[9] To this, the Headmaster replies: "The whole purpose of our school is to eradicate just such beliefs as that. Dead men do not require footpaths. The whole idea is just fantastic."[10] The village leader tells Obi that the path was there before either of them, or their fathers, was born. His parting words to Obi are: "What I always say is: let the hawk perch and let the eagle perch."[11] But tribal superstitions must be eradicated, so Obi blocks the path. A young woman in the village dies in childbirth shortly thereafter and the villagers trash the school premises. The last thing we learn is that Headmaster Obi's white superior, the colonial Government Education Officer, is deeply troubled by the 'tribal-war' situation in the village and will intervene by putting the blame 'in part' on the "misguided zeal of the new headmaster."[12]

The colonial world of the story is obviously one of domination and subordination and of binary oppositions: white/black, colonizer/colonized, modern/primitive, Western/African, and so forth, and people in this uneven power relations are put in positions of (in the discourse of empathy) opposing agents and targets. Under colonial dispensation empathy and perspective-shifting are rendered either inoperable or, if they do operate, take on twisted forms.

Take the three representative characters, the unnamed white Education Officer, Michael Obi, and the village leader. Positive empathy with Africans is out of the question for the white Officer in this context. His body is "the ultimate

---

9   Achebe, Chinua, "Dead Men's Path", in *Literature: A Pocket Anthology*, edited by R. S. Gwynn, 6th ed. (Boston: Penguin, 2015), 172–174.
10 *Ibid.*
11 *Ibid.*
12 *Ibid.*

barrier to empathy",[13] to use Steven Pinker's trenchant phrase in a different context. As a colonist, he cannot enact in-your-shoes perspective-shifting with Africans, yet he must relate to them in some way since he rules their lives. So he finds an unsuspecting surrogate black body, Michael Obi, to act as a buffer between him and Africans, which allows the white man to exercise control over the village by remote control, as it were. This relational move has a weird effect on Obi. Obi embodies as well as subverts the perspective-shifting model of relating. He becomes 'white' through a psychological-states manoeuvring. One cannot obviously take an in-your-shoes perspective-shifting with regard to oneself; neither can Obi, though he could with regard to his fellow Africans, but doesn't. Instead, he impersonates the white colonizer and functionally usurps his identity in his relations with fellow Africans. In other words, Obi performs the impossible; he does what Goldie calls 'empathetic perspective-shifting' of the first personal kind on his white superior; he enacts what is, for critical empathy theory, a conceptual conundrum and real-life impossibility. He was born Obi/African, but he's now Michael/British, and only Obi/African in name. This puts him in a no-win relational situation. The village blames him and his supervisor blames him. The consequences of Michael Obi's schizophrenia are dire on his people as well. A young mother dies in childbirth and their way of life is put in jeopardy.

The leader of the opposite camp, the village priest, may be seen as representing the potential transformative element in literature that I mentioned above. Unlike Obi and his white superior, he can put himself in Obi's shoes, even the white man's shoes. Recall that the racial binary under colonialism comes from whites, to which blacks react variously. The village leader's capacity for in-your-shoes perspective shifting is evident in what he tells Obi: *Let the hawk perch and let the eagle perch*. Let Brits and Africans, white and black, perch on the same tree of life. They are not the same bird, not birds of a feather, but birds nonetheless. Human beings of different colours and beliefs can share the same village/earth. The leader has noticed too that Africans are not all the same. There are Obis who turn Michaels, and they may yet have a role to play in his village – formal education perhaps – a role to be negotiated with the village in light of its cultural traditions, not imposed on it from the outside with the mission of eradicating its way of life, based on the conviction that the village is steeped in superstition and primitivism.

---

13 From Steven Pinker's *How the Mind Works* (1997), quoted in Coplan and Goldie, *Empathy: Philosophical and Psychological Perspectives*, 191.

If this is the complex of group relations under colonialism that Achebe's fictional narrative reveals, what can a discerning reader extrapolate from the controversy surrounding the superstition of the 'dead men's path'? One is that the story holds up a mirror to the colonizing society. The reader would realize that modern Western societies that believe 'dead men do not require footpaths' do have beliefs that might look like superstitions to a cultural outsider. Take Christianity's belief in the virgin conception of Jesus or his resurrection or the physical presence of Jesus in the Eucharist. Secondly, and this is as important, it will not do for the same discerning reader to reach for the atheist's automatic 'I-told-you-so-about-religions' conclusion. The village priest's position in the story may be pointing to another conclusion, that perhaps not all superstitions need be eradicated, that some may be worth preserving for those who find meaning in them, like the 'dead men's path' in a village, say, whose function is to foster beneficial empathic relations among the living and the dead, and act as a physical and symbolic path of life that connects the living with their ancestral roots; or the Eucharist, say, which enacts an empathic transcendental experience for the believers and which might transform the communicants into a living spiritual and social community. But, thirdly, if some 'superstitions' are worth preserving, some may not be, so how do we decide which to keep and which to throw out? A reader who has discerned the first two points about the story would have little difficulty understanding that that would depend on the function of the belief or practice. If a 'superstition' inculcates a sense of community and well-being, say, it's in, if it engenders division and hostility, it's out. But who gets to decide and how? That is to be negotiated among the people involved, not imposed by some on others. What Achebe's story seems to suggest, when it comes to the question of determining responsibility in group relations, then, is that diversity among peoples, cultures, and beliefs is a fact of life, hence negotiating differences is a necessary mode of being and becoming human together. The roles of the white supervisor, Michael Obi, and the village leader, taken together, offer us a copy of real-life conflict under colonialism in order to prise the conflict open for deeper exploration of why group relations fail, and how they may be transformed.

6 Relational Empathy in Individuals: Trial of Khmer Rouge Leader Duch

The trial of Khmer Rouge leader Duch for crimes against humanity, and the empathic understanding of his role that one of his former victims developed, offers a telling example for determining a basis for responsibility in empathy between individuals.

French ethnologist Francois Bizot was imprisoned by the Khmer Rouge in October 1971 while researching on Buddhism in the region. He was taken to the notorious S-21 torture and execution camp headed by Duch. He was released after three months and over the years thought much about those months in prison. He visited his former captor when Duch was arrested in the 1990s and he wrote a book on the events.[14] So when Bizot appeared as a witness at Duch's trial in Phnom Penh in 2008, he had processed the experience deeply. For Bizot, the issue was not about forgetting or forgiving Duch's crimes, which he could not, nor about finding proper punishment for Duch, which was not available, or giving justice to the victims, which was out of the question. It was about understanding how a committed idealist with personal integrity (which Duch was to begin with) turned into the vicious mass executioner that he became. Bizot was freshly reminded of other events in history, including the holocaust, and arrived at the understanding that inhumanity is human. This is how he put it: "But let's face the facts: this inhuman dimension is part of what's human. As long as we refuse to recognize that inhumanity is a human thing, we'll remain caught in a pious fraud."[15]

In the language of empathy, then, we could say that Bizot went through a process of deep in-your-shoes perspective-shifting with Duch as his target and found a matching inhumanity in himself – in potential. For Bizot, the trial of Duch for crimes against humanity, and others like it, would have meaning only if it allowed us to go beyond condemnation, which was necessary, on to examining the 'mechanisms of the production of evil',[16] which gets neglected. Bizot in his own words:

> I see the crime against humanity as a gaze that can be suddenly pointed at us. I'd like us to have the audacity to humanize the torturers – without trying to forgive them or minimize their crimes – to see in them what human beings are capable of being, what we are capable of being.[17]

---

14 Bizot, Francois, *Le Portail*, translated by Euan Cameron, as *The Gate* (New York: Alfred A. Knopf, 2003).
15 Todorov, Tzvetan, *Memory as a Remedy for Evil*, translated by Gila Walker (London: Seagull Books, 2010), 81.
16 *Ibid.*, 42.
17 *Ibid.*, 39.

7 Conclusion

I have entered the discourse of empathy from its peripheries of fictional literature and an extremely rare case of Bizot's empathic connection with his captor to raise a central question about responsibility in empathy. If empathy is an affective, cognitive, and imaginative in-your-shoes perspective-shifting on the part of an agent toward a target which may lead to, but does not need to find completion of any kind, either prosocial or antisocial, then it is difficult to render a responsible account for such a process. Is empathy Critical Empathy Theory's new noun without a referent? I've refrained from directly addressing the theoretical question, and instead assumed the presence of a referent for empathy and tried to explore a basis for determining responsibility in empathy at the collective and individual levels. I've tentatively deduced from my examples the basis for determining empathic responsibility to be a twin obligation: recognizing the supposed radical 'other' in oneself (the torturer living inside the victim – in potential, as Bizot discerned for himself and all humanity), and accepting human and cultural diversity, which would necessitate negotiating differences with Others as a salient way to become better human beings together.

Bibliography

Achebe, Chinua, "Dead Men's Path", in *Literature: A Pocket Anthology*, edited by R. S. Gwynn, 6th ed. (Boston: Penguin, 2015), 172–174.

Bizot, Francois, *Le Portail,* translated by Euan Cameron as *The Gate* (New York: Alfred A. Knopf, 2003).

Coplan, Amy and Goldie, Peter, *Empathy: Philosophical and Psychological Perspectives* (Oxford: Oxford University Press, 2014).

Goldie, Peter, "Anti-Empathy", in Coplan, Amy and Goldie, Peter, *Empathy: Philosophical and Psychological Perspectives* (Oxford: Oxford University Press, 2014), 302–317.

McFee, Graham, "Empathy: Interpersonal vs Artistic?", in Coplan, Amy and Goldie, Peter, *Empathy: Philosophical and Psychological Perspective* (Oxford: Oxford University Press, 2014), 185–208.

Stein, Edith, *On the Problem of Empathy* [1917], translated by Waltraut Stein (The Hague: Martinus Nijhoff, 1970).

Todorov, Tzvetan, *Memory as a Remedy for Evil* (London: Seagull Books, 2010).

CHAPTER 13

Empathy and Historical Understanding: a Reappraisal of 'Empathic Unsettlement'

Rosa E. Belvedresi

Abstract

'Empathy' is a key concept in epistemology of history usually applied to understand other's actions. The issue is linked to Dilthey's hermeneutical theory, the starting point where all the discussions about historical understanding are coming from. The aim of this paper is to consider the concept of 'empathy' and to explore its connections with notions like trauma and suffering of others. We will analyze LaCapra's 'empathic unsettlement' in order to see if it offers a plausible way to adopt empathy in history without falling in the typical misunderstandings (allegedly mindreading abilities, esoteric spiritual contact, and so on) and keeping the true-claims safe. Recovering some ideas connected to empathy would be helpful so as not to miss the point that history is a product of human agency. Obviously, historical processes involve contextual conditions which are difficult for agents to change. Some processes are so radically new, such as traumatic events, that alternative approaches are required to unfold their complex meanings. With the intention of assessing the fruitfulness of LaCapra's theory to reach historical (and empathic) understanding we will propose an example taken not from trauma studies but from Argentinean history in order to evaluate the possibility of a broader scope of the 'empathic unsettlement.'

Keywords

empathy – empathic unsettlement – historical understanding – LaCapra – trauma studies

1   Introductory Remarks

Wilhelm Dilthey considered history as a scientific discipline and, at the same time, stressed its specific character as a science of the human world. According to him, history must adopt the logical and argumentative tools that are characteristic of scientific knowledge but must also properly deal with the specific conditions of the historical world, which requires a particular approach. The historical world is, in part, an empirical object insofar as it is directly accessible to those who want to examine it. But its analysis cannot be restricted to a mere description of its observable characteristics since it is also an object that has meaning. Hence, to study the historical world is to interpret it.

Dilthey reformulated Hegel's notion of 'objective spirit' (*objektiver Geist*).[1] Instead of considering it as the objectification of a transcendent and infinite spirit he limited it to human productions. Human productions constitute a social, cultural and historical world shared by generations. They go beyond the particular time in which they were created, are presented as 'data' for the individuals in their communal life and constitute the true 'objective spirit' studied by the *Geisteswissenschaften*. To do so, these sciences must adopt a method that is appropriate to its object. An analysis of cultural productions focused only on observation and experimentation which are the emblematic methods used in natural sciences, would restrict these cultural productions to their condition of simple (empirical) phenomena and would thus eliminate the meaning they convey. Human productions that constitute the historical world are perceptible expressions of a meaning which manifests itself in these expressions but is not to be reduced to them.

A literary work, a painting, some handwritten lines and also body movements of people in their social routines (such as raising the hands to vote in an assembly or waving to greet someone) are empirical data accessible to any observer but they are also bearers of meanings that demand the development of the ability to 'read' them. It is not about 'hidden' meanings that require a parapsychological technique for their interpretation, such as a positivist epistemology could say, but about the semantic dimension that is essential to the objects of the social world, whether they are actions, communities, institutions or cultural artifacts of different kinds. For Dilthey, the historical world is the set of perceptible manifestations of the spiritual meanings that humanity has created and shared over the centuries.[2]

Dilthey formulates the methodological strategies of the *Geisteswissenschaften* based on the specific characteristics attributed to their object. Historical events are spiritual processes that have left different kinds of perceptible manifestations (documents, ruins, testimonies) whose meanings the historian

---

1 See his *The Formation of the Historical World in the Human Sciences: Selected Works*, vol. III, edited by R.A. Makkreel and F. Rodi (Princeton-NJ: Princeton University Press, 2002).
2 *Ibid.*, 229–231.

must understand. In order to interpret past events, the historian must evaluate them in their singularity by virtue of the particular context and conditions of their occurrence. An analysis of the historical events in terms of causal laws, which would be characteristic of the naturalistic approach to the cultural world, would distort their meaning.

2   History and Human Agency

Historical events, unlike natural events, are the result of human agency. Nonetheless, the link between human actions and the historical events that they cause cannot be traced in a linear manner. Singular actions occur in contexts whose elements are not always alterable by the historical agents themselves. In most cases, historical agents are not even conscious of these context-dependent factors. In fact, historical events result from the complex interaction between the resources available to the historical agents, their ability to generate a particular course of action and the actions of other agents with whom they share the social scene. In this way, the statement that history is the result of human actions must not be mistaken with the naive thesis that presents historical events as the direct and thoughtful result of agents' wishes. Nor does it force us to accept the idea of transparent and self-conscious historical agents. Feminist historiography of post-structuralism inspiration has shown that the construction of historical agents' subjectivity and agency results from the ways in which categories and identifications that occur in opaque social contexts operate.[3]

Agency is not a sort of inherent power of an individual before his social insertion; it is the result of the enactment of possibilities and the use of resources that are not equally available to all agents. Nonetheless, certain agents manage to build a particular subjectivity that allows them to recognize and use those possibilities and resources or even find alternatives to develop their own courses of action.

Agents are situated in a specific place in the social reality, which provides them with certain opportunities to act but, at the same time, imposes restrictions on the fulfillment of their wishes.[4] Once more, it is important to highlight

---

[3] A good analysis of social construction of subjectivity can be found in: Scott, J. W., "The Evidence of Experience", in *Critical Inquiry*, vol. 17, no. 4 (1991): 773–797.

[4] Giddens, Anthony, "Elements of the Theory of Structuration", in *The Constitution of Society: Outline of the Theory of Structuration* (Berkeley and Los Angeles: University of California Press, 1984).

the possibility that in concrete situations, social agents could manage to build a subjectivity that goes beyond the limits and conditions of a given historical context.[5]

Once history is conceived as a result of human agency, as we just have described it, the use of Dilthey's understanding in historical studies becomes indispensable. The process of understanding operates on an object that is a human product, because it is the result of what historical agents did in specific contexts in which they could generate, to a greater or lesser extent, their own alternatives of action.

3 Understanding and History

The discussion about the notion of understanding as an essential feature of the *Geisteswissenschaften* characterized the so-called 'critical' philosophy of history, that is, the philosophical thought that attempted to overcome the Hegelian metaphysical legacy that considered the development of world history as a result of the movement of the spirit in the search of self-consciousness. As we already mentioned, Dilthey retained the concept of 'objective spirit' of Hegel's theory of the spirit, but he got rid of its transcendental metaphysical meaning. The objective spirit is not the objectification of a universal substance but a human production of the shared socio-historical world. This world is the object of the *Geisteswissenschaften* and its knowledge is only possible through understanding.

The metaphysical perspective on history as well as the idea of a rational plan that would be carried out independently of the knowledge or desire of particular historical agents were abandoned when it became noticeable that they could not appropriately account for concrete historical processes. Historians, moreover, encountered real difficulties in writing a history that was truly global, since all attempts turned out to be, at best, European history.[6]

To avoid becoming a mere natural object, history needs to start from the world of lived experience (*Erlebnis*, according to Dilthey's terminology). Because human beings are, first of all, social beings, the basic source for the

---

5 And this is what allows us to understand historical contingency, that is, the emergence of novel events in history that are not exclusively engendered by the existing 'objective' or 'material' conditions, *vid.* Koselleck, Reinhart, "Transformations of Experience and Methodological Change: A Historical-Anthropological Essay", in *The Practice of Conceptual History: Timing History, Spacing Concepts* (California: Stanford University Press, 2002).
6 Koselleck, Reinhart, *historia/Historia* (Madrid, Trotta, 2006).

construction of the historical knowledge must be the experience of belonging to a community. Unlike psychology and sociology, which had not yet abandoned the positivist matrix at that time, Dilthey presented history as a model of knowledge of the world of lived experience and formulated a critique of historical reason that was intended to complete the Kantian trilogy.[7] According to his theory, history is an empirical science and thus shares some of the logical and argumentative principles of the natural sciences, but it has nonetheless a distinctive feature: the subject who studies history is the same who does history. This 'principle of continuity' between subject and object implies a fundamental epistemological assumption: historical knowledge is a more precise formulation, but is not different in nature, from the knowledge that social agents possess about the world of lived experience in which they are embedded. The use of understanding as a methodological strategy of historiography establishes its fundamental difference with the natural sciences, and in so far as historiography was the model of the *Geisteswissenchaften*, that methodology was extended to all social sciences.

In a Diltheyan perspective, human actions and their results constitute manifestations of life and, as such, expressions of meanings. At the elementary level, that is, in the world of everyday life, people understand gestures and behaviors of others with whom they share the world. Human actions and their results (from a scribbled note to a work of art or a testament) express the particular experiences that occur to us in our daily life. Understanding is the ability we have, as social subjects educated in a shared context, to access the experiences expressed under multiple modalities of manifestations of life. Dilthey considers that understanding is the ability to internally relive the experiences of others we want to understand. Understanding entails a progression from what is visible to the naked eye, which could be considered the empirical level, to the meaning it expresses, which can only be reached through a hermeneutic process of interpretation. The elementary understanding that we practice in our everyday social life serves as a model for more sophisticated levels of understanding that constitute the method of *Geisteswissenschaften* in general, and of history in particular.

---

7   Dilthey defended a kind of psychology that he called 'descriptive' opposed to the 'explanatory' psychology, which he considered dominated by a naturalistic ideal of knowledge (*vid.* Lorenzo, Luis M., "Vida, historia y psicología en Wilhelm Dilthey", in *Tópicos*, no. 21 (2011): 1–23). He couldn't accomplish his project of a critique of historical reason which was reconstructed by his interpreters, see for example Dilthey, Wilhelm, *Texte zur Kritik der historischen Vernunft*, edited by Lessing, H-U. (Göttingen: Vandenhoeck & Ruprecht, 1983).

The strong psychological hallmark of Dilthey's vocabulary, the darkness of his basic notion of 'experience' and the lack of precision of the idea of 're-experiencing,' were elements that cast doubt on the scientific character of understanding and its use as a reliable and (objectively) controllable method. The idea that science should follow a single method regardless of its purpose prevailed in the middle of the 20th century. Such methodological monism was reluctant to accept that understanding was the basic explanatory strategy of history. In fact, it is possible to identify two kinds of criticisms to Dilthey's thesis, both of positivist inspiration. First, there were some attempts to show that history, like all scientific knowledge, seeks to generate explanations of the events it studies, even if it could only provide a 'sketch' of these explanations.[8] The second strategy was to discredit understanding by considering it a dark psychological mechanism of mind-reading, similar to a kind of *Vulcan mental meld*.[9] This criticism arose from the characterization of understanding as an interpretation 'from within' as opposed to simple 'external' observation. The internal/external opposition, where the internal refers to the meaning and the external to the behavior or observable data, induced the confusing idea that understanding was a kind of access to other people's mind that requires the exercise of some strange psychic power.

Nonetheless, the idea that meanings are the 'inner side' of 'external' manifestations should be understood in a non-literal sense. This characterization only aims to point out that the simple empirical description (later considered by LaCapra as an 'objectifying' description) is not enough to capture the meanings expressed in the cultural diversity that constitute the social world. According to Geertz, the interpretation of meanings requires a thick description, a sheet of white paper with regular ink spots on its surface is actually a score and it should be considered as such if we do not want to lose sight of its purport as manifestation of life.[10] The historian should construct an interpretative hypothesis that would enable her to recover the perspective of the original actor and expose the meaning assigned to that score to other interpreters, who

---

8   Explanation was associated with the use of causal laws to account for individual cases, which were identified as particular instances of those.
9   We refer here to the ability of Mr. Spock, the Vulcan member of the starship *Enterprise*'s crew in the TV show *Star Trek*, to access other's people mind through a sort of trance. In a famous paper written in 1948, T. Abel criticized understanding as an unmediated form of pseudo-knowledge (Abel, Theodore, "The Operation called Verstehen", in *American Journal of Sociology*, vol. 54, no. 3 (1948): 211–218).
10 Geertz, Clifford, "Thick Description: Toward an Interpretive Theory of Culture", in *The Interpretation of Cultures: Selected Essays* (New York: Basic Books, 1973), 3–30.

would subsequently accept or refute her hypothesis. So, as we can see, understanding requires that the researcher (imaginatively) 'put herself in the place' of the agent under study. A description like that originates the common association between understanding and empathy.[11]

In order to overcome the risk of alleged psychologism that threatened Dilthey's theory, the identification between understanding and re-experiencing or empathy was subsequently questioned by several authors. Among them, R.G. Collingwood was a notorious case: he proposed to replace the concept of re-experiencing by that of re-enactment and avoided talking in terms of 'understanding.'[12]

4   LaCapra and the Recovery of the Notion of Empathy

In spite of these criticisms, LaCapra recovered the notion of empathy and assigned to it an important role in history especially in relation to trauma studies: "[e]mpathy is an affective component of understanding."[13] It allows us to pay attention to "the connection between historical understanding, social criticism, and ethico-political activity." However, it has not received due attention in specialized literature: "the problem of empathy is [...][an] indicator that there is much remaining to be done in the attempt of historians and others to write about -and in some sense write- trauma."[14]

For LaCapra, understanding historical agents and their manifestations of life, that is, understanding their actions and their results that, in many cases, persist as objects of the social world, requires establishing an empathic connection between historians and the historical agents under study. This

---

[11]   Dilthey did not use the word '*Einfühlung*' – the German term for 'empathy' – to characterize understanding, he conceived it as a re-experiencing (*Nacherleben*) of the original experience by virtue of the transposition (*Umstellung*) of the historian's self.

[12]   Collingwood's notion of *re-enactment* only applied to the rational contents (defined as 'thoughts') that were expressed in historical actions, unlike Dilthey's concept of '(lived)-experience' that could include irrational or emotional elements. Despite the conceptual closeness between these two notions, Collingwood scarcely mentioned Dilthey in his work. The theory of *re-enactment* was proposed by Collingwood to challenge the application of causal explanation to history. *vid.* Collingwood, Robin G., *The Idea of History*, revised edition by J. Van der Dussen (Oxford: Oxford University Press, 1994).

[13]   LaCapra, Dominick, *Writing History, Writing Trauma* (Baltimore: Johns Hopkins University Press, 2014), 102, footnote 10.

[14]   *Ibid.*, 219.

empathic connection accounts for the experiential dimension of the historical life: "I think that any historiographical, sociological, or theoretical appeal to experience is inadequate without an account of the problem of empathy as it bears on the relation of the inquirer to the experience of those studied."[15] Empathy does not suppose the uncritical identification between both historians and historical agents, but it does manifest the affective load that is displayed in the process of understanding. Far from being external factors to the research process, affects enable and hinder at the same time an adequate understanding of historical events. The involvement of historians with their objects of study, which are other human beings and not molecules or insects, is always present, although it is often hidden. It is generally believed that the affective bond that requires empathic understanding puts objectivity at risk. In fact, it is rather the opposite. When the historian does not pay attention to the affects operating in her work, she tends to consider as irrefutable data what could only be a projection of her own values.

LaCapra does not advocate a historiography flooded with uncontrolled affects. Historical empathy must be measured and controlled in order to avoid that our own subjectivity conceals that one of the agents studied. If as inquirers we want to gain knowledge about the role of active subjects performed by historical agents, even in conditions in which they faced extremely restrictive contexts, we cannot reject empathy. If we do so, we jeopardize our role as interpreters of the historical agents we seek to understand and we become their judges instead. Theoretical positions dominated by what we can characterized as 'objectivism' eliminate the experiential and lived dimensions of historical processes.[16]

LaCapra's notion of empathy, which is linked to his defense of the historian's intellectual and ethical commitment, allows him to argue against two positions that reject the normative and affective dimension of historical understanding. On the one hand, against the position that emphasizes a neutral and non-cathected approach to historical processes and phenomena, in order to fulfill the Rankean principle *to show what actually happened*. On the other hand, against the extreme constructivist proposals that reduce the historical

---

15   LaCapra, Dominick, *History in Transit: Experience. Identity. Critical Theory* (Ithaca: Cornell University Press, 2004), 64.

16   Unlike objectivity, objectivism focuses on the use of experimental techniques and supposes an extreme separation between the researcher and her object of study, which is another subject. LaCapra also refers to this strategy as 'objectification' (*vid.* LaCapra, *History in Transit*, 37–39).

evolution to a quasi-linguistic phenomenon.[17] Both perspectives lose sight of the historical subject as an agent that needs to be taken into account by the historian. This happens, in the first case, because all the strategies that suppose the development of certain sympathy are discarded, the historian must only take care of the actions and their results as they are duly documented, without recovering the perspectives of the agents involved, their wishes, anxieties and decisions. And in the second case, because the category itself of 'subject' vanishes, since it is simply considered as an effect of the texts.[18]

LaCapra considers that neither of the two perspectives mentioned before allows recovering the voice of the victims who are the central issue in studying trauma. Both positions silence the victims, either because they favor an external account of the processes that caused their victimization, or because the victims are over-determined by the conceptual apparatus of historiography and the rhetorical and stylistic decisions made by the historian.

Empathy accounts for the affective dimension that is involved in the historical understanding of traumatic events, that is, the 'transferential implication' of the historian with its object of study.[19] When the historian tries to account for situations that affected people's lives in ways that they could not imagine, such as slavery, concentration camps, or sexual abuse, they can set up different and more or less successful strategies. According to LaCapra, empathy represents the viable methodological alternative to recover the experience of the subjects who went through such extreme situations: "the problem of experience should lead to the question of the role of empathy in historical understanding."[20]

Historical empathy disagrees with two unsatisfactory modalities of understanding past traumas. First, the extreme objectification that denies the historian's affective commitment to its object of study.[21] Second, a disproportionate use of empathy that entails the illusion of a complete identification between the historian and the historical agents she studies: "[b]y identification I mean the unmediated fusion of self and other in which the otherness or alterity of

---

17   LaCapra characterizes the first position as a "documentary or self-sufficient research model", and the second as "radical constructivism." (LaCapra, *Writing History*, 1–11).

18   Although this perspective refers to the historical narrativism characteristic of H. White and F. Ankersmit, LaCapra makes a similar assessment of (certain theses of) post-structuralism.

19   For the definition of 'transferential implication' *vid.* LaCapra, *Writing History*, 39, 99, among many others.

20   *Ibid.*, 37–38.

21   *Ibid.*, 78–79.

the other is not recognized and respected."[22] The objects of trauma studies are subjects who have suffered a traumatic situation. Their study implies overcoming purely scientificist and objectifying strategies that reject the affective involvement of the researcher with those subjects and also avoiding identification strategies that suppose the fusion between the historian's self and the historical agents' selves, confusing thus their voices.

LaCapra's reintroduction of the notion of empathy is inspiring but disconcerting, because he presents it without taking into account its philosophical tradition or its possible objections.[23] It is true that he repeatedly questions the idea of empathy as a simple fusion or identification between the historian and the historical agents under study. His concept also seems closer to psychoanalysis than to the hermeneutic tradition to which it belongs.[24] But the use of empathy as a methodological strategy must reply serious criticisms such as: what criteria can allow us, as historians, to be sure that the empathy that we develop in our research is *the right one*? How can we determine the appropriateness of an empathic interpretation?[25] LaCapra's confidence in the ability of historians, as members of an academic field, to find the right balance in the use of the empathic method through the exchange among colleagues may not be sufficient, although it is difficult to find other criteria than those of the practice itself. As we will see later, it is the concept of 'empathic unsettlement' that will guarantee an adequate use of empathy.

Furthermore, another problematic question concerns the historical agents, that is, the objects of investigation, with whom the historian must empathize. The crimes of the past have left injuries in the present and historians must work through these painful traces. The victims of traumatic events, who have lost their families, their property and even their lives, must be recovered by historiography. Empathy is, for LaCapra, the most appropriate methodological strategy to do this: "[e]mpathy is important to try to understand traumatic events and victims". In addition, it allows the historian to write and represent the past by avoiding "fetishized and totalizing narratives that deny trauma [...][by] (re)turning to the pleasure principle, harmonizing events, and often

---

22 *Ibid.*, 27.
23 Moyn, Samuel, "Empathy in History, empathizing with Humanity", in *History and Theory*, vol. 45, no. 3 (2006): 398.
24 *vid.* also LaCapra, "History, Psychoanalysis, Critical Theory", in *History in Transit*, 72–105.
25 LaCapra, *Writing History*, 105. 'Appropriateness' does not refer here to a sort of adjustment criterion that requires a comparison with an external factor but to the possibility of establishing that the interpretation done through the use of empathy is the one that best fits the available evidence and the inter-subjective criticism.

recovering the past in terms of uplifting messages or optimistic and self-service scenarios."[26] In this way, the researcher dispenses with the positivist strategy that transforms the subjects studied into mere objects that do not affect, or are affected by, the scientist. At the same time, it also avoids the opposite risk: that the historian identifies herself with her object and produces thus self-satisfying explanations.

Understanding allows the historian to interpret the social world as the result of human actions, that is, as expressions and manifestations of life. Empathy, in turn, can be considered as a more specific modality of understanding to the extent that it makes explicit the affective aspect and the values involved in the scientific practices of the historian when she must consider those who suffered from traumatic historical events.[27] For LaCapra, historiography has to produce a critical knowledge that contributes to the public sphere and this requires a particular commitment of the historian to her object of study. In particular, when dealing with traumatic past events, empathy is the only modality of historical understanding that can facilitate its working-through, in order to avoid repetitions, repressions or victimizations.[28] The adequate use of empathy is guaranteed by what LaCapra calls 'empathic unsettlement.' In the next section we will briefly present its characteristics and make some proposals to expand its field of use.

5   Empathic Unsettlement

LaCapra introduces the concept of 'empathic unsettlement' to define a correct use of empathy. It prevents the simple identification between the historian and the subjects under study, especially when they are victims of traumatic events: "[b]eing responsive to the traumatic experience of others, notable of victims, implies not the appropriation of their experience but what would I call empathic unsettlement."[29] The critical analysis of the evidence and the use of the traditional conceptual apparatus of the historiography should be supplemented: "[o]pening oneself to empathic unsettlement, as I intimated, to a desirable affective dimension of inquiry which complements and supplements

---

26   *Ibid.*, 78.
27   LaCapra does not reject the possibility of an empathic connection in the study of perpetrators, which may even be desirable (LaCapra, *Writing History*, 41, 102). We will develop this idea further in the next section.
28   *Ibid.*, xvi.
29   *Ibid.*, 41.

empirical research and analysis."[30] The notion of empathic unsettlement establishes the difference between empathy and identification.[31]

The affective component of empathy that is activated when the historian studies subjects who suffered traumatic events does not justify her transformation into a surrogate victim: "[e]mpathy is, I think, a virtual but not a vicarious experience in that the historian puts him or herself in the other's position without taking the other's place or becoming a substitute or surrogate for the other who is authorized to speak in the other's voice."[32] The historian can become a secondary witness but must resist a complete identification with the victims and refuse to take their place.[33] The condition of surrogate victim occurs when empathy is confused with identification and the voice of the historian speaks, without any mediation, as the voice of the victims instead. LaCapra revisits Kaja Silverman's concept of heteropathic identification "in which emotional response comes with respect to the other and the realization that the experience of the other is not one's own."[34] In this way, the historian's experience is virtual but not vicarious.

LaCapra points out another use of the *empathic unsettlement* when the subjects under study are not the victims but the *perpetrators*. In this case, empathy can also operate because it enables the recognition of perpetrators and victimizers as human beings rather than as expressions of a irrational evil.[35] Recovering the perpetrator's point of view is also a purpose of historical research because it allows us to understand the subjective conditions that made traumatic events possible. The destructive violence of historical traumas does not operate as a force of nature but requires human executors whose particular subjectivity must be understood.[36]

In the case of an empathic connection with the victims, the empathic unsettlement provides the antidote against the risk that the historian merges

---

30   Ibid., 78.
31   LaCapra distinguishes empathy "from conventional or traditional associations with identification leading to a putative identity between self and other, whether through projection or incorporation" (*Ibid.*, 38, footnote 46).
32   LaCapra, *History in Transit*, 65.
33   LaCapra, *Writing History*, 70–71.
34   Ibid., 40.
35   LaCapra, *History in Transit*, 65, footnote 28.
36   Remember that LaCapra differentiates between 'historical trauma' that refers to precise historical situations that affect a specific group of people and 'structural trauma' that points to a generally imaginary situation that involves all of us (*vid.* LaCapra, *Writing History*, 76–82).

with them and becomes a surrogate victim. Concerning the victimizers, rather than the undifferentiated identification the opposite can occur, that is, an extreme objectification that prevents recovering their condition as agents with restrictions and possibilities of action in a specific context.[37]

Nonetheless, LaCapra's analysis does not consider a fundamental aspect that distinguishes the study of the victims from the study of their victimizers: the different 'scenarios' in which each of them utters their voice. The historiography of the recent past and especially trauma studies, have focused on the testimonies of the victims, their production and use within a research framework. Theories have been developed and research has been done to address the ethical dimension implicit in the treatment of victims, the role of the transferential implication and the risks of re-victimization. As for the perpetrators, however, the current reflection is much less structured particularly because, in contrast to the abundance of testimonies of victims – survivors and more or less direct witnesses –, the testimonies of the perpetrators are available to a lesser extent.[38] Furthermore, the testimonies of the perpetrators usually take place within the framework of judicial processes rather than as part of the recovery of social memory or academic research.

Empathic unsettlement generates rich alternatives for research that involves those with whom it is difficult to establish an affective connection because of their involvement in criminal actions. We may resist an empathic relation with the victimizer, probably because we fear that rescuing their voices would mean justifying atrocious actions that we do not want to forgive. For these reasons, we believe that the concept of empathic unsettlement is a powerful tool that allows us to carry out an 'epistemological surveillance' on the affects we mobilize in research, not only on the positive ones (compassion and affection for the victims) but also on the rejection and repugnance we may feel towards the perpetrators.

6   The Uses of Empathic Unsettlement: an Example

The notion of empathic unsettlement is proposed by LaCapra as a strategy in trauma studies that prevents from the excesses of identification in the

---

[37]   *Ibid.*, 41. Concerning the understanding of the actions taken by the perpetrators, *vid.* LaCapra's criticisms of the 'negative sublime' and the 'sacrificial purification' (*Ibid.*, 135).

[38]   On the willingness of the perpetrators to produce their own testimonies (*vid.* LaCapra, Dominick, "Trauma, History, Memory, Identity: What Remains?", in *History and Theory*, vol. 55, no. 3 (2016): 380).

understanding of victims. We believe, however, that its use could be extended to other subjects. Historiography could further explore the use of empathic unsettlement as a powerful antidote to self-satisfying interpretations not only of the *recent* past, from which there are still survivors and direct witnesses, but also of the most *distant* past, transmitted from generation to generation. In fact, LaCapra himself suggested this idea when he refers to the topic of slavery in the United States.

Concerning the history of Argentina, the use of the empathic unsettlement would be helpful to study the historical events of the 19th century that could be called 'wars for the border.' For a long time, Argentinian historiography characterized as 'conquest of the desert' the armed struggle to establish a national state by advancing on territories first inhabited by indigenous peoples.[39] Nowadays, this paradigm is under discussion. A new approach to the territorial consolidation characteristic of the national state formation could present a good opportunity for applying the methodological strategies of empathy and empathic unsettlement.

Criticisms to traditional historiographical interpretations also questions crystallized senses about national identity (which include vague ideas about Argentine as a non-racist country or as one of the most European country in Latin American, among others). A historiographical work according to LaCapra's proposal would have to take into account how the members of the indigenous peoples, and their descendants today, have processed the experience of the struggle against the white man as well as their defeat. The recovery of the voices of these victims of state's violence should be done on their own terms without imposing 'translations' that empty the experiential content that has been transmitted from generation to generation. In order to recover the status of social subjects of those victims, the historian would have to appeal to empathy, that is, to the transferential implication. At the same time, the historiographical work must also be able to identify the multiple layers of meanings that were embedded over time in the available testimonies, as well as their contexts of utterance and circulation. In many cases, the testimonies of the members of different

---

39   We are referring here to the military campaigns carried out between 1875 and 1885 to conquer the lands currently known as Argentinian Patagonia. For an analysis that criticizes the traditional historiographical version of these campaigns *vid.* Delrio, Walter; Lenton, Diana; Musante, Marcelo, and Nagy, Mariano, "Discussing Indigenous Genocide in Argentina: Past, Present, and Consequences of Argentinean State Policies toward Native Peoples", in *Genocide Studies and Prevention: An International Journal*, vol. 5, no. 2 (2010): 138–159; Pérez, Pilar, "Historia y silencio: La Conquista del Desierto como genocidio no-narrado", in *Corpus*, vol. 1, no. 2 (2011): 1–9.

indigenous peoples and of their descendants were generated to counteract the constant denial of the state's violence of which they were victims and facilitate the construction of a collective (and subordinate) identity. The real violence inflicted by the state, which led to the nearly complete extermination of native peoples, had as a necessary counterpart the construction of the historiographical metaphor of 'desert' a central image used in school history books not long ago. The empathic unsettlement provides the historian with the necessary tools to recognize, through the testimonies and other available sources of the indigenous peoples, their capacities and possibilities of action even in their condition of victims. At the same time, it would also be a useful antidote to the romantic idealization of the indigenous life as a kind of golden age in close connection with nature that would have come to an end with the arrival of the white man. Following LaCapra's ideas, we could argue that this new approach to the study of the 'conquest of the desert' should not be restricted to an intra-academic debate but should also try to answer to the demands of recognition of those subjects hitherto marginalized from constructions of socially shared meanings.

7 Conclusion

We believe that the methodological strategies of empathy and empathic unsettlement are useful and valuable tools for historiographical work in a broader sense than that proposed by LaCapra. Although they can be more suitable for trauma studies, their value is not only restricted to them. They may also be very effective for the study of other historical events, such as the example of the foundation of Argentine state borders we previously mentioned. Nonetheless there is a condition to be met in order to employ empathy and empathic unsettlement: both can only apply to those past events that still pose questions to the present. These events still need to be worked through on a social level, as LaCapra would say, and not just treated as if they were a new item on the historiographical agenda. They are events that belong to a past that is never gone and as such still asks for answers in the present to the whole society (Translated by Marina Trakas).

Bibliography

Abel, Theodore, "The Operation called Verstehen", in *American Journal of Sociology*, vol. 54, no. 3 (1948): 211–218.

Collingwood, Robin G., *The Idea of History*, revised edition by J. Van der Dussen (Oxford: Oxford University Press, 1994).

Delrio, Walter; Lenton, Diana; Musante, Marcelo, and Nagy, Mariano, "Discussing Indigenous Genocide in Argentina: Past, Present, and Consequences of Argentinean State Policies toward Native Peoples", in *Genocide Studies and Prevention: An International Journal*, vol. 5, no. 2 (2010): 138–159. Available at: https://scholarcommons.usf.edu/cgi/viewcontent.cgi?referer=https://www.google.es/&httpsredir=1&article=1101&context=gsp. Viewed on the 20th October 2018.

Dilthey, Wilhelm, *Texte zur Kritik der historischen Vernunft*, edited by H-U. Lessing (Göttingen: Vandenhoeck & Ruprecht, 1983).

Dilthey, Wilhelm, *The Formation of the Historical World in the Human Sciences: Selected Works*, vol. III, edited by R.A. Makkreel and F. Rodi (Princeton-NJ: Princeton University Press, 2002).

Geertz, Clifford, "Thick Description: Toward an Interpretive Theory of Culture", in *The Interpretation of Cultures: Selected Essays* (New York: Basic Books, 1973), 3–30.

Giddens, Anthony, "Elements of the Theory of Structuration", in *The Constitution of Society: Outline of the Theory of Structuration* (Berkeley and Los Angeles: University of California Press, 1984), 1–40.

Koselleck, Reinhart, "Transformations of Experience and Methodological Change: A Historical-Anthropological Essay", in *The Practice of Conceptual History: Timing History, Spacing Concepts*, translated by Todd Samuel Presner et al. (California: Stanford University Press, 2002),.

Koselleck, Reinhart, *historia/Historia*, translated by A. Gómez Ramos (Madrid: Trotta, 2006).

LaCapra, Dominick, *History in Transit: Experience. Identity. Critical Theory* (Ithaca: Cornell University Press, 2004).

LaCapra, Dominick, *Writing History, Writing Trauma* (Baltimore: Johns Hopkins University Press, 2014).

LaCapra, Dominick, "Trauma, History, Memory, Identity: What Remains?", in *History and Theory*, vol. 55, no. 3 (2016): 375–400.

Lorenzo, Luis M., "Vida, historia y psicología en Wilhelm Dilthey", in *Tópicos*, no. 21 (2011): 1–23. Available at: http://www.scielo.org.ar/scielo.php?script=sci_arttext&pid=S1666-485X2011000100005&lng=es&tlng=es. Viewed on the 20th October 2018.

Moyn, Samuel, "Empathy in history, empathizing with humanity", in *History and Theory*, vol. 45, no. 3 (2006): 397–415.

Pérez, Pilar, "Historia y silencio: La Conquista del Desierto como genocidio no-narrado", in *Corpus*, vol. 1, no. 2 (2011): 1–9.Available at: http://journals.openedition.org/corpusarchivos/1157. Viewed on the 20th October 2018.

Scott, Joan W., "The Evidence of Experience", in *Critical Inquiry*, vol. 17, no. 4 (1991): 773–797.

CHAPTER 14

Empathy with Future Generations?
A Historical Approach to Global Justice

Johannes Rohbeck

Abstract

The central idea of this paper is that our contemporary historical awareness, which is turning increasingly towards future, is accessible to philosophical reflection. This raises issues about the need for a new Philosophy of History that refers less to past but more primarily to present and future problems. If a moral responsibility and even empathy for future generations is addressed thereby, the Philosophy of History goes hand in hand with Future Ethics. From the perspective of the Philosophy of History, the 'responsibility for future generations' needs to be discussed by referring to the relationship between successive generations. In the current state of Future Ethics, differing models for the understanding of the relationship of the present people to those of the future have evolved. The most basic model is the one of family care, which has the advantage of proximity to the lifeworld and empathy with the relatives, but is limited to the three generations living at the same time. The model of a dialogue between the present and the future generations and the one for constructing an intergenerational contract are also extremely widespread; these models may be extended into the remote future, but they remain fictive and abstract. Therefore, the problem is to find a model that is less fictive and, at the same time, may be related to the remote future. To complement these approaches, I propose the model of intergenerational heritage. This transcends the limited timeline of family care, and it is also more realistic than the constructions of a dialogue or a contract. Additionally, this model permits an available opening for the empathic handling of the inherited in the future.

Keywords

philosophy of history – heritage – intergenerational justice – historical responsibility

Nowadays, the Philosophy of History only plays a marginal role in the canon of philosophical disciplines. If it is referred to at all, this merely concerns methodological problems of historical research and representation in most cases. Consequently, emphasis is placed on the question of how historians evaluate their sources so as to clarify the meaning of declaring some matter as a historical fact. Thus, the problem arises what historiography refers to and how representations of the historic work. If historians do not simply depict events, they interpret history. In addition to the understanding of human action, this goes along with explaining historical processes, since the traditional contrast between these patterns of interpretation may be considered to be overcome by now. There is also a broad consensus that historical representation is basically narration, which is accessible for narratological analysis. In the course of the *linguistic turn*, interest is concentrated on the analysis of language and discourse. Complementing this, there are studies on collective memory and the culture of remembrance.

As this review shows, this is a reduction in the philosophical thinking about history. Some even speak of *atrophied stages* or of *leftover functions*.[1] However, this serves as a reminder that the Philosophy of History originally has faced further challenges. Here, the object is a philosophical discipline that developed almost exactly in the middle of the 18th century and that still has its adherents today. With regard to terminology, the difference between these two types of thinking may be expressed in calling the historical form a *Philosophy of History* [*Geschichtsphilosophie*] contrary to the current variant of a *philosophy of history* [*Philosophie der Geschichte*], which is restricted to methodological problems.[2]

There is no doubt that modern discourse analysis provided important methodological insights, but one should not conceal the losses accompanying this narrow perspective. On the contrary, the classical Philosophy of History,

---

1 Marquard, Odo, *Schwierigkeiten mit der Geschichtsphilosophie* (Frankfurt a.M.: Suhrkamp Verlag, 1973), 23-ff.; Nagl-Docekal analysed these 'atrophied stages' [*Schwundstufen*] in detail: Nagl-Docekal, Herta, "Ist Geschichtsphilosophie heute noch möglich?", in *Der Sinn des Historischen*, edited by H. Nagl-Docekal (Frankfurt/M.: Fischer Verlag, 1996), 7-ff.; Cf. with Lübbe, Hermann, *Geschichtsphilosophie. Verbliebene Funktionen* (Erlangen-Jena: Palm und Enke Verlag, 1993).
2 See, to that effect in Baumgartner, Hans Michael, *Kontinuität und Geschichte* (Frankfurt a.M.: Suhrkamp Verlag, 1972), 151-ff. The foundation of this reduction is the usual criticism relating to the Philosophy of History, which I have systematically summarised and rejected recently. *vid.* Rohbeck, Johannes, "Rettende Kritik der Geschichtsphilosophie, Immanuel Kant im historischen Kontext", in *Zeitschrift für kritische Sozialtheorie und Philosophie*, vol. 1, no. 2 (2014), 350–376; *vid.* Rohbeck, Johannes, *Aufklärung und Geschichte* (Berlin: Akademie Verlag, 2010), 54-ff.

stands out due to the reflection of content-related aspects of history. These include topics like the relationship between nature and history, the succession of generations and heritage, contingency and continuity, Enlightenment and the modern age, world history and globalisation, or global and intergenerational justice. This raises issues regarding the relation between historical times and spaces, as well as the specific direction of the historical process such as regression, stagnation, and progression, with their corresponding symbols of cycle, wave, and upward-pointing arrow. Essential to this analysis is a prospect for the future with practical intentions.

This classification gives rise to a distinction between a material *Philosophy of History* dealing with the content as described above, and a formal *philosophy of history* that is focused on methodological problems. Considering this, it might be conceivable that both types could coexist or be complementary with each other, just as the classical type – for example the Kantian – already knew how to combine content-related and methodological issues. Considering this patently obvious connection seriously, this strict separation into a material and a formal option does not appear to be very meaningful. In fact it seems natural to strive for a Philosophy of History that is both materially and methodically well reflected.

Provided that the described Philosophy of History is related less to events of the past but, rather, more to actions in the present with regard to the future, the problem arises regarding which way the future presents itself as a projection space ('*Projektionsraum*') and whether that may be considered as history at all. Indeed, it should be pointed out that the modern notion of future has emerged in the context of the Philosophy of History in the 18th century.[3] The Historicism of the 19th century teaches us that neither the future nor the past can be accessed directly. Rather, it is necessary to consider one's own standpoint and connection to the future, so as to obtain a reflexive relation to the future. In this manner, our relationship, not only to the past but also to the future, may be perceived as a hermeneutic circle. We project our present experiences onto the past and the future, just as the concepts about the future and the past influence our orientation in the present. This is also the background of Reinhart Koselleck's two notions of *space of experience* and *horizon of expectation*.[4] If a

---

[3] Hölscher, Lucian, *Die Entdeckung der Zukunft* (Frankfurt/M.: Fischer Taschenbuch Verlag, 1999), 9-ff.

[4] Koselleck, Reinhart, *Vergangene Zukunft* (Frankfurt/M.: Suhrkamp Verlag, 1979), 349-ff., 356; Koselleck, Reinhart, *Zeitschichten. Studien zur Historik* (Frankfurt/M.: Suhrkamp Verlag, 2003), 249; Rüsen, Jörn, *Historische Orientierung* (Köln-Weimar-Berlin: Wochenschau Verlag, 1994), 6-ff.

moral responsibility for future generations is thus addressed, the Philosophy of History goes hand in hand with *Future Ethics*.

This implies, according to Future Ethics, that this philosophical discipline opens itself to considerations from the perspective of the Philosophy of History and includes certain insights concerning the structure and the function of historical consciousness in its own theoretical basis. According to the *Philosophy of History*, this means that the discipline must, due to its future perspective, participate in solving current problems and ally with Practical Philosophy. This, I will now address the Practical Philosophy of History.

First, I assume history to be a time sequence of generations that is mediated by heritage. Because heritage enables a versatile approach, a horizon opens for a cultural change and an open process. This is linked to the ethical principle of autonomy, which shall be guaranteed by preventative measures. To structure the timeframe of such actions, I use the concept of the *deadline* (*'Frist'*) that allows a gradation of the ranges of moral responsibility in scope and time, relative to their *fields of action*. Because this leads to the global dimension, the question also arises as to whether the often-demanded catch-up development of disadvantaged peoples can be justified. For this purpose, I analyse the historical structure of such a development and formulate an ethical norm that is genuine based on the Philosophy of History, a norm that I consider to be the request for greater autonomy and development.

1 Generation and Heritage

From the perspective of the Philosophy of History, the 'responsibility for future generations' needs to be discussed by referring to the relationship between successive generations. In the current state of Future Ethics, differing models for the understanding of the relationship of the present people to those of the future have evolved. The most basic model is the one of *family care*, which has the advantage of proximity to the lifeworld, but is limited to the three generations living at the same time.[5] In this area we are able to perceive empathy

---

5 Jonas, Hans, *Das Prinzip Verantwortung* (Frankfurt/M.: Suhrkamp Verlag, 1979), 84, 197-ff.; Laslett, Peter, "Is There a Generational Contract?", in *Justice between Age Groups and Generations*, edited by P. Laslett and J. S. Fishkin (New Haven-London: Yale University Press, 1992), 24-ff.; Höffe, Otfried, *Moral als Preis der Moderne* (Frankfurt/M.: Suhrkamp Verlag, 1993), 182; Unnerstall, Herwig, *Rechte zukünftiger Generationen* (Würzburg: Königshausen und Neumann, 1999), 66; Leist, Anton, "Ökologische Gerechtigkeit", in *Angewandte Ethik. Die Bereichsethiken und ihre theoretische Fundierung. Ein Handbuch*, edited by J. Nida-Rümelin (Stuttgart: Alfred Kröner Verlag, 2005), 459-ff.; Birnbacher, Dieter, "Langzeitverantwortung – das

with future generations. The model of a *dialogue*⁶ between the present and the future generations and the one for constructing an *intergenerational contract*⁷ are also extremely widespread; these models may be extended into the remote future, but they remain fictive and abstract. Therefore, the problem is to find a model that is less fictive and, at the same time, may be related to the remote future.

To complement these approaches, I propose the model of *intergenerational heritage*. This transcends the limited timeline of family care, and it is also more realistic than the constructions of a dialogue or a contract. Additionally, this model permits an available opening for the handling of the inherited in the future.

In addition to the concept of generations, the model of heritage originates from the Philosophy of History of the 18th century.⁸ With this, there is a necessary combination of generation and heritage.

As far as the concept of the generation may be understood, not only synchronously⁹ but also in diachronically, the notion of heritage characterises the connection within the succession of generations.

Accordingly, a generation is a social group that preserved a heritage from the preceding group bequeathing it to the next. There is no generation that

---

Problem der Motivation", in *Langzeitverantwortung. Ethik – Technik – Ökologie*, edited by C. F. Gethmann and J. Mittelstraß (Darmstadt: Wissenschaftliche Buchgesellschaft, 2008), 33; Böhler, Dietrich, *Zukunftsverantwortung in globaler Perspektive* (Bad Homburg: VAS Verlag, 2009), 29.

6   Gethmann, Carl Friedrich, "Langzeitverantwortung als ethisches Problem im Umweltstaat", in *Langzeitverantwortung im Umweltstaat*, edited by C. F. Gethmann, M. Kloepfer and H. G. Nutzinger (Bonn: Economica-Verlag, 1993), 12; Ott, Konrad and Döring, Ralf, *Theorie und Praxis starker Nachhaltigkeit* (Marburg: Metropolis Verlag, 2008), 92; Böhler, *Zukunftsverantwortung*, 28-ff., 84-ff.

7   Rawls, John, *Eine Theorie der Gerechtigkeit* (Frankfurt/M.: Suhrkamp Verlag, 1979), 319-ff.; see also Laslett, "Is There a Generational Contract?", 24-ff.; Höffe, *Moral als Preis*, 183; Veith, Werner, *Intergenerationelle Gerechtigkeit* (Stuttgart: W. Kohlhammer Verlag, 2006), 127; Heubach, Andrea, *Generationengerechtigkeit – Herausforderung für die zeitgenössische Ethik* (Göttingen: V&R Unipress, 2008), 136-ff.; Ott and Döring, *Theorie und Praxis*, 96-ff.; Tremmel, Jörg, *Eine Theorie der Generationengerechtigkeit* (Münster: Mentis Verlag, 2012), 221-ff.

8   Turgot defined history as the tradition of a cultural treasure that is given from one generation to the next, like a heritage, *vid.* Turgot, Anne Robert Jacques, *Über die Fortschritte des menschlichen Geistes* (Frankfurt/M.: Suhrkamp, 1990), 140; See Rohbeck, *Aufklärung und Geschichte*, 126-ff.; Rohbeck, Rohbeck, Johannes, *Zukunft der Geschichte. Geschichtsphilosophie und Zukunftsethik* (Berlin: De Gruyter Akademie Forschung, 2013), 130-ff.

9   This synchronic understanding of the term *generation* dominates in the 20th century; see, for example Mannheim, Karl, "Das Problem der Generation", in *Wissenssoziologie*, edited by K. Mannheim (Berlin: Neuwied Verlag, 1964), 509-ff.

does not inherit and transmit, just as there is no heritage that is not bestowed by one generation to the next. Heritage is constitutive for a cultural process, because the following generations are heirs, and the present generations are testators who both, each in their own way, have to assume a special responsibility for that heritage.

First, the relation between the generations is connected by an inheritance that is legally regulated. However, the collective heritage is essential for Future Ethics.[10] It refers to the heritage between the generations that may be understood as a historical sequence of populations, including regional or ethnic groups, peoples, or nation states, culminating in a world community, so that national heritages can be distinguished from global inheritance.

This permits the specifying of intergenerational heritage. This clarification includes economic prosperity and material goods such as public buildings, traffic systems and communication systems. In addition, cultural heritage appears in the form of traditional knowledge, education, language, art, and religion. The social heritage consists of institutions or, rather, several kinds of social rules.[11] Since the beginning of the ecological crisis, the natural environment is also understood as a heritage that is given to the next generation.[12] Admittedly, this inheritance often turns out to be anything but positive. The negative examples include the tremendous indebtedness of several countries, world poverty, the polluted environment, the shortage of natural resources,

---

10   Hauff, Volker (ed.), *Unsere gemeinsame Zukunft. Der Brundtland-Bericht der Weltkommission für Umwelt und Entwicklung* (Greven: Eggenkamp Verlag, 1987), 259-ff.; Compare with Jonas, *Das Prinzip*, 72; Meyer, Lukas, *Historische Gerechtigkeit: Ideen und Argumenten* (Berlin-New York: Walter De Gruyter Verlag, 2005), 135-ff.

11   The notion of capital is quite often used in this context. Thus, this notion is larger than the traditional concept of capital and contains both social and cultural aspects, and the economisation of all life areas is quite problematic. This can be shown with regard to the term of social capital and within the following debate: Putnam, Robert D. (ed.), *Gesellschaft und Gemeinsinn* (Gütersloh: Bertelsmann Stiftung Verlag, 2001), 19, 24; *vid.* Kopfmüller, Jürgen; Brandl, Volker; Jörissen, Juliane; Paetau, Michael; Banse, Gerhard; Coenen, Reinhard, and Grunwald, Armin (eds.), *Nachhaltige Entwicklung integrativ betrachtet: Konstitutive Elemente, Regeln, Indikatoren* (Berlin: Edition Sigma, 2001), 68-ff.; Ott and Döring, *Theorie und Praxis*, 145; Tremmel, *Eine Theorie der Generationengerechtigkeit*, 119-ff.; Tremmel is criticised in Bourdieu, Pierre, "Ökonomisches Kapital, kulturelles Kapital, soziales Kapital", in *Soziale Ungleichheiten*, edited by R. Kreckel (Göttingen: Schwartz, 1983), 183, 190.

12   See the agreement of the cultural and natural world heritage of UNESCO in 1972: Weikard, Hans-Peter, *Wahlfreiheit für zukünftige Generationen* (Marburg: Metropolis Verlag, 1999), 130; Heubach, *Generationengerechtigkeit*, 61-ff.

and climate change. In these cases, a collective-character evil becomes inherited as well.

Again, I utilise the contrast of the model of heritage compared to the models of family care, dialogue, and intergenerational contract so as to analyse the structure of this kind of transmission. The latter models indeed have their own 'subject' but, apart from that, only feature a two-member relationship. The model of family care is based on the immediate interaction of people existing at the same time. In comparison, the model of heritage does not imply a direct communication between the generations, but represents a form of *mediation*. With heritage, a real *middle* occurs between the successive generations. This dynamic constitutes a *three-member relationship* that cannot be reduced to two members. This involves goods that exist, independent from their specific testators and heirs, as discrete entities. This induces an idiosyncratic ambivalence.

On one hand, the inherited goods are not neutral objects; specific ways of use and, therefore, certain ways of life are embodied in these goods. Within their thingness, they represent certain human lifeforms and values. Atomic power mediates a different attitude towards nature than alternative forms of energy generation. A city that is car-friendly means a different lifestyle compared to a city with a developed system of public transport. With respect to such a heritage, the testators not only create the conditions of future lifeworlds, but they also affect the preferences of future people.

Contrarily, it is optional for the future generations, to a certain extent, how they handle the inherited goods. That the heritage works like an objective *means* that it can be used in several ways. The legacy comes along with restrictions, as well as with new potential for the user. That is why this model permits the making of free access to the heritage thinkable and desirable. This format opens a horizon of real possibilities that can be exhausted by the descendants at their own discretion. Thus, the heritage is an *ethical* category. For the people living at present, this nuance implies an imperative to leave behind a 'good' heritage and to allow scopes for an autonomous assuming of the inherited goods.

2   Limited Openness of History

This ambivalent function of the heritage may be generalized with regard to history. Behind this idea of the most flexible use of the heritage is the concept of history as an *open historical process*. Provided that autonomy is desirable in general, this implies the moral imperative that future generations are not only allowed to change their way of living, but that this should be facilitated by specific measures. The enabling of cultural change must be considered to be the moral obligation to recognise the right to the self-determination of every generation. For the very reason that we cannot know the preferences of future generations, we are obligated to guarantee the conditions for their greatest possible freedom of choice.

However, to support such living conditions, it is necessary to introduce *limitations* to the openness of history as well. The future must not enable all prospects, if this will lead to certain danger. That would, in fact, lead to a radical kind of liberalism and, as a result, to the loss of every long-term responsibility. Actually, the principle of the openness of history and the idea of responsibility for future generations would then be contradictory. The limitation of history refers to the surrounding lifeworld, to the conservation of natural resources, to the infrastructure, and to adequate public finances. Thus, the relationship between openness and limitation of history must be redefined.

On the other side, the principle of openness of history prohibits the projection of the current development of the modern scientific-technological civilisation into future.[13] The historical experience of the transformation of modern societies leads to the expectation that there will be such cultural change in the future as well. This suggests ensuring the conditions for the possibility of this development. For example, we should not only inherit certain kinds of transport systems, but the freedom to revise these systems and, in general, to redefine the value of mobility. Intergenerational cooperation projects like space travel should be designed flexibly, so that future generations have the possibility to change plans or even to stop projects. Following Niklas Luhmann's Theory of Double Contingency, I want to formulate a *triple contingency*. The double contingency results from simultaneous communicative interaction.[14] It consists of the uncertainty of reciprocal interpretations, when

---

13 Traditional Future Ethics persist with the common historical process by assuming that future generations will have new technologies, but would have the same desires, so that the aggregate benefit of all people could be defined. *vid.* Birnbacher, Dieter, *Verantwortung für zukünftige Generationen* (Stuttgart: Reclam, 1988), 101-ff.; Criticized in Höffe, *Moral als Preis*, 184; Weikard, *Wahlfreiheit*, 10; Leist, "Ökologische Gerechtigkeit", 470; Sturma, Dieter, "Die Gegenwart der Langzeitverantwortung", in *Recht, Gerechtigkeit und Freiheit*, edited by C. Langbehn (Paderborn: Mentis Verlag, 2006), 230. It is also problematic to measure the 'benefit' of future generations by referring to the Human Development Index (HDI): Tremmel, *Eine Theorie der Generationengerechtigkeit*, 153, 193-ff.

14 Luhmann, Niklas, *Soziale Systeme* (Frankfurt/M.: Suhrkamp Taschenbuch Verlag, 1984), 154.

one person cannot be sure if she/he was understood correctly by the other. This contingency belongs to the present, where the options are discussed and the decisions concerning precautionary policies are made. The third contingency originates from the additional time dimension of the future, meaning with reference to the people involved in the future. The uncertainties of the present are increased, due to the contingencies of the people living in the future and their interpretations and actions. It remains uncertain which future generations will handle the legacies and how they will evaluate them. This implies discontinuity.

Conversely, the principle of openness of history needs to be placed into perspective, as the principle of autonomy should not be absolutized. Every free choice is constituted by the historical conditions in which the decision occurs. These conditions *limit* the horizon of possibilities, as well as certain conditions that are needed to enlarge the radius of action. This gives rise to the task of formulating an alternative model of openness of the historical process according to the principle of autonomy and, also, to practical implementation.

The freedom of choice is not to be confused with arbitrariness. It would be a misunderstanding to postulate an 'open' future with no regulations at all. In contrast, it might be unavoidable, under certain circumstances, to limit options in the future. This is exemplified by the fictive choice, for example, that people of future epochs would give up nature and prefer air-conditioned rooms. This would miss the point, to argue that it cannot be ruled out that future individuals may value untouched nature. Rather, it is particularly necessary to ensure that environmental protection remains a moral concept in the future so as to prevent such an absurd alternative from occurring.

The fact that every choice depends on conditions implies that appropriate circumstances must be created, so as to guarantee as many options as possible. This, in turn, leads to an avoidance of specific conditions that are dangerous and would impair the realisation of particular needs and interests. Only on these terms, can the scope of options be preserved at all, or changed for in order to permit progress. In addition to the openness of history, it is necessary to avoid risks. For these reasons, a *limited openness* is appropriate.

This plea is consistent with the postulate of *continuity* in history that prevents rendering contingency into an absolute.[15] We need alternatives to the present course of action that leave the failed paths of unquestioned

---

15   In opposition to the transcendental-philosophical analysis in Baumgartner, Hans Michael, *Kontinuität und Geschichte* (Frankfurt a.M.: Suhrkamp Verlag, 1972); linked to this Zwenger, Thomas, *Geschichtsphilosophie. Eine kritische Grundlegung* (Darmstadt: Wissenschaftliche Buchgesellschaft, 2008).

industrialisation, yet this goal, an economic and ecologic turn, needs to be grounded in binding agreements that are valid over longer periods, national and global.[16] If, for example, governments commit to certain climate objectives, this can only succeed if there are long-term guarantees to ensure this. For that reason, long-term responsibility presupposes historical continuity, and actions that are followed continuously can only make this kind of responsibility even possible.

3 Deadlines of Historical Responsibility

From the previous discussion, history could be understood as a diachronic succession of generations mediated by heritage. This results in the challenge to maintain concern for the conditions that determinate a free handling of heritage. Certain measures are meant to create historical continuities that continue well into future periods. Diachronic bridges need to be achieved through future-oriented actions.

This imperative is even more demanding because the depth of intervention by new technologies has enlarged drastically. The questions are how far-reaching human actions may become and to what extent humans are responsible for them. In the context of ethics that not only consider the 'near', but also

---

[16] An example of this continuity is the question of whether future living people do have a right to self-determination or if they do 'have' rights at all. The answer that we 'attribute' certain rights is still unsatisfactory if there is no anticipation of a continuity within our social and cultural praxis. *vid.* Baier, Annette, "The Rights of Past and Future Persons", in *Responsibilities to Future Generations: Environmental Ethics*, edited by Ernest Partridge (New York: Prometheus Books, 1980), 171-ff.; Plechter, Galen K., "The Rights of Future Generations", in *Responsibilities to Future Generations. Environmental Ethics*, edited by E. Partridge (New York: Prometheus Books, 1980), 167-ff.; Feinberg, Joel, "Die Rechte der Tiere und zukünftigen Generationen", in *Ökologie und Ethik*, edited by D. Birnbacher (Stuttgart: Reclam, 1980), 170; Warren, Mary Anne, "Do Potential Persons Have Rights?", in *Responsibilities to Future Generations: Environmental Ethics*, edited by E. Partridge (New York: Prometheus Books, 1980), 261-ff.; De George, Richard T., "The Environment, Rights, and Future Generations", in *Responsibilities to Future Generations: Environmental Ethics*, edited by E. Partridge (New York: Prometheus Books, 1980), 157-ff.; Birnbacher, *Verantwortung für zukünftige Generationen*, 98-ff.; Beckerman, Wilfred, "Intergenerational Justice", in *Intergenerational Justice Review*, no. 2 (2004), 4; Tremmel, Jörg, "Is a Theory of Intergenerational Justice Possible?", in *Intergenerational Justice Review*, no. 2 (2004), 6; Meyer, *Historische Gerechtigkeit*, 29; Heubach, *Generationgerechtigkeit*, 111-ff.; Gesang, Bernward, *Klimaethik* (Frankfurt/M.: Suhrkamp Verlag, 2011), 136.

the 'remote' and 'distant' future,[17] the problem of the range of responsibility and empathy for future generations arises.

However, this is not only an ethical issue, but also one regarding the Philosophy of History, as the period between the present and the future living generations is not an abstract time unit: it must be understood as a tangible, *historical time period*. Human actions are constitutive to specific historical scopes that depend on the temporal and spatial structure of the respective fields of activity.

It is particularly important in this regard to specify a responsibility for the future that is understood as a part of history. For this purpose, I suggest the term *deadline*, which is taken from the Philosophy of History as well. In addition, I apply to the future specific categories that come from the phenomenological theory of history.

To emphasise the historical dimension of responsibility for future generations, I differentiate my perspective from two contrary positions. Ethical universalism suggests the postulation of unlimited responsibility concerning all people in all times and places.[18] However, irrespective of how justified this universalist formulation may be, it is questionable to conclude that no time specifications might be allowed concerning the ascription of responsibility. The limitation of responsibility to a 'median' length, or to the three generations, remains abstract as well.[19] The choice between an unlimited responsibility and a limited responsibility relative to the near future is not convincing at all.

17　Future Ethics distinguish between a 'near' and a 'remote' future. While traditional ethics are limited to the 'near' future, Future Ethics refer to the 'remote' future. *vid.* Jonas, *Das Prinzip Verantwortung*, 215; Birnbacher, *Verantwortung für zukünftige Generationen*, 24, 156; Birnbacher, Dieter, "Verantwortung für zukünftige Generation – Reichweite und Grenzen", in *Handbuch Generationengerechtigkeit*, edited by Stiftung für die Rechte zukünftiger Generationen (München: Ökom Verlag, 2003), 81; Heubach, *Generationgerechtigkeit*, 13, 134; Veith, *Intergenerationelle Gerechtigkeit*, 12, 153-ff.

18　Jonas, *Das Prinzip Verantwortung*, 9, 89, 245. Against the preference of time: Rawls, *Eine Theorie der Gerechtigkeit*, 319-ff.; *vid.* Parfit, Derek, "On Doing the Best for Our Children", in *Ethics and Population*, edited by M. Bayles (Cambridge-MA: Schenkman Publishing Co., 1976), 100-ff.; Parfit, Derek, "Future Generations: Further Problems", in *Philosophy & Public Affairs*, vol. 11, no. 2 (1981), 113-ff.; Laslett, "Is There a Generational Contract?", 24-ff.; Veith, *Intergenerationelle Gerechtigkeit*, 127. According to temporal neutrality, see: Ekardt, Felix, *Das Prinzip Nachhaltigkeit. Generationengerechtigkeit und globale Gerechtigkeit* (München: C. H. Beck, 2005), 59, 83; Veith, *Intergenerationelle Gerechtigkeit*, 156.

19　To avoid this opposition of responsibilities, other theories refer to a temporal 'limitation' of responsibility: Gethmann, "Langzeitverantwortung als ethisches Problem ...",

In contrast, my thought is to phase the scope of responsibility in space and time. Provided that the temporal extension of ethics is prompted by the new effectiveness of modern technologies, these scopes of action are decisive for the shifting of responsibility towards the future. Responsibility for future generations may well be limited in some cases, so as to achieve a frequently demanded reduction of distress. Furthermore, the time periods must certainly be extended, as far as the consequences of technical practice and its dangers determine appropriate behaviour. This proposal encourages advances toward those who are afraid of excessive moral demands of humans, but rejects an absolute demarcation of moral responsibility.

The term of *deadline* is suitable for this differentiation. This notion is, with modifications, taken from Günter Anders' Philosophy of History in his essay *Endzeit und Zeitende [The Final Hours and the End of All Time]*.[20] According to Anders, with the end of the Cold War, there is no *single* deadline for *the* catastrophe to occur or to be prevented. Rather, *several deadlines* occur. There are several dates or even deadly marks (literally *dead-lines*) that must not be exceeded. While history had been designated *unlimited* during the epoch of Enlightenment,[21] certain *limits* now exist within history.

Deadlines *are scopes of action* within which certain effects must be realised. People in the present are responsible for them. Consequential, there are deadlines of *actions*, of *effects*, and of *responsibilities*. *Deadlines of action* are those limits of history within which we must act to protect or to achieve desirable conditions in, or to prevent danger from, the future. The *deadlines of effects* result from the deadlines of action. There is a need to precisely specify the time periods toward which the effects of actions, as defined by the temporal ranges of technological practices, are aimed. The relationship between actions and effects is predicated by *deadlines of responsibility*. As people are concerned with certain effects or focus on particular results, they are responsible. This implies a content-, time-, and space-related horizon: A person, or an institution, is responsible for events related to certain places and times, insofar as these events belong to the person's sphere of action. Within this precondition, it is possible to vary responsibilities for the future corresponding to deadlines.

This notion of the deadline is concurrently *descriptive* and *normative*. First, deadlines refer to certain *situations* that are defined by a constellation of particular *facts*. Their temporal dimension depends on the scopes of human

---

15; Birnbacher, "Verantwortung für zukünftige Generation ...", 82; Leist, "Ökologische Gerechtigkeit", 4; Sturma, "Die Gegenwart der Langzeitverantwortung", 221-ff.
20   Anders, Günther, *Die atomare Bedrohung* (München: C.H. Beck, 1986), 170, 203.
21   Blumenberg, Hans, *Lebenszeit und Weltzeit* (Frankfurt/M: Suhrkamp Verlag, 1986), 180-ff.

actions and on the prospects of certain effects. Due to the remote effects of technology and ecology, future is structured according to the contents of these factual fields. Various spatial and temporal deadlines may be identified relative to these fields. Moreover, deadlines refer to certain *objectives* that must be accomplished within specified time periods, because deadlines represent expected, feared, or desired conditions for which people or institutions are responsible. Deadlines consist of an agenda for what must be done, and when. When they are defined in this way, they are morally charged and ethically connoted.

The categories developed by the historian Ferdinand Braudel, following the phenomenology of Edmund Husserl and Henri Bergson, are relevant in this context.[22] Just as a 'short', a 'medium' and a 'long' duration of time with regard to past history may be differentiated, different future periods may be forecasted as well; this depend on various fields of action, each with regard to their specific objects.

Long-lasting deadlines are generated by technological and ecological praxis. The long-term orientation is less related to preventive actions that take place within a few decades, but more to the effects of these actions that, due to technology, extend far into the future. We are responsible for these effects even if, at such time, measurement is involved. We are obligated to these delineations even though we do not imagine the affected people and have no empathic relationship with them. Extremely long durations result from the management of radioactive waste; they must be kept away from the biosphere for actually immeasurable time periods.[23] With respect to these durations, the three hundredth or even the thousandth future generation is definitively real and tangible.

Despite the enormous temporal distance, the present people are, with a doubt, responsible for such long-lasting effects. This responsibility is not just based on universalist ethics, which attribute the fundamental interest concerning health and the appropriate moral rights to all people at all times, making we people of the present responsible. This is also, necessarily due to the actual far-reaching effects and long-distance dangers of modern nuclear technologies. If present action can minimize this risk, there is a concrete obligation that

---

22 Braudel, Ferdinand, *Schriften zur Geschichte 1. Gesellschaften und Zeitstrukturen* (Stuttgart: Klett-Cotta, 1992), 49-ff.; Cf. with Koselleck, Reinhart, *Zeitschichten. Studien zur Historik* (Frankfurt/M.: Suhrkamp Verlag, 2003), 287-ff.

23 Kornwachs, Klaus, *Das Prinzip der Bedingungserhaltung: Eine Ethische Studie* (Münster: LIT Verlag, 2000), 106; Böhler, *Zukunftsverantwortung*, 44-ff.; Leggewie, Klaus and Welzer, Harald, *Das Ende der Welt, wie wir sie kannten* (Frankfurt/M.: Fischer Verlag, 2009), 11.

definitely transcends the limits of the previously mentioned three generations, or the medium reach. Limitations of responsibility, in general, would even be negligent in this case.

The short periods refer to specific events within history, mostly regarding the reach of political decisions. This applies equally to short duration deadlines in the future. Insofar social systems are affected, these periods primarily concern financial crises, which necessitate a rapid response: within just a few months, weeks, days, or hours. In such cases, the people are responsible for the next generation affected, which explicitly means not for the people following after that generation. The abstract obligation towards this time limitation is not practically relevant in this case.

Similarly, different fields of action define the *medium-duration deadlines* as well. Their temporal background depends on natural and social systems that inherit specifically historic time lengths. Medium-duration periods are exemplified by natural resources. As the oil crises of 1973 – 1974 and 1979 – 1980 caused a great wave of discovery of new oil reserves, the global oil peak will occur (about 35 years later) within this decade or in the near future. If consumption levels remain the same, fossil fuels, especially oil, will deplete in 2050 or its use will be at least submarginal.[24] The time left to avoid the negative effects of climate change, which should last up to hundreds of years, are in the medium term as well.[25] According to these fields, actions within the next one to two decades are unavoidable. However, the deadlines of responsibility last beyond this, because we are responsible for those generations directly affected. On this occasion, moral responsibility must be extended beyond the realm of the three generations.

This is especially problematic, insofar as that the deadlines not only refer to the future, but to the *past* as well.[26] Certain climate objectives do have a *prospective* as well as a *retrospective* aspect, because they are geared to a former stage of industrialisation. If it is necessary to return to former stages, this means a demand for *revisions*.

For example, climate researchers require reducing the global emission of greenhouse gases to its 1990 levels by the middle of the 21th century. The year

---

24 *Ibid.*, 12.
25 Welzer, Harald, *Klimakriege. Wofür im 21. Jahrhundert getötet wird* (Frankfurt/M.: S. Fischer Verlag, 2008), 57; Leggewie and Welzer, *Das Ende der Welt*, 27, 68, 167; Gesang, *Klimaethik*, 15-ff.
26 At this point, I cannot discuss the complex problem of *if and how* the cause of damage in the past could be compensated in the present and the future. *vid.* Rohbeck, *Zukunft der Geschichte*, 92-ff.

1990 is important because, since then, most of the traditional industrialized nations have not increased emissions significantly.[27] Other examples that are more realistic and already indicate success are the recovery of polluted waters, the cleaning of air, the reduction of spreading desert areas, the prevention of soil erosion, the reforestation of cleared woodlands, and the recovery of fish populations in the oceans – with the objective of restabilising natural systems, such as the climate, or reclaiming ecological systems, such as in the case of resources, within certain time periods. The evaluation criteria formulated in these cases aim to re-establish previous conditions.

These phenomena refer to the *principle of reversibility*. This means not only reversing specific technologies, but also creating new technologies that enable their own self-correction.

This principle, applied to history as a whole, leads to a *cyclical understanding of history*.[28] However, the absolutisation of the circle conflicts with our modern awareness of the uniqueness of historical times. The contraposition between the natural cycle and the progress of civilization is problematic as well, as nature implies not only cycles but also unidirectional processes, like the chain of successive generations. Conversely, certain cycles, like the reproduction of humans or the processes of social institutions, are embodied within history. Although history contains partial cycles, it remains, from this perspective, an irreversible process. Therefore, it is important to integrate the principle of reversibility into future processes of history.

4   Justice in World History

Deadlines indicate not only temporal but also spatial dimension. There is a need to more precisely define which generations, in which places, and in which times that we need to sustain by creating certain types of living conditions,[29]

---

27   Ott and Döring, *Theorie und Praxis*, 336.
28   According to the concept of 'strict sustainability', the cycle of nature and the linear process of industrialisation seem to exclude each other: Enge, Kristin, *Zeit und Nachhaltigkeit. Die Wiederentdeckung der Naturzeiten als Ausgangspunkt für den Übergang zu einer Nachhaltigen Entwicklung* (Berlin: Akademische Abhandlungen zur Raum- und Umweltforschung, 2000), 68. More useful is the term 'Wiederholungsstruktur' in Koselleck, Reinhart, *Vom Sinn und Unsinn der Geschichte* (Frankfurt/M., Suhrkam Verlag, 2010), 96-ff.
29   The thesis must, therefore, be dismissed in that there is an ecological globalization that 'mankind' is affected by. *vid.* Lienkamp uses the term 'catastrophic-egalitarianism'

as the prognosticated ecological and financial crises will certainly show significantly different impacts on certain peoples living in different geographical territories. This results in a *historical map of the future*, on which certain areas indicate desired, critical, or threatening conditions. If one includes the historical past, the situations marked on this map may be understood as the results of different developments, whereby the less developed countries deserve the maximum support.

This phenomenon may be described using a category from the Philosophy of History called the *simultaneity of the non-simultaneous* [*Gleichzeitigkeit des Ungleichzeitigen*]. Following Ernst Bloch, non-simultaneity is not simply understood as backwardness, but as a *disallowed* historic possibility, more precisely, as the historical *undone* and *unfinished*.[30] With respect to the diverging processes of the present, the objective is to synchronize the non-simultaneity. This *synchronization* refers to ecological divergences within the relationship between nature and culture, as well as to global non-simultaneities of modernisation between different peoples and cultures.

A problem arises, as to whether less developed countries may claim the right to catch up regarding developments that have been already executed by the industrialised countries. The notions of 'catch-up development' and the ideas of 'sustainable development' are, therefore, up for discussion.[31] However, if countries are to exercise the right to catch-up development, this implies a synchronisation of divergent levels of progress. The foundation for this right is related to the Philosophy of History. I will illustrate the theoretical implications and then provide a normative foundation.

The Philosophy of History during the epoch of *Enlightenment* addressed 'mankind' as analogous to an individual that progresses and develops its

---

(Lienkamp, Andreas, *Klimawandel und Gerechtigkeit* (Paderborn: Ferdinand Schoningh Verlag, 2009), 340).

30 Bloch, Ernst, *Das Prinzip Hoffnung*, 4 Band (Frankfurt/M.: Suhrkamp Verlag, 1977), 104-ff.; with reference to Benjamin, Walter, *Gesammelte Schriften*, Band I.2 (Frankfurt/M.: Suhrkamp Verlag, 1974), 697.

31 With regard to this term, see: Paehlke, Robert C., *Environmentalism and the Future of Progressive Politics* (New Haven-London: Yale University Press, 1989), 113; Bartelmus, Peter, *Environment, Growth and Development: The Concepts and Strategies of Sustainability* (London: Routledge, 1994), 78-ff.; Enge, *Zeit und Nachhaltigkeit*, 9, 65; Ekardt, *Das Prinzip Nachhaltigkeit*, 29; Veith, *Intergenerationelle Gerechtigkeit*, 167-ff.; Grunwald, Armin and Kopfmüller, Jürgen, *Nachhaltigkeit* (Frankfurt/M.: Campus Studium, 2006), 49-ff.; Ott and Döring, *Theorie und Praxis*, 41-ff.; Böhler, *Zukunftsverantwortung*, 16; Heintel, Peter and Krainer, Larissa, "Geschichtlich-kulturelle Nachhaltigkeit", in *Erwägen Wissen Ethik*, vol. 4, no. 21(2010), 438.

'perfectibility.'[32] Universal history means, in this case: The downfall of certain peoples serves the progress of the human species.

Whereas single peoples rise and fall, as in the model of the age of life, mankind as a whole is not damaged at all because it develops continuously. A completely different interpretation of this progress is achieved by *historicism,* which rejected the perspective of world history and, thereby, the idea of a comparable development at all. This implies that earlier epochs, which seem to be less developed from the perspective of the present, should not be devaluated because every people and every culture have the same right to happiness.[33] According to this perspective, it would be unjust for a people to be favoured due to their participation in 'progress.' The *concept of catch-up development* presents itself as a synthesis of these two types of historical thinking. It combines classical Philosophy of History and its perspective on progress – though with no group of people considered to be a real subject – with historicism and its national standpoint, but without its radical critique of civilisation. According to this perspective, all people have the right to participate in the process of global civilisation.

Furthermore, to give a normative foundation to the right postulated above, the question arises whether this foundation is limited to the project applying common theories of justice, which are well-established at the time being, to the near, far, or even remote future. Instead, are there specific *norms* from the *Philosophy of History* to be asserted in this case?

Classical Philosophy of History was characterised by its future-orientation and, therefore, by its action-orientation. Its purpose was not only to philosophically reflect upon past events and processes, but also to give functional orientation to a forward-looking praxis.

The concept of progress was not restricted to the description of developments, but contained the positive assessment of achievements of civilisation. This focus was linked with the hope for future progress, like the imperative to improve future conditions for the living.

Today, the idea of progress may seem problematic, due to its contribution to aberrations, but it is still an important concern to address the welfare of future generations and strive for better conditions for the living or, at least, to provide that there will be no major deterioration.

---

32   In detail: *vid.* Rohbeck, *Aufklärung und Geschichte,* 54-ff.
33   With Jonas, I refer to the dictum that every nation is 'actual with god': von Ranke, Leopold, *Über die Epochen der neueren Geschichte* (München-Wien: Oldenbourg Verlag, 1971), 59; see also Jonas, *Das Prinzip Verantwortung,* 287.

This includes the creation of conditions for the possibility of more autonomy and further developments. This may be considered a genuine norm of the Philosophy of History, one that can claim validity even at the present time.

The absolution and the teleological superelevation of the concept of progress may be avoided by limiting the expectation of progress to certain areas and by differentiating it due to its spatial and temporal aspects. This demand for an improvement in a global, historical context is at the essence of a reason for justice in world history as achieved by the Philosophy of History.

This demand contains the historical consciousness that the conditions of possibility for human praxis extend within the historical process and that modern civilisation is, thereby, open for new horizons.[34] Provided that interest in this progress may be presupposed, this implies that the practical intention not to be satisfied with absolute and often minimal standards,[35] as soon as they assume prerequisites for the enhancement of their quality of live.[36] When they believe that these prerequisites permit an improvement in their standards of living, people will articulate this recognition and make appropriate demands. Citizens of less developed nations will claim this right, particularly as they recognise their possibilities being realised as tangible realities in rich countries. A corresponding appeal is justified as far as it can be realised according to the contingent conditions, and as far as it is coherent with a system that preserves

---

34 See Ernst Bloch's category of 'realen Möglichkeit' [*real possibilities*] in Bloch, *Das Prinzip Hoffnung*, 258, 278-ff.; Cf. with Rohbeck, Rohbeck, Johannes, *Technik – Kultur – Geschichte* (Frankfurt a.M.: Suhrkamp Verlag, 2000), 105-ff.; Rohbeck, *Zukunft der Geschichte*, 35-ff.

35 If historic comparison is denied, this leads to concepts like 'Suffizienz' [*sufficiency*] or 'Schwellenwert' [*threshold value*]. *vid.* Partridge, Ernest, "The Future – For Better or Worse", in *Environmental Values*, vol. 11, no. 1 (2002), 75-ff.; Meyer, *Historische Gerechtigkeit*, 3, 23, 36-ff.; Cf. with Ekardt, *Das Prinzip Nachhaltigkeit*, 190; Heubach, *Generationgerechtigkeit*, 116, 125; Gesang, *Klimaethik*, 52-ff., 60, 136-ff.

36 If historic comparison is made, two positions can be distinguished: 1. At least as high as, or perhaps even better. *vid.* Pogge, Thomas W., *World Poverty and Human Rights* (Malden-MA: Blackwell Publishers, 2002), 143-ff.; Tremmel, *Eine Theorie der Generationengerechtigkeit*, 291; Ekardt, *Das Prinzip Nachhaltigkeit*, 25-ff.; Ott and Döring, *Theorie und Praxis*, 101, 138; Caney, Simon, "Climate Change and the Duties of the Advantaged", in *Critical Review of International Social and Political Philosophy*, vol. 13, no.1 (2010), 203-ff.; 2. Of equal value: Epstein, Richard A., "Justice across the Generations", in *Justice between Age Groups and Generations*, edited by P. Laslett and J. S. Fishkin (New Haven-London: Yale University Press, 1992), 84-ff.; Heubach, *Generationgerechtigkeit*, 44; 3. Perhaps, worse: Fishkin, James S., "The Limits of Intergeneral Justice", in *Justice between Age Groups and Generations*, edited by P. Laslett and J. S. Fishkin (New Haven-London: Yale University Press, 1992), 62-ff.; Sturma, "Die Gegenwart der Langzeitverantwortung", 230.

nature and respects social justice. This, justice means the enabling of autonomy and development.

A model of progress that is modified in this way has a threefold meaning: According to the *poor countries*, 'progress' means nothing more and nothing less than achieving a minimum standard of conditions of living that satisfies the basic needs.[37] On the contrary: first of all, the *industrialised countries* are not eligible for unlimited 'progress.' They are, moreover, obligated to renounce progress as long as the emerging countries have realised the required proceedings. This exemplifies those models of history of stagnation and even downfall in the meaning of a controlled decline. Finally, the plea for 'proceedings' in the less-developed countries is not to be confused with an optimism that is naïve, because these desires address these alternative developments. The disadvantaged countries especially have the chance for alternative modes of modernisation.

5 Why the Philosophy of History?

Finally, there remains the question regarding the function of the Philosophy of History with regard to the discourse on responsibility for future generations. Thus, it was shown that terms like 'developing' or 'emerging countries', as well as the concept of 'catch-up development', have meanings related to the issues of the Philosophy of History. The concept of 'development' contained therein presupposes the theorems of the 'simultaneity of the non-simultaneous' and 'synchronization of the non-simultaneity.' To understand history as both a limited and open process, the categories of 'historic contingency' and 'practical continuity' have been formulated relative to each other in a new way. As demonstrated, even basic concepts such as 'generation' and 'heritage' as well as 'future' and 'deadline' originate from the Philosophy of History. This holds true for the norm of a desire for improvement.

---

[37] While the concept of basic needs refers more to material aspects, the concept of realisation opportunities refers to the aggregate of satisfaction of needs and to live a self-determinate life. *vid.* Sen, Amartya, *The idea of justice* (Cambridge-MA: Harvard University Press, 2009), 231, 271; Nussbaum, Martha Craven, *Women and Human Development* (Cambridge-New York-Melbourne: Cambridge University Press, 2001), 87-ff.; Cf. with Weikard, *Wahlfreiheit*, 163-ff.; Ott and Döring, *Theorie und Praxis*, 83. The debate on egalitarianism has shown that the demand for absolute standards and for the same comparative standards are essentially the same. *vid.* Krebs, Angelika, "Wieviel Natur schulden wir der Zukunft?", in *Zukunftsverantwortung und Generationensolidarität*, edited by D. Birnbacher and G. Brudermüller (Würzburg: Königshausen&Neumann, 2001), 157-ff.; Ott and Döring, *Theorie und Praxis*, 78-ff.; Gesang, *Klimaethik*, 48, 93-ff.

In general, these terms, theorems, and images of history are interpretative patterns of the historical. They may be understood as representations in which gained experiences, subjective attitudes, values and norms, and worldviews or concepts are integrated. If history is meant to be the area 'created' by human beings under particular circumstances, these are self-interpretations of their own history. In this context, it is vital that these interpretative patterns not only have the capacity to describe and value the historical past and current situations, but that they also play a major role in discourses about the future.

Discourses about the future describe an historic action framework that is not finished but has to be designed first. Thus, they are part of the planning of actions and, ultimately, of elements of actions. These representations of realistic possibilities receive their historical character not only because they are collective and far-reaching, but also through the generation of interpretative patterns that reflect current developments that refer to today's ideals. This gives an orientation to our praxis in the present and defines the way in which we are able to affect the future.

For example, the model of cycles in nature calls for the conservation of the natural environment. The historical image of stagnation leads equally to the cessation of the process of civilisation in order to protect nature and conserve the existing culture. As with the Philosophy of Enlightenment, stagnation and downfall are negative assessments, and today's circumstances call for their re-interpretation and appreciation. The concept of process demands the hope be maintained that, at least, the conditions of living for the disadvantaged people can be improved and that technological progress can rehabilitate the destruction of nature. Based on this prerequisite, I strongly believe that the reflexive use of interpretative patterns of the historical is not only justified, but also essential, for there is evidence now that these structures play an important role in discourses about the future. As far as they are used in political discourses, one may declare this a policy of history. In this way, they support the re-politicisation of the future. Thus, the Philosophy of History's prospect is to address the future as an action framework of possible history and, in conjunction with Future Ethics, to develop ethical standards for future-oriented and responsible praxis.

Bibliography

Anders, Günther, *Die atomare Bedrohung* (München: C.H. Beck, 1986).
Baier, Annette, "The Rights of Past and Future Persons", in *Responsibilities to Future Generations: Environmental Ethics*, edited by Ernest Partridge (New York: Prometheus Books, 1980), 171–183.

Bartelmus, Peter, *Environment, Growth and Development: The Concepts and Strategies of Sustainability* (London: Routledge, 1994).

Baumgartner, Hans Michael, *Kontinuität und Geschichte* (Frankfurt a.M.: Suhrkamp Verlag, 1972).

Baumgartner, Hans Michael, "Philosophie der Geschichte nach dem Ende der Geschichtsphilosophie", in *Der Sinn des Historischen: Geschichtsphilosophie Debatten*, edited by Herta Nagl-Docekal (Frankfurt/M.: Fischer, 1996), 151–167.

Beckerman, Wilfred, "Intergenerational Justice", in *Intergenerational Justice Review*, no. 2 (2004), 1–5.

Benjamin, Walter, *Gesammelte Schriften*, Band I.2 (Frankfurt/M.: Suhrkamp Verlag, 1974).

Birnbacher, Dieter, *Verantwortung für zukünftige Generationen* (Stuttgart: Reclam, 1988).

Birnbacher, Dieter, "Verantwortung für zukünftige Generation – Reichweite und Grenzen", in *Handbuch Generationengerechtigkeit*, edited by Stiftung für die Rechte zukünftiger Generationen (München: Ökom Verlag, 2003), 81–103.

Birnbacher, Dieter, "Langzeitverantwortung – das Problem der Motivation", in *Langzeitverantwortung. Ethik – Technik – Ökologie*, edited by C. F. Gethmann and J. Mittelstraß (Darmstadt: Wissenschaftliche Buchgesellschaft, 2008), 23–39.

Bloch, Ernst, *Das Prinzip Hoffnung*, 4 Band (Frankfurt/M.: Suhrkamp Verlag, 1977).

Blumenberg, Hans, *Lebenszeit und Weltzeit* (Frankfurt/M: Suhrkamp Verlag, 1986).

Böhler, Dietrich, *Zukunftsverantwortung in globaler Perspektive* (Bad Homburg: VAS Verlag, 2009).

Bourdieu, Pierre, "Ökonomisches Kapital, kulturelles Kapital, soziales Kapital", in *Soziale Ungleichheiten*, edited by R. Kreckel (Göttingen: Schwartz, 1983), 183–198.

Braudel, Ferdinand, *Schriften zur Geschichte 1. Gesellschaften und Zeitstrukturen* (Stuttgart: Klett-Cotta, 1992).

Caney, Simon, "Climate Change and the Duties of the Advantaged", in *Critical Review of International Social and Political Philosophy*, vol. 13, no.1 (2010): 203–228.

De George, Richard T., "The Environment, Rights, and Future Generations", in *Responsibilities to Future Generations: Environmental Ethics*, edited by E. Partridge (New York: Prometheus Books, 1980), 157–165.

Ekardt, Felix, *Das Prinzip Nachhaltigkeit. Generationengerechtigkeit und globale Gerechtigkeit* (München: C. H. Beck, 2005).

Enge, Kristin, *Zeit und Nachhaltigkeit. Die Wiederentdeckung der Naturzeiten als Ausgangspunkt für den Übergang zu einer Nachhaltigen Entwicklung* (Berlin: Akademische Abhandlungen zur Raum- und Umweltforschung, 2000).

Epstein, Richard A., "Justice across the Generations", in *Justice between Age Groups and Generations*, edited by P. Laslett and J. S. Fishkin (New Haven-London: Yale University Press, 1992), 84–106.

Feinberg, Joel, "Die Rechte der Tiere und zukünftigen Generationen", in *Ökologie und Ethik*, edited by D. Birnbacher (Stuttgart: Reclam, 1980), 140–179.

Fishkin, James S., "The Limits of Intergeneral Justice", in *Justice between Age Groups and Generations*, edited by P. Laslett and J. S. Fishkin (New Haven-London: Yale University Press, 1992), 62–83.

Gesang, Bernward, *Klimaethik* (Frankfurt/M.: Suhrkamp Verlag, 2011).

Gethmann, Carl Friedrich, "Langzeitverantwortung als ethisches Problem im Umweltstaat", in *Langzeitverantwortung im Umweltstaat*, edited by C. F. Gethmann, M. Kloepfer and H. G. Nutzinger (Bonn: Economica-Verlag, 1993), 1–21.

Grunwald, Armin and Kopfmüller, Jürgen, *Nachhaltigkeit* (Frankfurt/M.: Campus Studium, 2006).

Hauff, Volker (ed.), *Unsere gemeinsame Zukunft. Der Brundtland-Bericht der Weltkommission für Umwelt und Entwicklung* (Greven: Eggenkamp Verlag, 1987).

Heintel, Peter and Krainer, Larissa, "Geschichtlich-kulturelle Nachhaltigkeit", in *Erwägen Wissen Ethik*, vol. 4, no. 21(2010): 435–446.

Heubach, Andrea, *Generationengerechtigkeit – Herausforderung für die zeitgenössische Ethik* (Göttingen: V&R Unipress, 2008).

Höffe, Otfried, *Moral als Preis der Moderne* (Frankfurt/M.: Suhrkamp Verlag, 1993).

Hölscher, Lucian, *Die Entdeckung der Zukunft* (Frankfurt/M.: Fischer Taschenbuch Verlag, 1999).

Jonas, Hans, *Das Prinzip Verantwortung* (Frankfurt/M.: Suhrkamp Verlag, 1979).

Kopfmüller, Jürgen; Brandl, Volker; Jörissen, Juliane; Paetau, Michael; Banse, Gerhard; Coenen, Reinhard, and Grunwald, Armin (eds.), *Nachhaltige Entwicklung integrativ betrachtet: Konstitutive Elemente, Regeln, Indikatoren* (Berlin: Edition Sigma, 2001).

Kornwachs, Klaus, *Das Prinzip der Bedingungserhaltung: Eine Ethische Studie* (Münster: LIT Verlag, 2000).

Koselleck, Reinhart, *Vergangene Zukunft* (Frankfurt/M.: Suhrkamp Verlag, 1979).

Koselleck, Reinhart, *Zeitschichten. Studien zur Historik* (Frankfurt/M.: Suhrkamp Verlag, 2003).

Koselleck, Reinhart, *Vom Sinn und Unsinn der Geschichte* (Frankfurt/M., Suhrkam Verlag, 2010).

Krebs, Angelika, "Wieviel Natur schulden wir der Zukunft?", in *Zukunftsverantwortung und Generationensolidarität*, edited by D. Birnbacher and G. Brudermüller (Würzburg: Königshausen&Neumann, 2001), 157–182.

Laslett, Peter, "Is There a Generational Contract?", in *Justice between Age Groups and Generations*, edited by P. Laslett and J. S. Fishkin (New Haven-London: Yale University Press, 1992), 24–47.

Leggewie, Klaus and Welzer, Harald, *Das Ende der Welt, wie wir sie kannten* (Frankfurt/M.: Fischer Verlag, 2009).

Leist, Anton, "Ökologische Gerechtigkeit", in *Angewandte Ethik. Die Bereichsethiken und ihre theoretische Fundierung. Ein Handbuch*, edited by J. Nida-Rümelin (Stuttgart: Alfred Kröner Verlag, 2005), 426–513.

Lienkamp, Andreas, *Klimawandel und Gerechtigkeit* (Paderborn: Ferdinand Schoningh Verlag, 2009).

Lübbe, Hermann, *Geschichtsphilosophie. Verbliebene Funktionen* (Erlangen-Jena: Palm und Enke Verlag, 1993).

Luhmann, Niklas, *Soziale Systeme* (Frankfurt/M.: Suhrkamp Taschenbuch Verlag, 1984).

Mannheim, Karl, "Das Problem der Generation", in *Wissenssoziologie*, edited by K. Mannheim (Berlin: Neuwied Verlag, 1964), 509–565.

Marquard, Odo, *Schwierigkeiten mit der Geschichtsphilosophie* (Frankfurt a.M.: Suhrkamp Verlag, 1973).

Meyer, Lukas, *Historische Gerechtigkeit: Ideen und Argumenten* (Berlin-New York: Walter De Gruyter Verlag, 2005).

Nagl-Docekal, Herta, "Ist Geschichtsphilosophie heute noch möglich?", in *Der Sinn des Historischen*, edited by H. Nagl-Docekal (Frankfurt/M.: Fischer Verlag, 1996), 7–63.

Nussbaum, Martha Craven, *Women and Human Development* (Cambridge-New York-Melbourne: Cambridge University Press, 2001).

Ott, Konrad and Döring, Ralf, *Theorie und Praxis starker Nachhaltigkeit* (Marburg: Metropolis Verlag, 2008).

Paehlke, Robert C., *Environmentalism and the Future of Progressive Politics* (New Haven-London: Yale University Press, 1989).

Parfit, Derek, "On Doing the Best for Our Children", in *Ethics and Population*, edited by M. Bayles (Cambridge-MA: Schenkman Publishing Co., 1976), 100–112.

Parfit, Derek, "Future Generations: Further Problems", in *Philosophy & Public Affairs*, vol. 11, no. 2 (1981): 113–172.

Partridge, Ernest, "The Future – For Better or Worse", in *Environmental Values*, vol. 11, no. 1 (2002): 75–85.

Plechter, Galen K., "The Rights of Future Generations", in *Responsibilities to Future Generations. Environmental Ethics*, edited by E. Partridge (New York: Prometheus Books, 1980), 167–179.

Pogge, Thomas W., *World Poverty and Human Rights* (Malden-MA: Blackwell Publishers, 2002).

Putnam, Robert D. (ed.), *Gesellschaft und Gemeinsinn* (Gütersloh: Bertelsmann Stiftung Verlag, 2001).

Rawls, John, *Eine Theorie der Gerechtigkeit* (Frankfurt/M.: Suhrkamp Verlag, 1979).

Rohbeck, Johannes, *Technik – Kultur – Geschichte* (Frankfurt a.M.: Suhrkamp Verlag, 2000).

Rohbeck, Johannes, *Aufklärung und Geschichte* (Berlin: Akademie Verlag, 2010).

Rohbeck, Johannes, *Zukunft der Geschichte. Geschichtsphilosophie und Zukunftsethik* (Berlin: De Gruyter Akademie Forschung, 2013).

Rohbeck, Johannes, "Rettende Kritik der Geschichtsphilosophie, Immanuel Kant im historischen Kontext", in *Zeitschrift für kritische Sozialtheorie und Philosophie*, vol. 1, no. 2 (2014), 350–376.

Roldán, Concha; Brauer, Daniel; Rohbeck, Johannes (eds.), *Philosophy of Globalization* (Berlin: Walter De Gruyter Verlag, 2018).

Rüsen, Jörn, *Historische Orientierung* (Köln-Weimar-Berlin: Wochenschau Verlag, 1994).

Sen, Amartya, *The idea of justice* (Cambridge-MA: Harvard University Press, 2009).

Sturma, Dieter, "Die Gegenwart der Langzeitverantwortung", in *Recht, Gerechtigkeit und Freiheit*, edited by C. Langbehn (Paderborn: Mentis Verlag, 2006), 221–238.

Thomson, David, "Generations, Justice, and the Future of Collective Action", in *Justice between Age Groups and Generations*, edited by P. Laslett and J. S. Fishkin (New Haven-London: Yale University Press, 1992), 237–235.

Tremmel, Jörg, "Is a Theory of Intergenerational Justice Possible?", in *Intergenerational Justice Review*, no. 2 (2004): 6–9.

Tremmel, Jörg, *Eine Theorie der Generationengerechtigkeit* (Münster: Mentis Verlag, 2012).

Turgot, Anne Robert Jacques, *Über die Fortschritte des menschlichen Geistes* (Frankfurt/M.: Suhrkamp, 1990).

Unnerstall, Herwig, *Rechte zukünftiger Generationen* (Würzburg: Königshausen und Neumann, 1999).

Veith, Werner, *Intergenerationelle Gerechtigkeit* (Stuttgart: W. Kohlhammer Verlag, 2006).

Von Ranke, Leopold, *Über die Epochen der neueren Geschichte* (München-Wien: Oldenbourg Verlag, 1971).

Warren, Mary Anne, "Do Potential Persons Have Rights?", in *Responsibilities to Future Generations: Environmental Ethics*, edited by E. Partridge (New York: Prometheus Books, 1980), 261–273.

Weikard, Hans-Peter, *Wahlfreiheit für zukünftige Generationen* (Marburg: Metropolis Verlag, 1999).

Welzer, Harald, *Klimakriege. Wofür im 21. Jahrhundert getötet wird* (Frankfurt/M.: S. Fischer Verlag, 2008).

Zwenger, Thomas, *Geschichtsphilosophie. Eine kritische Grundlegung* (Darmstadt: Wissenschaftliche Buchgesellschaft, 2008).

Index of Subjects

admiration   1, 49
altruism   20, 32, 40, 65, 74, 153
amour de soi   54, 56, 56n, 59, 59n, 60, 61, 63, 65
amour-propre   55–56, 56n, 58–60, 60n, 61–62, 62n, 63, 63n, 64–66, 66n, 67, 70
Anti-utilitarianism   82–85, 87–89
appraisal   4–5
axiom of interest   83

benevolence   45, 47n, 67n, 74
bon sauvage   57

caring   13, 21, 33
catch-up development   181, 193–194, 196
character   50–51, 58, 68n, 79, 83, 107–109, 111–118, 122–123, 126–129, 135–140, 147, 149, 155–157
cognitive performance historiography   107, 111
compassion   28–29, 31, 33–37, 39, 42n, 44n, 47, 47n, 48, 53, 55–57, 61, 64, 68–69, 74, 83, 93, 108, 133, 138, 174
Critical Empathy Theory (CET)   153, 154n, 158, 161

decolonization   87, 89
dédoublement   110
development of language (proto-language)   12, 12n, 15, 54, 67

egotism   139
Émile   53, 54, 54n, 56, 56n, 63, 63n, 65, 66–70
empathisation   12
Empathy
   (affective)   100–101
   (cognitive)   8–9, 11–13, 17, 100, 117
   (connection)   108, 152, 161, 168–169, 172n, 173
   (didactics)   75
   (egocentric)   114
   (emotional)   8, 9, 10–11, 13, 21
   (higher-level)   154–155
   (historical)   169–170

(projection)   107, 107n, 111–112, 114, 117, 119
(somatic)   8, 10–11, 100
(theatrical)   106, 107, 111–112, 117–118, 120, 123
empathetic art   94–95, 97, 99, 101–104
empathic unsettlement   171–176
enact(ment)   108, 111, 122–123, 158–159, 164, 166
encephalisation   14
Erlebnis   165
expression   20, 33, 48, 133, 145, 150, 163, 166, 172–173
extended consciousness   17

fictional truth   129, 132, 135–136, 139, 143, 146, 150
flipped classroom   79–80
fMRI (functional magnetic resonance imagery)   9, 12
Frist (deadline)   181, 187–192, 196
Future Ethics   181, 183, 185n, 188n, 197

Geisteswissenschaften   163, 165–166

historical (agents)   164–165, 168–171
   (events)   163–164, 169, 172, 175–176
   (responsibility)   187
historicism   180, 194
historiography   107, 111, 164, 166, 169–172, 174–175
homo empathicusnarrativus   12
homo oeconomicus   84
homo sapiens   7, 17
hospital artwork   93
hubris   122
humiliation   5, 122–123
humility   108–109, 121n, 122–123

intergenerational contract   182, 184
   heritage   182–183

mechanical animals   23
metaphor   54, 112–114, 119, 176
metatheatre   106–107, 109–111, 117n, 120

moral imagination 145, 149
moral obligation 149, 185
moral right 149, 190

narratives
   (conventional) 127–128, 140
   (fictional) 126–129, 139–140
   (first-person) 128–129
   (third-person) 129
   (traditional) 128

páthos 3, 74
Philosophy of History 165, 179, 179n, 180–182, 188–189, 193–197
Pity 3, 4, 44n, 56–58, 60n, 61, 61n, 62–65, 68, 68n, 69, 109, 119, 138, 150
Pitié 55, 60, 62, 64, 68
pragmatic contradiction 145, 147–149
principle of reversibility 192
process of learning 73
promissory logic 145, 147

resilience 115

Self
   (*self*-appraisal) 122
   (self-concept) 53
   (self-consciousness) 11, 13, 17, 21, 55, 62, 74, 165
   (self-determination) 185, 187n, 196
   (diminished-self/small self) 121, 121n
   (self-estrangement) 61–62
   (*self*-interest) 44–45, 65n, 83–85
   (self-other distinction) 61, 64
   (self-perspective) 17
   (self-preservation) 55–56, 59–60, 61, 64
   (self-reference) 16, 59, 61
   (*self*-representation) 17, 108, 114–115, 121, 123
   (self-talk) 120
sympathetic concern 8, 10–11, 42n
Sympathy 3–4, 10–11, 21, 30, 30n, 41, 43, 47, 47n, 50–51, 55, 83, 107n, 109, 146, 170

Terror Management Theory (TMT) 120–121, 121n
theatre studies 107, 111, 116–117, 120
Theatre of War 116
Theory of Double Contingency 185
Theory of Triple Contingency 185–186
thick evaluative concepts 4

virtue epistemology 149
volonté générale 70
esprit de commerce 70

Index of Authors

Achebe, Chinua   156, 159
Anders, Günter   189
Ansell-Pearson, Keith   64
Arendt, Hannah   70
Aristotle   115, 144, 149
Arsuaga, Juan Luis   16

Bergson, Henri   190
Berry-Dee, Christopher   38
Bizot, Francois   160–161
Bloch, Ernst   193, 195n
Bloom, Paul   36–39, 46n, 47n
Borges, Jorge Luis   110
Braudel, Ferdinand   190

Caillé, Alain   83–84
Cohen, Joshua   68–69
Collingwood, Robin G.   168, 168n

Davidson, Donald   5, 28–29, 31, 35
De Sousa Santos, Boaventura   89
Deleuze, Gilles   146, 147
Dennett, Daniel   29, 31–33
Dilthey, Wilhelm   162–163, 165–166, 166n, 167–168, 168n
Drescher, Joan   95, 97–100

Falkner, Thomas   109–111, 114, 118–119
Fowles, John   129, 135
Fried, Charles   145, 147

Geertz, Clifford   167
Glover, Jonathan   42, 42n
Goldie, Peter   154, 154n, 155, 158
Goleman, Daniel   74

Hare, Robert B.   37
Hesk, Jon   109–111
Hobbes, Thomas   55
Hume, David   30, 30n, 42, 42n, 43–46, 46n, 47n, 49, 50–51

Husserl, Edmund   155, 190

Kemp, Rick   114
Koselleck, Reinhart   180

LaCapra, Dominick   167–169, 169n, 170, 170n, 171, 171n, 172, 172n, 173, 173n, 173n2, 174, 174n, 175–176
Lakoff, George (and Johnson, Mark)   112–114, 119
Luhmann, Niklas   185

Mauss, Marcel   83–85, 88
McFee, Graham   155–156
Meineck, Peter   107n, 111, 116–117, 119–120
Melville, Hermann   144–145
Mencius   46–47, 47n, 48, 48n, 49
Mignolo, Walter   89
Minchin, Tim   73, 78
Murdoch, Iris   135

Obama, Barack   29, 29n
O'Hagan, Timothy   68

Pinker, Steven   42n, 158

Rogers, Carl   84–85
Ronson, Jon   37–38
Rousseau, Jean-Jacques   48, 48n, 53–54, 54n, 54n2, 55, 55n, 56, 56n, 57–61, 63, 70

Shay, Jonathan   115–116, 120
Smith, Adam   30, 30n, 44n
Stein, Edith   74, 155

Wegman, William   102–103
Whitman, Walt   79
Williams, Bernard   4, 42–43, 46

Printed in the United States
By Bookmasters